AMERICAN
PRESIDENTIAL
ELECTIONS

*Copublished with the
Eagleton Institute of Politics,
Rutgers University*

AMERICAN PRESIDENTIAL ELECTIONS

Trust and the Rational Voter

Jeffrey A. Smith

American Political Parties
and Elections

general editor:
Gerald M. Pomper

PRAEGER SPECIAL STUDIES • PRAEGER SCIENTIFIC

Library of Congress Cataloging in Publication Data

Smith, Jeffrey A
   American presidential elections.

   (American political parties and elections)
   Bibliography: p.
   Includes index.
   1. Political participation--United States.
2. Presidents--United States--Election. 3. Trust
(Psychology) I. Title. II. Series.
JK1764.S55   324.973   80-17228
ISBN 0-03-056143-4

Published in 1980 by Praeger Publishers
CBS Educational and Professional Publishing
A Division of CBS, Inc.
521 Fifth Avenue, New York, New York 10017 U.S.A.

© 1980 by Praeger Publishers

0123456789 145 987654321

Printed in the United States of America

PREFACE

*T*his is a book about democracy, both the classical ideal and the contemporary American variation on that theme. It is also a book about trust, rationality, and citizen participation in American presidential elections. These diverse themes are brought together in the central thesis of this work: that trust is an essential component of the rational decisions of voters to participate in elections and is crucial to the candidate preference decision. By "trust" I understand attitudes—toward both the political system and its agents—reflecting evaluations of honesty, reliability, competence, responsiveness, and related qualities, as well as very broad political values. Although it may vary in importance with the circumstances of particular elections and voters' perceptions of the quality of their government's performance, rational voters' concern with trust has its basis in the alienation of popular sovereignty to representative institutions in the political system.

The voting behavior of American citizens is perhaps the most extensively studied aspect of human activity among contemporary political scientists. Yet there are surprisingly few works in the voting literature that concern themselves to any significant extent with the bonds of faith between the people, their political system, and their political leadership. Indeed, until quite recently the predominant theoretical orientations of voting researchers have offered little room for a serious treatment of this topic. Instead, trust appears as a mere reflection of more fundamental psychological attachments or issue-based judgments. I propose to establish that trust is a primary and essential element of voting behavior, with regard to both the decision to vote or abstain and the choice of candidates, and that casting electoral concerns in terms of trustworthiness is a rational response to the context of national elections.

The question of faith in the political system has not been a major preoccupation of voting analysts. Since the postwar boom in the technology for accumulating and processing massive quantities of data, the focus of research has been on the individual voter and not on the political system. While the performance of the electorate was measured against standards of model democratic citizenship, the performance of political institutions was not problematic for voting studies. On the contrary, the assumptions implicit in *The American Voter* and common to most voting behavior

v

research are that the political system is democratic, responsive, and effective, and that elections present voters with distinguishable, relevant alternatives, which in turn grant them effective control of public policy.

The present understanding of voters has been developed largely within this assumption set, with consequent expectations of full, informed citizen participation in elections and emphasis on issue-based notions of rationality. My own argument is that the gap between the behavior of American voters and that of the ideal democratic citizen is largely explained not by the want of rationality on the part of the electorate, but rather by disparities between the democratic ideal and normal American politics. Naturally, this argument has implications for proposals to reform the political system as well as for evaluations of the American voter.

The development of this thesis necessarily entails a critical examination of the extant models of voter behavior. Specifically, it seems that the failure of three decades of extensive voting research to recognize such a potent factor as trust as central to voting behavior is evidence of limitations common to the prominent approaches. These limitations lie in certain unexamined assumptions that have unnecessarily and inappropriately narrowed the scope and relevance of their understanding of the electoral process. A major portion of the task at hand is the exposition and replacement of these assumptions.

The arguments contained in this work share two broad assumptions about the nature of voting behavior. First, I assume that the individual members of the electorate are characterized by political rationality. I have in mind a rather precise notion of rationality: one that implies that voting behavior can be understood in terms of its relationship to specific political ends, but that implies nothing about the selection of those ends. In making this assumption, I depart from the tradition that produced impressive evidence of the irrationality of the electorate, but I have not assumed that which I attempt to prove. Instead, the success of this work must depend on the extent to which the model developed here can account for the vast body of empirical data on voter behavior.

Second, I assume that whatever constitutes rational behavior cannot be defined a priori. Instead, rational behavior is conditioned by its context, which in this case would be the values and goals of the individual; the specific alternatives that the political system offers the voter; the quality, quantity, and accessibility of the information available to voters; and the costs associated with various strategies. While this assumption may seem quite harmless and even intuitively obvious, the implications of this approach have largely evaded the voting literature. In particular, the debate about the quality and rationality of the American electorate is misguided in evaluating voters according to standards defined independently of the context of American elections.

The analysis of the role of trust in elections begins in Chapter 1 with consideration of what is perhaps the most significant indicator of the performance of our political system: the consistent decline in turnout in national elections since 1960. Although the voting literature offers a plethora of approaches to the explanation of turnout, none of these is adequate for treating the most recent trends. Instead, a rational account of the turnout decision, incorporating a reformulation of the notion of citizen duty and placing political system performance evaluation at the heart of the participation decision, is developed in this chapter. The implications of the analysis are that voters will not support institutions that fail to meet qualitative performance standards, and that recently declining turnout is directly associated with a widespread, general loss of faith in elections as vehicles for providing democratic control of public policy.

In Chapters 2 and 3 the focus of the study shifts to a critical review of the various models that psephologists have employed in their work during the era of survey-based voting research, with particular attention to the assumptions that characterize each. This review identifies four distinct but related models of voting behavior:

(1) The Naive Model of the Democratic Citizen: the body of prescriptions for good citizenship (in elections), with roots predating survey research, which has exerted a powerful but rarely acknowledged influence on subsequent voting research and contemporary thinking about democratic politics.

(2) The Social-Psychological Model: the account developed in the classic voting study, *The American Voter*, that offers a nonrational explanation of voter behavior that contrasts sharply with the standards of the naive model and relegates the bulk of the electorate to the status of mere spectators to a political process they do not really understand.

(3) The Rational Voter Model: the approach that emphasizes the instrumentality of voter behavior, producing an image of the voter as a consumer choosing among competing products in the political marketplace.

(4) The New Issue Voter: the contemporary hybrid of rational and nonrational models that evolved during the early 1970s.

In all of these models the emphasis is on the central role of issues in elections and the extent to which voters do or do not base their choices on those issues.

An alternative to these, developed in Chapter 4, is the investor-voter model, which departs from earlier models in placing the candidate at the center of the voter's preference decision. The individual's vote is viewed as an investment in the political system and the candidates as the agents whose performance will determine the value of that investment. Voters are assumed to be rational and to share the dominant culture's evaluation of political participation. The influence of distinguishing features of the American political system—for example, the dominance of elections by two major parties and the role of the president—on the rational behavior of voters is explicitly considered. In addition, the costs associated with participation, including information costs, limit and direct the approaches of voters to critical decisions in the model. The incorporation of these elements of the context of American elections leads, inter alia, to a nontraditional analysis of the role of nonissue-specific criteria, including trust and other performance values.

With the matter of trust thus placed in a general account of voter decision making, the emphasis shifts in Chapters 5, 6, and 7 to a narrower focus on the specific nature and role of trust as an element of voter decisions in elections. Theoretical arguments and empirical evidence are combined in exploring the salience, meaning, and independence of trustworthiness evaluations of candidates. Then the relative importance of trust in the voter's calculus is examined using various methodologies, including simulation, to compare trust with more traditional objects of research attention such as party identification and issue positions.

A systematic treatment of the broader issues raised by this work is reserved for the concluding chapter. The investor-voter model provides a more meaningful basis for analyzing dynamic elements of political context and particular elections that is afforded by other models. More important, however, is that the investor-voter model, if it is an appropriate representation of American voters, necessitates a reexamination of some of the basic empirical underpinnings of modern democratic theory. Finally, the investor-voter model, because it does explicitly incorporate elements of the context of elections in a rational model of voter behavior, can serve as a means of estimating the impact of institutional reform of the political system.

Watergate, the Agnew resignation, the conduct of the war in Vietnam, Cambodia, and Laos, questions surrounding the adequacy of the official reports on the assassinations of key political figures, evidence of FBI and CIA abuses of power, the credibility gap, Koreagate, and countless additional instances of official deception and corruption have focused public attention on the broad issue of trust in government. Thus, the present work is, at least, topical. But the thrust of the arguments to follow is that trust is not a transient issue in American politics raised by events like those above only to fade away again when the proper reforms are introduced and the rascals thrown out. Rather, the issue of trust is inherent in a representative political system. Beyond this, the concern of voters with the trustworthiness of candidates is derived from particular structural characteristics of the

American political system, especially the role of the chief executive and the nature of the issues. Public reaction to the exposure of contradictions within the political system merely affirms the central role of trust.

On the other hand, it is not my purpose to argue that all of the electoral politics can be reduced to the single dimension of trust. I have merely chosen to focus upon one element, albeit the most important one, of a larger set of performance evaluation criteria. Performance evaluation in turn is only one part (along with issues, of course) of the broader field of voter concerns. But the emphasis on trust in this study does permit the generation of some interesting hypotheses about modern democratic politics.

The present work would have been impossible, in a very literal sense, without the contributions of a number of individuals. I wish to thank and publicly acknowledge Larry Dodd and Gerald Pomper for their commitment to this work, Joe Oppenheimer and Sam Popkin for the training they gave me, Joe and Jim Miller for their painstaking readings of earlier drafts and numerous criticisms, Jim and Sam for the inspiration, and Patricia Tierney for countless hours of manuscript preparation, as well as inspiration of a different sort.

Jeffrey A. Smith

ACKNOWLEDGMENTS

*T*he author gratefully acknowledges permission to reprint passages from the following:

Berelson, Bernard R., Paul F. Lazarsfeld, and William M. McPhee. *Voting.* Chicago: University of Chicago Press, 1954.

Campbell, Angus T., Philip E. Converse, Warren E. Miller, and Donald E. Stokes. *The American Voter.* New York: John Wiley & Sons, 1960.

Downs, Anthony. *An Economic Theory of Democracy.* New York: Harper & Row, 1957.

Miller, Arthur H., and Warren E. Miller. "Partisanship and Performance: 'Rational' Choice in the 1976 Presidential Election." Paper presented at the 1977 annual meeting of the American Political Science Association, Washington, D.C., September 1–4.

Miller, Warren E., and Teresa E. Levitin. *Leadership and Change: The New Politics and the American Electorate.* Cambridge, Mass.: Winthrop, 1976.

Pomper, Gerald M. *Voters' Choice: Varieties of American Electoral Behavior.* New York: Dodd, Mead, 1975.

Schumpeter, Joseph A. *Capitalism, Socialism and Democracy.* New York: Harper & Row, 1950.

The data utilized in this book were made available by the Inter-University Consortium for Political Research. The data for the 1960–76 American national election studies were originally collected by the Survey Research Center/Center for Political Studies of the Institute for Social Research, the University of Michigan, under grants from the National Science Foundation, the John and Mary R. Markle Foundation, and the Carnegie Corporation. Neither the original collectors of the data nor the consortium bear any responsibility for the analyses or interpretations presented here.

CONTENTS

LIST OF TABLES

1

VOTER PARTICIPATION IN AMERICAN ELECTIONS

*T*he 1976 election saw fewer than 55 percent of eligible voters exercise their options to participate in the selection of the president. This proportion continued a consistent decline in the rate of turnout in national elections that is unbroken since 1960 (see Table 1.1). If the present trend continues, the 1980s will see a presidential election marked by the participation of less than half of the eligible electorate, a situation long characteristic of midterm congressional elections. Jimmy Carter's popular mandate in 1976 was constructed from the votes of only slightly more than one-fourth (about 27 percent) of the potential voters. The rate of participation in American elections stands in sharp contrast to that observed in other Western industrialized nations, where the turnout figures are both absolutely higher (see Table 1.2) and relatively stable.

Students of politics are far from unanimous that these data bode ill for the American political system. Numerous authors, particularly in the post-World War II era, have argued—explicitly or implicitly—that a high rate of participation is not an essential characteristic of an efficient political system.[1] On the contrary, the evaluation of nonparticipation in these works may range from a matter of indifference to a functional necessity for maintaining the stability of the political system. The latter view is expressed by Berelson in one of the first voting studies to make extensive use of survey data:*

*Bernard R. Berelson, Paul F. Lazarsfeld, and William N. McPhee, *Voting*, 1954. This and all following quotes from Berelson et al. reprinted by permission of The University of Chicago Press, Chicago, Ill.

1

TABLE 1.1: Voter Turnout in Presidential and Off-year Congressional Elections (percent)

	Vote for President	Vote In Off-year Congressional Elections
1960	62.8%	
1962		45.4%
1964	61.9%	
1966		45.4%
1968	60.9%	
1970		43.5%
1972	55.5%	
1974		36.3%
1976	54.3%	
1978		36.0%

Sources: U.S. Bureau of the Census, Statistical Abstract of the United States: 1978, 99th ed. (Washington, D.C.: U.S. Government Printing Office, 1978), p. 520. 1978 figures based on Statistics of the Congressional Election (Washington, D.C.: U.S. Government Printing Office, 1979).

TABLE 1.2: Voter Turnout in National Elections: Percentage of Eligible Voters Casting Ballots

Australia	97	1972
Italy	93	1972
W. Germany	91	1972
Netherlands	83	1972
France	82	1973
Canada	74	1972
Great Britain	71	1970
United States	55	1972

Source: Congressional Record, April 10, 1973, p. 7,030.

Extreme interest goes with extreme partisanship and might culminate in rigid fanaticism that could destroy democratic processes if generalized throughout the community. Low affect toward the election—not caring much—underlies the resolution of many political problems.[2]

Obviously this perspective provides no basis for viewing declining turnout with alarm.

On the other hand, there is an earlier tradition that views democracy as an ideal model of political organization rather than as a decision-making process, and holds the active participation of the citizenry to be an essential characteristic of democracy.[3] The standards of participation in these theories demand more than the mere registration of preference through voting, for example, public discussion of issues, a minimum level of information, or even the personal assumption of positions of public responsibility. In the United States, where voting is virtually the only active form of participation for most citizens, and only a small portion of the public votes with any regularity, even this portion is falling. All this must be regarded with greater concern by those who ascribe to participatory ideals.

The vast literature dealing with the voting behavior of American citizens devotes relatively little attention to explanations of the decision to vote. The lack of emphasis on turnout may be accounted for in part by the widespread adoption of the modern, realist notions of democracy that relegate citizen activism to a peripheral role in the political process. A contributing factor is the general acceptance of the view that the turnout decision is not a decision at all, but rather the product of the internalization of participatory norms at a prerational stage of the life cycle. These are not the positions taken here.

This work begins by considering turnout for two reasons. First, it is assumed that the decision to vote may be understood as an investment decision on the part of the voter. It is, in effect, a decision to absorb certain costs, many of which are associated with the determination of preference (rather than with voting per se). Specifically, the maximum effort that a voter is willing to expend to make the appropriate choice is limited by the overall motivation to participate in the election. The second reason is the determining influence of context on behavior. Voting takes place in the context of a particular political system, which is in turn imbedded in a particular culture. The institutional structure of the political system and its cultural setting shape the attitudes and values that the individual brings to both the turnout and preference decisions and define the parameters of rational behavior with respect to each. The turnout and preference decisions are thus intimately linked in the model of voting behavior developed in these pages, and the analysis of one is central to understanding the other.

The remainder of this chapter outlines an explanation of the turnout decision that combines the rational approach implied in the conceptualization of the vote as an investment with explicit consideration of the context of that investment. The product of this marriage is an account that focuses on voters' evaluations of the performance of the political system, for which turnout is a useful barometer.

ELEMENTS OF A RATIONAL MODEL OF THE TURNOUT DECISION

Behavioral Assumptions

Any account of turnout that is to explain the trends noted at the beginning of this chapter must have a dynamic quality, that is, a single model must account for varying levels of turnout as a function of specified explanatory variables. A rational model of the turnout decision is capable of incorporating change because it begins with behavioral assumptions that do not themselves depend upon a particular context. The next step is the specification of the aspects of context that influence the outcome of the turnout decision. Then, because the predictions of the model are a function of the values that the relevant contextual parameters assume at any point, the model—if adequately specified—should properly reflect a changing world.

The set of behavioral assumptions necessary to build this explanation of voting behavior is quite simple. It is assumed throughout that the electorate is composed of rational, self-interested, utility-maximizing individuals, whose political activities exhibit political rationality. Rationality implies that individuals perceive alternatives, order them, and choose the most preferred.[4] Self-interest implies that the ordering of preferences is based on personal criteria. More formally, self-interest implies the independence of any two individuals' utility functions. Utility maximization implies that preferences are based on the satisfaction an individual derives from a particular alternative and that the alternative most satisfying will be most preferred. (This assumption is of greatest interest when combined with consideration of the declining marginal utility of various activities and of opportunity costs, as noted in the chapters following.) Political rationality implies that the goals of political behavior have a political content, or, in other words, that the case of the man who votes in order to please his wife will not be explained in the present context. These assumptions taken together imply a great deal about human behavior, including that it is moderately reflective and purposive rather than instinctive, random, or arbitrary, and that it is guided by the individual's own values (within the bounds of a given context) rather than being other directed or merely traditional or habitual. It is important to note that these assumptions bear no implications for the selection of goals or the character of individual preferences. In particular, it is not assumed that people are wise, well informed, practical, selfish, or altruistic, or that they exhibit good taste.

Everyone has observed human behavior that violates these assumptions. Nevertheless, the author believes that they are the most appropriate and fruitful assumptions to guide a theory of voting behavior, a position that distinguishes the present approach from many (but not all) of the others considered throughout this work. Combined with a careful specification of the context of the behavior to be explained, these assumptions are adequate to account for much of voting behavior. Naturally, they are part of every hypothesis tested here.[5]

Liberal Individualism and Opportunity Costs

One contextual determinant of American political behavior that has not received its due consideration in the voting literature is the set of values, assumptions, and concepts that comprises the dominant American culture. In particular, the place of politics in the lives of the individuals under study must be the starting point for any analysis that attempts to understand their responses to political stimuli. Unfortunately, this primary concern is typically handled by an implicit assumption that politics—and in particular, elections—are of such centrality to people's lives that one is compelled to explain not why some people participate, but why others fail to devote the resources necessary to meet the standards of model democratic citizenship.

The liberal notion of individualism runs directly counter to the assumption of the centrality of politics. Americans by and large accept the premise that, except for the occasional interference of fate, people are individually responsible for success or failure in their own lives.[6] This liberal individualism has direct consequences for attitudes toward politics because it lends itself to the compartmentalization of one's life experience into separate and relatively independent spheres, with politics substantially isolated from one's social and economic fortunes.

Any theory that places politics at the center of human activity must involve a conceptual integration of various spheres of activity, since human needs that are met through work and interpersonal relationships must have at least as high a priority as any concern that is purely political. In the dominant culture of the United States, this condition is not satisfied. While political institutions are often employed to deal with social or economic problems, the latter are not generally felt to be political per se. Similarly, issues are rarely conceptualized in terms of class conflicts or inequalities, but are addressed rather to vague notions of the "public Interest."[7]

This is not the place to argue the centrality of politics; it is sufficient for the present purpose to point out that, for the overwhelming majority of the American electorate, politics occupies a place, at best, alongside the other concerns of their lives.[8] In spite of this basic datum of the cultural context of American elections, voters are typically measured against standards based on an expectation of full participation by the electorate, meaning not only actual voting, but also the prefacing of the voting act by careful, informed consideration of a wide range of issues. A more realistic expectation, given the analysis here, is that the potential voter will weigh the costs and benefits of participation in the political system against the potential returns from the investment of the same resources in other spheres of activity—including, perhaps, leisure. In other words, one ought to expect participation to be conditioned by consideration of opportunity costs.

The Vote as an Economic Good

The notion of opportunity costs associated with the act of voting is appropriate to a broader conception of political participation in economic terms. In this respect, political activity differs from more conventional concerns of economic analysis mainly in the material nature of the latter.[9] Otherwise, it is not misguided to appropriate many of the tools of micro-economics to analyze voters' political purchases or investments. Thus attention is directed to such questions as: What are the costs associated with political activity? What are the returns from participation? How do opportunity costs affect the evaluations of these costs and returns?

The benefits that rational voters receive for their efforts are comprised of two distinguishable payoffs: the expected value of the vote, based on the probability of affecting policy outputs from the political system as a consequence of having a preference recorded for one or another alternative, and the immediate payoffs from the act of participation in the electoral process per se. The returns associated with having one's vote tallied are universally recognized as one payoff to participation, although it is generally stipulated as well that this payoff by itself is not sufficient to motivate voting. In fact, the probability of a single vote actually making a difference in the outcome of an American presidential election (even in the decentralized election format institutionalized in the electoral college) is so small that the expected value of the vote for most people is probably incalculable.*

If one cannot reasonably expect to affect the outcome of an election by voting, and if this fact is apparent to most voters, then those who do vote must be motivated largely by the returns from voting per se.[10] Not surprisingly, voting analysts disagree on the precise nature of these returns, although there is near consensus on their importance. The phenomena of half of the adult population of the United States turning out to vote in the 1964 and 1972 presidential elections, even though the outcome of each election was virtually a foregone conclusion, demand explanation.

Citizen Duty

This attempt to identify the returns from voting can be facilitated by considering first the most likely nonrational payoff. A preponderance of voting analysts would endorse some variation of the notion of citizen duty

---

*The expected value of the vote is the probability of affecting the outcome (making or breaking a tie) times the differential returns from the preferred alternative. Thus, if the probability of making a difference were one in a million, the differential return from the preferred alternative would have to be worth the equivalent of $100,000 in order to justify ten cents worth of effort.

as the motivating force in turnout. According to this school of thought, part of the common socialization of most Americans is indoctrination in the duty of a citizen to cast informed votes in elections, and the payoff for voting derives from compliance with the participatory norm. It has been repeatedly demonstrated empirically that many people profess a sense of citizen duty, and that people actually vote in proportion to their felt responsibility.[11]

Although the notion of citizen duty is useful for predicting turnout, by itself it is inadequate as an explanation of the decision to vote. A citizen's duty to vote is a moral principle that is unlikely to be an independent premise in one's system of values, if only because the effects of the behavior that it compels are mediated by social institutions. If this is correct, then the duty to vote must be deduced from other premises and the strength of the obligation must be in proportion to the moral force of the principles that command it.

In the American context various notions of democracy are called upon both to legitimize the political system and to underscore the meaningfulness of participation in elections. One's duty to vote in elections is based on the assumption that elections are democratic institutions, that is, that the outcomes of elections permit control of, or have some impact on (in a predictable direction), the quality of one's political environment or the people and policies that shape it. Although the linkages may not be explicit for the voters, it would seem unlikely that an individual could hold dissonant attitudes on citizen duty and the political system's democratic claims for long. To argue otherwise is to transform citizen duty from a moral concept to one of habit or ritual. To those who would argue that citizen duty is precisely an expression of habit or ritual, a similar response would apply. A habit or ritual without an underlying rational justification would not be sustained by positive reinforcement and would itself want explanation.

The linkage—at least temporally—of the citizen's obligations to be informed and to vote with the assumption that such behavior will have political influence is confirmed in this description of the socialization process:

> The young child's trust in the political system is expressed not only by a view of figures and institutions as benign, but through a view of the obligation of the citizen primarily to be a good person. This image of the citizen persists, but the obligations to vote and express interest in governmental affairs become more dominant elements of the norms of adult citizenship as the child grows older. The belief that the citizen should be interested in political matters is apparent in the behavior reported by elementary school children; by the end of the eighth grade most children have acquired some interest in governmental activities and have participated in discussions about political issues and problems. . . . The elementary-school child's view of the election process and of the mechan-

isms of influence on governmental action is dominated by an image of the citizen as powerful and the individual vote as the most effective force in the political process. The sense of efficacy in influencing political processes increases with age.[12]

The notion of a citizen's duty to vote that is independent of attitudes toward the political system is at least problematic. Specifically, citizen duty is a moral principle derived from the democratic nature of the American political system. Although citizen duty alone cannot explain voting, it is incorporated in the account of turnout developed below.

Returns from Participation

One interpretation of citizen duty that temporarily circumvents the problems arising from the moral nature of duty is to focus upon the external social sanctions attached to compliance with the norm of participation. Thus, the nonvoter may be reproached by friends and in other ways made to feel guilty, that is, to bear costs for noncompliance, so that a rational individual may vote even though it were meaningless in itself. But in the United States, where there are no official sanctions attached to voting, one's compliance is typically a private matter, so that social sanctions may be easily avoided. Moreover, such sanctions are properly regarded as consequences of the acceptance of the norm, and not as the basis for it. Although sanctions may be effective in the short run independently of the social meaning of elections, the view of citizens' rationality here is such that there must be social benefits from elections in the long run. External sanctions then may be understood as mechanisms enforcing contributions to a collective good (the election), and the individual's vote as one's fair share of the cost.

Citizen duty is transformed in the work of Anthony Downs and others from a moral concept to a purely pragmatic contribution to system maintenance:*

> Although the benefits each citizen derives from living in a democracy actually accrue to him continuously over time, he can view them as a capital sum which pays interest at each election. This procedure is rational because voting is a necessary prerequisite for democracy; hence democracy is in one sense a reward for voting. We call the part of this reward the citizen receives at each election his *long-run participation value.*

---

*Specified excerpts from *An Economic Theory of Democracy* by Anthony Downs. Copyright © 1957 by Harper & Row, Publishers, Inc., New York, N.Y. Reprinted by permission of the publisher.

Of course, he will actually get this reward even if he himself does not vote as long as a sufficient number of other citizens do. But we have already shown that he is willing to bear certain short-run costs he could avoid in order to do his share in providing long-run benefits. The maximum cost he will bear for this reason in any given election is that which just offsets his long-run participation value.[13]

According to Downs's formulation, the total turnout in an election is a collective good for the electorate and each vote is a unit contribution toward the guarantee of future elections. The voter's turnout decision is based in part on a comparison of long-run participation value with the costs associated with voting.

A careful consideration of the long-run participation value reveals it to be of dubious weight in the voter's calculus. The critical level of participation that guarantees the stability of political institutions for the near future (insofar as voting per se provides such a guarantee) is probably considerably less than even the most recent turnout rates in presidential elections. Above this critical level, each vote provides only a minuscule and rapidly declining marginal contribution to system maintenance. It seems unlikely that any noticeable costs of voting would fail to outweigh the expected value of the increased probability of future elections associated with a single vote.

Finally, Riker and Ordeshook combine the notion of citizen duty with rational calculation of costs and benefits of turnout in a more promising effort to explain why people vote.[14] Rejecting the assumption that voting per se is an onerous task with costs but no associated benefits, they suggest that many voters may find personal rewards in the act of voting irrespective of any instrumental policy-shaping value. These benefits include:

the satisfaction from compliance with the ethic of voting;
the satisfaction from affirming allegiance to the political system;
the satisfaction from affirming a partisan preference;
the satisfaction of deciding, going to the polls, etc.;
the satisfaction of affirming one's efficacy in the political system: the theory of democracy asserts that individuals and voting are meaningful and for most people the only chance to fulfill this role is in the voting booth.[15]

A limited test of the proposition that turnout varies with the evaluation of these considerations offers some support for this argument.

The Riker and Ordeshook formulation of the motivation for voting differs in two important respects from Downs's long-run participation value: the returns from voting are immediate and personal, rather than remote, and the returns are independent of the actions of others. Thus, the voter can estimate relatively easily the satisfaction to be derived from voting, and a positive decision does not depend upon some grossly inaccurate estimate of one's efficacy in influencing the outcome of the election or stabilizing the political system. (Riker and Ordeshook, however, include influence on the outcome as a major consideration in the voter's calculus.) In addition, the vote decision is based on a rational calculation of costs, benefits, and opportunity costs, rather than politically irrational habit or duty.

Given earlier assumptions, a theoretically sound accounting of the turnout decision must satisfy the criteria of rationality. It also must posit rewards that are actually realized in the voter's experience; otherwise, one is obliged to suppose that millions of people periodically engage in behavior that is irrational and/or is directed toward a goal (making a difference in the outcome) that is, for virtually all of them, never realized. In these respects, the list above is a plausible schedule of benefits to be derived from voting. But, once again, one is faced with the necessity of ascribing to those who vote certain attitudes preceding the decision to vote. The items on the Riker-Ordeshook list may be considered to be rewards for voting only if the votes that the electorate cast are perceived by voters to be meaningful. In the modern American context, the meaning of elections is bound up with notions of democracy. These connections will be considered next.

American voters who see elections as a manifestation of democracy in the political system receive a number of political returns from voting per se. First and most important, democracy, which claims an exalted position among American values, has content for individuals only through their participation in it. In this respect democracy is no different from any number of consumer goods that must be used rather than merely possessed to generate utility for their holders. For most Americans elections are of the essence of democrary, and voting is thus an extremely important actualization of democracy in their experience.* In addition, voters gain a stake in politics, a claim on the attention of those they support, and a part in the policymaking process. One may even posit certain returns that incorporate the notion of citizen duty as an intervening variable, that is, returns not from compliance with the norm of voting per se, but from the voter's contribution to the collective social experience of democracy. The voter's contribution is not only a vote, which increases the popular base of government, but also an opinion, which affects the quality of the outcome.

---

*In the modern American context, it is probably safe to say that democracy typically means some combination of the subservience of the state to the popular will and the observance of certain civil liberties. It is with respect to the former that democracy gives meaning to elections. Since the continued observance of fundamental civil liberties is rarely raised as a general issue in elections, voting in order to guarantee freedom is subject to the same analysis applied above to Downs's long-run participation value.

It is important to note that these rewards from voting do not depend on the voter actually affecting the outcome of the election. It is sufficient that a vote be counted, that it be weighed equally with the votes of others, and that the votes collectively have some minimum influence on policy. It is impossible to be more precise about the degree of influence that elections are expected to bear in modern democracies. Certain conflicts among students of politics on the nature of democracy were noted earlier; it is not more likely that the lay public has reached a consensus. Thus the expectations that voters hold may range from a conceptualization of elections as a referendum on specific policy issues, to the opportunity for a retrospective pat-on-the-back or kick-in-the-pants for one's representative. In any case, the election itself acquires meaning through its actualization of some notion of democracy in the sense of public control or oversight of government. In other words, the election is meaningful only if the outcome of the election can be related to some impact on the output of the political system, even if indirectly through the selection of representatives. The specific meaning (policy content) of a given vote may be distinguished from the meaning of voting in general.

This conceptualization of the meaning of participation to the voter in terms of the actualization of democracy places the performance of the political system at the center of the explanation of turnout. Those who perceive the political system to be unresponsive to the registration of their preferences in elections have no rational basis for voting and will not do so. Those who operate according to naive assumptions about the benevolence and responsiveness of public officials and the general democratic nature of American politics will vote whenever they have any policy or candidate preferences. In between these categories are many more potential voters who discount their expected returns from voting according to the quality of the performance of the political system, and who may or may not vote. In the following section, the relationship between turnout and system performance is further developed and tested empirically.

TURNOUT AND POLITICAL SYSTEM PERFORMANCE

The foregoing may be summarized as follows: in the United States, the crucial legitimating ideology, intervening and defining the relationship between the citizen and the state, is democracy. Although there is no single theory of democracy to which the entire society subscribes, a common element in the various notions of democracy extant is some form of popular oversight of the state, of which the most important institutional expression is the system of elections. Thus the citizen is encouraged to participate in elections on the ground that one's voting facilitates, in one way or another, one's control over the course of social policy.

For the citizen, participation in elections is a marginal activity; one may or may not vote, depending upon one's estimate of the net benefits and opportunity costs of doing so. In this sense the vote represents an investment of certain resources—time and effort at a minimum—in the election. As a rational investor, the voter can be expected to base a turnout decision in large measure upon the quality of elections as investments. The relevant qualities of elections are those that are defined by the voter's expectations of democracy. Further, because the election of an American president is an event that occurs within and has its effects mediated by the larger political system, the scope of the voter's evaluation of personal investment naturally extends beyond elections per se to the effect of elections on the performance of the political system.

If turnout may be represented as a function of the perceived performance of the political system, it remains to specify the aspects of performance that influence voters' decisions. This task is complicated by the fact that individuals can be supposed to vary in their expectations of democracy; thus, no particular list of performance qualities would be both exhaustive and universally applicable. In the conclusion to this chapter, some general dimensions of democratic performance are proposed. In the meantime, it is possible to proceed with the empirical testing of the present argument on a limited basis.

Because much of the policymaking process and day-to-day operation of government is hidden from the typical citizen due to the sheer size and complexity of the institutional apparatus, technological barriers, secrecy, and inattention, voters may be expected to employ rather crude and generalized measures of political system performance. Recent surveys of the electorate record attitudes on a number of dimensions where widespread agreement could doubtless be obtained as to which positions are more democratic. For example, without being specific about the expectations of individuals, it is safe to say that the U.S. political system is more democratic when public officials care what people think than when they do not care, or when fewer public officials, more likely to feel that important decisions are influenced by elections, and are, as a group, more concerned about the outcome of the current election. All of this tends to confirm the primacy of performance evaluations.

A more direct indication of the association between such attitudes and voting is the comparison of attitudes among voters and nonvoters in the 1976 presidential election in Table 1.4. Again, two minor qualifications should be noted. First, the group of voters includes a number of respondents who simply lied about having voted. The SRC/CPS sample, for

TABLE 1.3: Citizen Duty, Turnout, and Voter Attitudes, 1976 (percent)

	Citizen Duty	No Citizen Duty
Turnout	83.0	32.1
People like me don't have any say about what the government does.	36.4 Agree	68.6 Agree
I don't think public officials care much what people like me think.	48.9 Agree	74.7 Agree
Do you think there are any important differences in what the Republicans and Democrats stand for?	56.2 Yes	39.0 Yes
Do you think that quite a few of the people running the government are crooked, not very many are, or do you think hardly any of them are crooked? (Modal Response)	44.7 Not Many	52.2 Quite a Few
Would you say the government is pretty much run by a few big interests looking out for themselves or that it is run for the benefit of all the people?	72.1 Few Big Interests	84.3 Few Big Interests
Over the years, how much attention do you feel the government pays to what the people think when it decides what to do—A good deal, some, or not much? (Modal Response)	59.4 Some	45.8 Not Much
And how much do you feel that having elections makes the government pay attention to what the people think—A good deal, some, or not much? (Modal Response)	54.9 A Good Deal	42.6 A Good Deal
Generally speaking, would you say that you personally care a good deal which party wins the presidential election this fall, or that you don't care very much which party wins?	63.2 A Good Deal	36.0 A Good Deal

Source: Data based upon Survey Research Center, Center for Political Studies of the Institute for Social Research, University of Michigan.

TABLE 1.4: Attitudes of Voters and Nonvoters, 1976 (percent)

	Voters	Nonvoters
People like me don't have any say about what the government does.	36.1 Agree	57.8 Agree
I don't think public officials care much what people like me think.	47.3 Agree	70.2 Agree
Do you think there are any important differences in what the Republicans and Democrats stand for?	56.8 Yes	41.1 Yes
Do you think that quite a few of the people running the government are crooked, not very many are, or do you think hardly any of them are crooked? (Modal Response)	43.3 Not Many	47.7 Quite a Few
Would you say the government is pretty much run by a few big interests looking out for themselves or that it is run for the benefit of all the people?	72.5 Few Big Interests	72.3 Few Big Interests
Over the years, how much attention do you feel the government pays to what the people think when it decides what to do—a good deal, some, or not much? (Modal Response)	58.3 Some	48.9 Some[a]
And how much do you feel that having elections makes the government pay attention to what the people think—a good deal, some, or not much? (Modal Response)	56.7 A Good Deal	43.2 A Good Deal
Generally speaking, would you say that you personally care a good deal which party wins the presidential election this fall, or that you don't care very much which party wins?	63.8 A Good Deal	41.8 A Good Deal
Sample Size	1,546–1,705[b]	572–648[b]

[a] Voters: 30.2 Not Much; Nonvoters: 42.0 Not Much.
[b] Sample size varies due to exclusion of inappropriate responses. Source: Data based upon Survey Research Center, Center for Political Studies of the Institute for Social Research, University of Michigan.

example, always overreports its compliance with the norm of voting. In 1976, 71.6 percent of their sample reported voting. Second, the group of nonvoters includes those regular voters whose reasons for not voting were specific to the 1976 election. (In tests that discriminate on the basis of turnout, it is assumed that costs of voting are randomly distributed with respect to each variable.) Still, the same trends are evidenced, supporting the argument that voting is a reflection of attitudes toward the electoral system.

It has been argued in the foregoing, and demonstrated empirically, that there exists an intimate connection between individuals' decisions whether or not to vote and their evaluations of their participation as meaningful. In particular, as elections come to be viewed as less effective instruments of public control over policy outputs—that is, as parties appear less distinct, or as the policymaking process seems to be captured by crooks or big interests while public opinion bears less weight—the rewards for participation decline in value, the sense of citizen duty is eroded, and members of the electorate are less inclined to bear the costs of participation. It remains only to show that recently declining turnout is correlated with a recent shift in public opinion toward more negative evaluations of system performance. Some typical trends are reported in Table 1.5.

TURNOUT AND SOCIAL POSITION

At this point it is appropriate to examine a hypothesis, which while not essential to the present concerns, is of considerable interest in the general explanation of turnout and which, if correct, lends a certain plausibility to the broader argument. It is indisputable that various groups in the society receive, for whatever reasons, different portions of the flow of benefits of membership in the society. It is reasonable to suppose that those groups that perceive themselves as disproportionately excluded from those benefits (or as bearing a disproportionate share of the costs) would be more sensitive to any gaps between performance and promise in the political system. It would follow that such groups generally will evidence more negative appraisals of system performance, will be less likely to have a sense of citizen duty, and will be less likely to vote.

The demographic classification of voters and nonvoters is the most characteristic approach to turnout. Milbrath explains:

> The greatest quantity of research on political participation has related that behavior to social-position variables. In part, this is because social-position and other demographic variables are so visible and so readily measured. They are included in nearly every study as a matter of custom and

TABLE 1.5: Trends in Voter Attitudes and Turnout in Presidential Elections, 1964-76 (percent)

How much of the time do you think you can trust the government in Washington to do what is right—just about always, most of the time, or only some of the time?

	1964	1968	1972	1976
Always	14	8	7	3
Most of the time	62	53	45	30
Only some of the time	22	37	45	62
Don't know/Not ascertained	2	2	3	4

Would you say the government is pretty much run by a few big interests looking out for themselves or that it is run for the benefit of all the people?

	1964	1968	1972	1976
For benefit of all	64	52	43	24
Few big interests	29	39	48	66
Other/Depends/Both	4	5	3	3
Don't know/Not ascertained	3	4	6	8

Do you think that quite a few of the people running the government are a little crooked, not very many people are, or hardly any of them are crooked at all?

	1964	1968	1972	1976
Hardly any	18	18	16	13
Not many	48	49	46	40
Quite a few	28	25	34	41
Don't know/Not ascertained	5	8	4	7

	1964	1968	1972	1976
Turnout	63	60	55	53

Source: Data based upon Survey Research Center, Center for Political Studies of the Institute for Social Research, University of Michigan.

convenience. A related reason is that social-position variables "stand for" many of the attitudinal and personality variables . . . which are so difficult to measure.[16]

This research has firmly established that the American voter is character-ized by higher income, more education, and a higher status occupation than the nonvoter. The voter is also more likely to be a professional, middle-aged, married, white, male, urban resident who is involved in organizations that take political positions.[17] Overall, it is safe to say that voters tend to be more successfully integrated into the American social system than nonvot-ers in the sense of having more advantages and stronger institutional ties to the center of society.

The observation of differential rates of political participation by various groups has given rise to the dilution thesis as an explanation of relatively low turnout in modern elections. The potential electorate has been expanded in this century by the enfranchisement of women, efforts to make voting rights for minorities a reality, and the 18-year-old vote. Each of these groups has traditionally shown less interest and lower levels of participation than older, white males. Thus the more highly motivated pre-1900 electorate has been systematically diluted by the inclusion of lesser-motivated citizens. The dilution thesis is immediately plausible, but it cannot meet the test of the most recent trends in turnout. Since 1960 turnout has declined despite increased participation by blacks and women in the wakes of the civil rights and women's movements.[18] The dilution argument breaks down because it is founded on nothing more than the continued observance of traditional relationships.

The demographic sorting of the electorate is interesting for its heuristic value, but it is an incomplete approach to turnout because it leaves unexamined the relationship between attributes and behavior. Thus it lends itself to inferences that certain groups possess a participatory capacity. A theoretical account of turnout must specify the intervening variables.

A stronger entry among demographic accounts cites the relationships among education, attitudes, and turnout, and has the form of a theoretical explanation:*

> The greater an individual's education, the more likely he is to attend to
> sources of political information and hence to know "what is going on." His
> view of political objects and events will be more specific and more highly
> differentiated. . . . Our data provide a fairly clear picture of the types of
> motivation to participate that distinguish the more highly educated people

*Angus T. Campbell, Phillip E. Converse, Warren E. Miller, and Donald E. Stokes, *The American Voter*, © 1960. This and all following quotes from Campbell et al. reprinted by permission of John Wiley & Sons, Inc., New York, New York.

and that hence may be presumed to intervene between education and higher turnout at the polls. We have indicated that interest and involvement in the outcome of the current election vary strongly as a function of education. We have assumed extensive interplay between these motivational correlates of education and the cognitive differences mentioned previously. The more meaning an individual can find in the flow of political events, the more likely it is that these events will maintain his interest. The person who makes little sense of politics will not be motivated to pay much attention to it. And, of course, the more interested the individual, the richer the cognitive background which he accumulates for subsequent political evaluation. . . . With more formal schooling an individual is more likely to feel that he has influence on political events. And he is more likely to feel a sense of civic responsibility about voting, however hopeless the cause and however small his vote against the total number cast.[19]

In other words, education facilitates the comprehension of politics and the perception of important differences between alternative positions. The latter in turn heightens involvement, defined operationally as caring about the outcome of the election and being interested in the campaign.[20] Also with education comes a greater sense of efficacy and responsibility, and the combination of these with involvement leads to voting.

It is important to note that this formulation of the turnout decision places the burden of nonparticipation on the individual. To be more precise, the burden is assigned to attributes of the individual. While the society's institutions of socialization and education may be blamed for failure to prepare the individual properly, the exclusive emphasis on education implies that all educated observers will reach the same conclusions about the value of elections. It is implicitly assumed that elections offer meaningful avenues of participation in meaningful decisions. The individual who is intellectually prepared to meet the task will develop "a characteristic degree of interest and involvement in political affairs, which varies widely among individuals but which exhibits a good deal of stability for the same person through successive election campaigns."[21] In sum, the relevant determinants of turnout are internal to the members of the electorate.

The argument from education to turnout is again incomplete. It implies that any sufficiently capable individual will find voting worthwhile; in other words, it specifies a particular alternative as the rational preference. In so doing, the argument ignores much of the context of the turnout decision. In particular, it ignores the sociocultural context of elections, the various costs associated with participation, and the structuring of participation by the political system. It assumes that elections are the institutional expression of democracy. Finally, the education argument fails the empirical test, at least insofar as formal education continues to impart political sophistication.

Despite the ever higher levels of educational achievement of the electorate, turnout has declined.[22]

The hypothesis offered at the beginning of this section is a more promising account of the relationships between demographics and turnout. The argument here is that groups that are more successfully integrated into the center of American society have more at stake in elections and are more likely to view the political system as trustworthy, competent, and responsive to them, and thus to find their participation in it meaningful. Alternatively, individuals who receive a greater portion of social benefits may discount the importance of any otherwise negative feedback on system performance. The data in tables 1.6 and 1.7 compare groups differentiated by two measures of success: education and income. Those on the high end of each measure also have higher turnout, stronger sense of citizen duty, and more positive political system performance evaluations in the aggregate. The data are consistent with the relationships hypothesized above, and additional corroboration is provided by the relatively greater participation of those groups, such as blacks and women, that are receiving increased attention from the political system.

CONCLUSION

The declining turnout in American presidential elections since 1960 can be explained by a dynamic model of the turnout decision that incorporates defining characteristics of the contexts of those elections. The model proposed in this chapter begins with the relative isolation of politics in American liberal culture, an element of context that leads to dropping the traditional assumption of the centrality of politics and raising in turn the consideration of opportunity costs for participation. For rational voters, turnout may be understood in the terms of traditional microeconomic analysis.

The vote is at once a consumption and an investment good. The voter realizes immediate personal benefits from participation in elections, but the positive valuation of those returns is derived from the expectations of future dividends generated by the (collective) outcome of the election. The benefits are purchased at the price of the costs of voting per se and the investment of resources in the determination of preference.

This formulation of the turnout decision is capable of subsuming most traditional accounts. Variations in registration requirements are reflected in the costs of voting. Citizen duty is a moral expression of the institutional function that transforms the activity it compels (informed voting) into collective goods (policies based on the wills of the people) for the society.

TABLE 1.6: Education, Citizen Duty, Turnout, and Voter Attitudes, 1976 (percent)

	No Academic Training beyond High School	At least some College
Citizen Duty	90.8	96.7
Turnout	64.5	85.0
People like me don't have any say about what the government does.	49.2 Agree	29.2 Agree
I don't think public officials care much what people like me think.	62.0 Agree	38.7 Agree
Do you think there are any important differences in what the Republicans and Democrats stand for?	48.2 Yes	60.4 Yes
Do you think that quite a few of the people running the government are crooked, not very many are, or do you think hardly any of them are crooked? (Modal Response)	48.9 Quite a Few	49.4 Not Very Many
Would you say the government is pretty much run by a few big interests looking out for themselves or that it is run for the benefit of all the people?	75.1 Few Big Interests	70.2 Few Big Interests
Over the years, how much attention do you feel the government pays to what the people think when it decides what to do—a good deal, some, or not such? (Modal Response)	51.2 Some[a]	63.6 Some[a]
And how much do you feel that having elections makes the government pay attention to what the people think—a good deal, some, or not much? (Modal Response)	51.2 A Good Deal[b]	56.2 A Good Deal[b]
Sample Size	1,472–1,750[c]	806–927[c]

[a] High School: 38.7 Not Much; College: 23.8 Not Much.
[b] High School: 12.2 Not Much; College: 7.6 Not Much.
[c] Sample size varies due to exclusion of inappropriate responses and respondents without postelection interviews.

Source: Data based upon Survey Research Center, Center for Political Studies of the Institute for Social Research, University of Michigan.

TABLE 1.7: Family Income, Citizen Duty, Turnout, and Voter Attitudes, 1976 (percent)

	Family Income	
	$0 – 5,999	$20,000 +
Citizen Duty	85.4	98.0
Turnout	57.0	86.5
People like me don't have any say about what the government does.	55.9 Agree	30.1 Agree
I don't think public officials care much what people like me think.	71.8 Agree	37.1 Agree
Do you think there are any important differences in what the Republicans and Democrats stand for?	53.3 Yes	56.8 Yes
Do you think that quite a few of the people running the government are crooked, not very many are, or do you think hardly any of them are crooked? (Modal Response)	47.3 Quite A Few	51.1 Not Many
Would you say the government is pretty much run by a few big interests looking out for themselves or that it is run for the benefit of all the people?	74.4 Few Big Interests	70.0 Few Big Interests
Over the years, how much attention do you feel the government pays to what the people think when it decides what to do—a good deal, some, or not much? (Modal Response)	46.1 Some[a]	64.6 Some[a]
And how much do you feel that having elections makes the government pay attention to what the people think—a good deal, some, or not much? (Modal Response)	50.1 A Good Deal[b]	60.0 A Good Deal[b]
Sample Size	485–560[c]	491–568[c]

[a] $0–5,999: 42.4 Not Much; $20,000+: 23.8 Not Much.
[b] $0–5,999: 14.0 Not Much; $20,000+: 7.1 Not Much.
[c] Sample size varies due to exclusion of inappropriate responses and those with no postelection interviews.

Source: Data based upon Survey Research Center, Center for Political Studies of the Institute for Social Research, University of Michigan.

Variations in the turnout proclivities of different groups are accounted for by variations in the perceived stakes (investment value) of elections for these groups.

It also follows that evaluations of the performance of the political system that tend to attenuate the essential function of elections will similarly decrease the incentive to vote. It is impossible to be precise about the nature of the performance that voters expect from the political system in order to give meaning to their participation.* For most Americans this performance clearly has something to do with democracy, and this gives a name to the relevant qualities. Beyond this, if it is the presumption of democracy that lends meaning to elections, then there is some direction to the search for defining characteristics.†

Given the broad contours of the present institutional arrangement, it would seem that at least three general qualities must characterize the American political system to some degree in order for it to qualify as democratic: responsiveness, competence, and trustworthiness.

Responsiveness: The central argument for support of and participation in political systems that partake of democratic legitimization is that the activities of the state are in some way derived from the wills of its citizens. Without responsiveness, elections are meaningless.

Competence: The political system must be at least minimally effective in implementing the public will, moving policy in a predictable direction, or else the registration of preferences in elections is merely symbolic.

Trustworthiness: The importance of trust in the political system increases in direct proportion to the gap between direct democracy and modern political institutions. As direct control of various aspects of policy shifts from individuals to complex representative institutions, and thence to executive agencies even further removed from public control, greater responsibility to secure the public interest accrues to the political system. Elections invest trust in public agents.

Trustworthiness is the most important of these three qualities, in part because it subsumes to some degree both responsiveness and competence, and in part because trust is necessary for the voluntary alienation of individual autonomy to the state, as well as for voluntary compliance and

---

*The problem is analogous to specifying the qualities that must characterize a religion in order to justify participation in its rituals by its adherents. But one would expect voluntary participation to cease at the point when the adherent determines that the god being worshipped is a false one.

†The concern here is not with developing a theory of democracy, but rather with identifying underpinnings of democratic legitimization in the American political system. It is presumed that the qualities described are sufficiently broadly defined to be capable of achieving popular consensus, yet sufficiently meaningful to permit the generation of interesting hypotheses.

support. Trust, broadly defined, seems to be at the heart of the indicators of system performance evaluation considered above. In addition, many of the most significant political events since 1960 have had important implications for the bonds of trust between the people and their government, quite apart from their implications for the direction of public policy. It is clear that these events have contributed to an erosion of trust in the political system that has in turn contributed to declining turnout, among other consequences. In addition to the exposure of contradictions within the political system through events such as Watergate, there are more subtle but perhaps more significant implications arising from the impact of technology on normal politics, which are treated in Chapter 4.

The matters of trust, responsiveness, and competence concern voters not only in their evaluations of participation in elections, but also in the candidate preference decision as well. The ensuing chapters will argue that basing the preference decision on estimates of the trustworthiness of the candidates is both a rational response to the institutional context of American presidential elections and a more characteristic response of American voters than has been recognized heretofore by voting analysts. The consequences of this perspective for modern notions of democracy are considered in the concluding chapter.

NOTES

1. The most important work in the modern revision of democratic theory is Joseph A. Schumpeter, *Capitalism, Socialism, and Democracy* (New York: Harper & Row, 1950), esp. pp. 232–302. This and related works are reviewed in the following chapter.

2. Bernard R. Berelson, Paul F. Lazarsfeld, and William N. McPhee, *Voting* (Chicago: University of Chicago Press, 1954), p. 314.

3. For a much more elaborate analysis of participatory and nonparticipatory democratic theories, see Carol Pateman, *Participation and Democratic Theory* (Cambridge: Cambridge University Press, 1970), esp. pp. 1–44.

4. These assumptions are treated in more detail at the beginning of Chapter 4. On the rationality assumption in particular, see also the discussion in Anthony Downs, *An Economic Theory of Democracy* (New York: Harper & Row, 1957), pp. 4–11.

5. An excellent and more formal treatment of the use of such assumptions in explaining behavior is Norman Frohlich and Joe A. Oppenheimer, *Modern Political Economy* (Englewood Cliffs, N.J.: Prentice-Hall, 1978), esp. Chapter 1.

6. Much to the chagrin of social reformers, liberal individualism repeatedly emerges as a cornerstone of American thought. Cf., for example, Robert E. Lane, "The Fear of Equality," *American Political Science Reivew* 53 (March 1959): 35–51. An excellent review of American thought with emphasis on the dominance of the peculiarly American notion of liberalism is contained in Louis Hartz, *The Liberal Tradition in America* (New York: Harcourt, Brace, and World, 1955). Hartz traces the historical development of "Americanism" as an "irrational liberalism" with roots in the United States' uniquely nonfeudal past. His analysis not only stresses the peculiar isolation of politics from other spheres of activity in our culture, but also calls attention to the broader issue of contextual determinants of political behavior.

7. These observations on American culture are common themes in any comprehensive examination of the subject, for example, Kenneth M. Dolbeare and Patricia Dolbeare, *American Ideologies: The Competing Political Beliefs of the 1970's* (Chicago: Rand McNally, 1976), pp. 38–55.

8. This analysis is corroborated by Milbrath:

> . . . the smooth meshing of political roles (i.e., various levels of participation) likely is enhanced if *politics play only a limited role* in the overall functioning of society. Limited constitutional democracies have evolved painfully over centuries of political learning; by consensus they place boundaries on politics and rulers. In constitutional democracies it is deemed proper that political considerations should not determine a person's opportunities for an education, a job, advancement on the job, a place to live, goods to enjoy, the friends one makes, the thoughts one utters, the religion one follows, one's chance for justice, and so forth. People have found that life is happier if politics are kept out of the above areas.

Lester W. Milbrath and M. L. Goel, *Political Participation* (Chicago: Rand McNally, 1977), pp. 154–55. The issue of the centrality of politics is raised again in the concluding chapter of this work.

9. There are other obvious and important distinctions between economic and political goods. For example, political goods are typically collective goods, where the same good—say, national defense—is shared by a group, up to the whole society. A more precise classification of collective goods is in Frohlich and Oppenheimer, *Modern Political Economy*, pp. 32–36. Another important distinction is that political activity, especially voting, is often directed toward goals that will be realized only in the future, giving political goods the character of investments rather than purchases. Also, the number of supplies and variety of goods available simultaneously are often limited in the political sphere. All of these distinctions are incorporated in the further development of the model in Chapter 4.

10. Ferejohn and Fiorina argue that rational voters are not necessarily expected value maximizers, and that alternative assumptions may yield more reasonable criteria for rational voting. Their argument is not convincing, however, because the alternative they suggest—the "minimax regret" criterion—clearly is not applied by individuals in most other aspects of their lives. John A. Ferejohn and Morris P. Fiorina, "The Paradox of Not Voting: A Decision Theoretic Analysis," *American Political Science Review* 68 (June 1974): 525–36.

11. Angus T. Campbell, Philip E. Converse, Warren E. Miller, and Donald E. Stokes, *The American Voter* (New York: John Wiley & Sons, 1960), pp. 105–6.

12. Robert D. Hess and Judith V. Torney, *The Development of Political Attitudes in Children* (Chicago: Aldine Publishing, 1967), p. 215.

13. Downs, *An Economic Theory of Democracy*, p. 270.

14. William H. Riker and Peter C. Ordeshook, "A Theory of the Calculus of Voting," *American Political Science Review* 62 (March 1968): 25–42.

15. Ibid., p. 28.

16. Milbrath and Goel, *Political Participation*, p. 86.

17. The studies supporting these findings are too numerous to mention. An excellent summary profuse with references is ibid., pp. 86–122.

18. Analyzing data through the 1972 election, Gerald Pomper summarizes:

> While Americans still express a duty to vote, even this ritualistic action is performed less frequently. Turnout has increased recently only in social groups that have been restricted from the ballot in the past, such as blacks and women. Among the general population, particularly youth, the felt duty to participate has been displaced by skepticism and alienation.

Gerald M. Pomper, *Voter's Choice: Varieties of American Electoral Behavior* (New York:

Dodd, Mead, 1975), p. 212. Pomper's conclusion is based on elaborate analysis of sex and voting (pp. 69–76), race and voting (pp. 120–28), and new voters (pp. 97–105). Census bureau data for the 1976 election indicate that the gap in participation rates between male and female declined from 2.1 percent in 1972 to 0.8 percent in 1976; the gap between blacks and whites closed slightly from 12.4 percent to 12.2 percent; and the participation rate of the youngest group of voters (ages 18–21 years) declined 10.3 percent over the same period. *Current Population Reports*, U.S. Bureau of the Census, Series P-20, No. 307 (April 1977), p. 23.

19. Campbell et al., *The American Voter*, pp. 476–79.

20. Ibid., pp. 102–3.

21. Ibid., p. 102.

22. It is further argued that increasing education has not had the anticipated effects on the voters' sophistication in dealing with electoral preferences in Samuel Popkin, John W. Gorman, Charles Phillips, and Jeffrey A. Smith, "Comment: What Have You Done for Me Lately?: Toward an Investment Theory of Voting," *American Political Science Review* 70 (September 1976): 779–805.

2

THE VOTER AS SPECTATOR: THE NAIVE MODEL OF THE DEMOCRATIC CITIZEN AND THE SOCIAL-PSYCHOLOGICAL MOOD

*T*he close of World War II marked a significant reorientation in the academic study of politics. There was, first, a serious reexamination of the political organization of society, spurred in large measure by the recent histories of the German and Russian states. The behavioral revolution within the discipline saw the attention of political scientists shift from the analysis of political institutions to the analysis of political attitudes and activities. There also was a technological revolution of sorts, as technologies and resources that had been devoted to the war effort became available at its conclusion for application to the new questions that political scientists were asking.

Among the many products of this era that had profound impacts on the larger society, two are of particular relevance for this work. The first is the reformulation of the meaning of one of the animating symbols of the American consciousness: democracy. In effect, the popular commitment to a vaguely understood democracy was reconciled with the reality of American politics by an exercise that simply laid classical notions of democracy to rest—along with their accompanying ideals—and redefined democracy in terms of modern political institutions. A key element in this process was the specification of the expectations that the classical theory held for members of democratic societies. Comparison of these expectations with the actual behavior of modern democratic citizens established the contemporary irrelevance of the classical theory and opened the way for a new under-standing of democracy. The standards of good democratic citizenship purportedly derived from classic theory and the more sophisticated formu-lations employed in many voting studies are treated here in the section dealing with the naive model of the democratic citizen.

The extensive application of survey technology to national samples of eligible voters, and the computer processing of the data collected, also began in earnest during the postwar period. The fruits of that research are captured here in the social-psychological model of the voter. The image of the citizen that emerged from these studies is a dismal one; far from being rational and independent, the citizen appeared as distinctly nonrational and dependent. The limited capacity for political autonomy evidenced by members of the electorate seemed to relegate them to the role of specta-tors, cheering on favorites in the game of politics. Social science thus entered a symbiotic relationship with contemporary political philosophy; the empirical analysis of voting behavior lent scientific legitimacy to the inter-ment of the classical ideal, while the revision of democratic theory provided a ready framework for the interpretation of the psephologists' findings.

The interaction of these developments on apparently separate intellec-tual fronts is essential to any exegesis of the pessimistic conclusions about democratic citizens that characterize contemporary political thought. The influence of that interaction for both the scientific understanding of voting behavior and the theoretical role of the modern citizen is traced in this chapter.

THE NAIVE MODEL OF THE DEMOCRATIC CITIZEN

The reformulation of democratic theory, with a limited empirical base, antedated and anticipated the evidence of survey research of voters. To some extent, this correspondence may be understood as a combination of coincidence and the insight of the modern philosophers into the behavior of their fellow citizens. More significantly, however, the findings of voting analysts corroborated the assertion that citizens were not fit for direct participation and political autonomy because both were founded on the failure of their subjects to measure up to arbitrary and inappropriate standards of fitness.

The most significant aspect of the revisionist arguments for voting analysis is the identification of rational voter behavior with the naive model of the democratic citizen. This is an umbrella term for the efforts of various authors to articulate the demands that classical democratic theory makes of democratic citizens. In general, the standards of the naive model of the democratic citizen are treated as expectations or minimum conditions for the success of democracy rather than as ideals or ethical imperatives. Similarly, they are applied to American voters as if one should expect them to model themselves after the ancient Athenians, that is, without regard to the implications for rational behavior of the context within which it occurs. The failure of voters to exhibit rational behavior so defined forced analysts to turn to nonrational explanations of the electorate's attitudes and actions.

The most prominent statement of the naive model of the democratic citizen is contained in Joseph Schumpeter's *Capitalism, Socialism, and Democracy,* first published in 1942.[1] Actually, the relevant discussion is tangential to Schumpeter's larger concern with the confrontation of socialism and capitalism; not surprisingly, the subject of democracy occupies a central role in his analysis. Schumpeter argues that while modern democracy is a bourgeois ideology that is directly linked historically and in practice with capitalist institutions, the successful operation of democracy depends not on the presence of those capitalist institutions but rather upon certain social preconditions.[2] The implication is that democracy can survive under socialism if the preconditions for its operation are maintained.

Schumpeter's argument turns on his redefinition of democracy in a reformulated democratic theory. This reformulation in turn begins with a demonstration of the deficiencies of "the classical doctrine of democracy."[3] In part, the classical doctrine fails because of:*

> . . . the practical necessity of attributing to the will of the *individual* an independence and a rational quality that are altogether unrealistic. If we are to argue that the will of the citizens *per se* is a political factor entitled to respect, it must first exist. That is to say, it must be something more than an indeterminate bundle of vague impulses loosely playing about given slogans and mistaken impressions. Everyone would have to know definitely what he wants to stand for. This definite will would have to be implemented by the ability to observe and interpret correctly the facts that are directly accessible to everyone and to sift critically the information about the facts that are not. Finally, from that definite will and from these ascertained facts a clear and *prompt* conclusion as to particular issues would have to be derived according to the rules of logical inference—with so high a degree of general efficiency moreover that one man's opinion could be held, without glaring absurdity, to be roughly as

---

good as every other man's. And all this the model citizen would have to perform for himself and independently of pressure groups and propaganda.[4]

In general, Schumpeter finds these demands to exceed the capacities of the typical citizen. In fact, the actual structure of the political system is a response to the fact that "the electoral mass is incapable of action other than a stampede."[5]

Schumpeter's pessimistic conclusions about voters do not extend to democracy in general, however. Instead, he reverses the priorities of the classical doctrine to emphasize democratic method, that is, "that institutional arrangement for arriving at political decisions in which individuals acquire the power to decide by means of a competitive struggle for the people's vote."[6] The success of democracy in this sense requires "no more than that the democratic process reproduce itself steadily without creating situations that enforce resort to non-democratic methods and that it cope with current problems in a way which all interests that count politically find acceptable in the long run."[7] This stability is insured by a set of social conditions that, it is argued, may exist as readily under socialism as under capitalism.

The details of Schumpeter's reformulation are, for the present purpose, secondary to his notions of democratic citizenship. It is important to note, however, that in his necessary conditions he lays down the foundations for what has been called "the elitist theory of democracy."[8] Thus he argues that sufficient quality in public officials requires that they be recruited from a social stratum of those successful in private affairs; that "the range of political decision should not be extended too far," especially not into the realm of technological issues where specialists must reign; and that the administration—along with, to a considerable extent, the determination—of public policy must reside in a powerful and independent, professional bureaucracy, similarly recruited from an "official class."[9] The role of the citizen is spelled out under the heading of "Democratic Self-control":

> The voters outside of parliament must respect the division of labor between themselves and the politicians they elect. They must not withdraw confidence too easily between elections and they must understand that, once they have elected an individual, political action is his business and not theirs. This means that they must refrain from instructing him about what he is to do.[10]

Democratic citizens thus exercise their wills only at election times, otherwise restricting themselves to the role of spectators.

Some years later Bernard Berelson gave an even more explicit account of the implications of classical democratic theory for voting behavior.[11] In concluding remarks to the milestone work *Voting*, Berelson outlines the expectations for citizens raised by democratic theory, contrasting these expectations with the picture of the actual citizen that emerges from his own research.[12] Ultimately he hopes that "empirical research can help to clarify the standards and correct the empirical presuppositions of normative theory."[13]

There are, according to Berelson, expectations of democratic citizens in four broad categories of behavior related to voting:

(1) *Interest, discussion, motivation:* The democratic citizen is expected to be interested and to participate in political affairs. . . .

(2) *Knowledge:* The democratic citizen is expected to be well informed about political affairs. He is supposed to know what the issues are, what their history is, what the relevant facts are, what alternatives are proposed, what the party stands for, what the likely consequences are. . . .

(3) *Principle:* The democratic citizen is supposed to cast his vote on the basis of principle—not fortuitously or frivolously or impulsively or habitually, but with reference to standards not only of his own interest but of the common good as well. . . .

(4) *Rationality:* The democratic citizen is expected to exercise rational judgment in coming to his voting decision. He is expected to have arrived at his principles by reason and to have considered rationally the implications and alleged consequences of the alternative proposals of the contending parties.[14]

Again, in Berelson's as in Schumpeter's work, the failure of American voters to measure up to the classical standards necessitates a reorientation of theorists toward a new understanding of democracy:

Individual voters today seem unable to satisfy the requirements for a democratic system of government outlined by political theorists. But the *system of democracy* does meet certain requirements for a going political organization. . . . This suggests that where the classic theory is defective is in its concentration on the *individual citizen.* What are undervalued are certain collective properties that reside in the electorate as a whole and in the political and social system in which it functions.[15]

Among the collective properties that Berelson identifies is a heterogeneous electorate characterized by a distribution of qualities ranging from conformance with the naive model of the democratic citizen to low interest and "the moderate indifference that facilitates compromise."[16] The stability and flexibility of the political system are enhanced by chronic nonparticipants exhibiting the latter qualities.

Two characteristics of these arguments ought to be emphasized. First, the information and position requirements contained in the naive model are formulated in terms of more-or-less specific policies. This is consistent with the direct, personal responsibility of citizens for deciding policy questions in classical democratic theory. It is not clear that the same requirement ought to apply where this responsibility lies with representatives or bureaucratic institutions and not with the people themselves. Nevertheless, voting analysts generally employ standards of voter rationality defined exclusively in terms of policy issues.

The second characteristic worthy of note is the fundamental conservatism of these reformulations. The quality of citizen participation in politics is taken as a parameter in the political system. The authors' functionalist approach to theoretical questions leads them to redefine democracy in terms of existing institutions and to focus on the conditions for system stability. Thus the extent to which the behavior of voters is shaped by those same institutions does not arise as a significant concern. Unfortunately, the influence of political institutions on voting behavior has remained in the background for most analysts.

Berelson's representation of the model democratic citizen is the most elaborate to be found in the major voting studies. In general, the authors of subsequent works have resisted the systematic confrontation between empirical findings and normative theory, restricting themselves to an occasional reference to theoretical implications.[17]

Similarly, the impact of the naive model of the democratic citizen on subsequent voting studies has been subtle and indirect. It appears most prominently in the form of the various expectations that researchers hold for rational voters, which frequently are embodied in turn in methodological devices such as the index of ideological constraint considered below.

THE SOCIAL-PSYCHOLOGICAL MODEL

The Sociological Approach of the Columbia School

The quantitative analysis of voting behavior is a relatively modern phenomenon that only became feasible with the simultaneous development of modern survey methods, sophisticated scaling techniques, and electronic data-processing hardware and software.[18] Previous efforts in this area inevitably displayed methodological limitations that relegated them to the status of exploratory studies. A major portion of this early research combined official vote records with census data to examine the ecological correlates of voting trends.[19] Although these pioneering efforts were necessarily limited in scope and tentative, they provided the direction for subsequent analysis employing more sophisticated methodology.

Ecological analyses identified a set of consistent relationships between certain demographic characteristics and voting patterns, and research along these lines has continued to produce evidence of the party preferences and turnout inclinations of various groups. While this body of data only records empirical correspondence and does not constitute an explanation of voting, it provided the historical starting point for attempts at explanation. It is not surprising, then, that the initial research into individual voting behavior engaged in the sociological analysis of voting.

The first milestone in the microlevel analysis of voting behavior was the 1944 publication of *The People's Choice* by an interdisciplinary group from Columbia University under the direction of Paul Lazarsfeld.[20] The context of the research was the 1940 presidential election in Erie County, Ohio.

The Columbia approach may be designated sociological because of the predominant focus upon group membership and group dynamics as determinants of voting behavior. In *The People's Choice*, particular emphasis is placed on the roles of religion, socioeconomic status, and urban or rural residence as independent variables predicting voting decisions. When these are combined in an index of political predisposition, the relationship with vote is sufficiently strong to prompt the authors to remark that "social characteristics determine political preference."[21]

Political attitudes were treated as intervening variables in the study, that is, the authors argued that membership in groups determined the content of attitudes toward parties, issues, and candidates. Two important findings supported the causal priority of social variables. One was the identification of a two-step flow of communication. Political information passed from the media to the majority of the community's electorate indirectly through more politically involved opinion leaders, who served as catalysts for the homogenization of attitudes within groups. Thus personal contact and interaction proved to be powerful events in the campaign period. Perhaps more important was the analysis of those individuals whose voting intentions changed during the course of the campaign. The study showed that changers constituted a very small proportion of the electorate and that they generally changed in a direction that was consistent with the members of groups with which they were affiliated. The latter finding was part of a broader analysis of cross-pressured individuals, that is, those with politically conflicting affiliations. As often as not, such conflict was resolved simply by withdrawing from participation in the election.

The findings in the Erie County study were extended and amplified in

Voting, an analysis of the 1948 presidential campaign in Elmira, New York.[22] *Voting* is more comprehensive in several respects: a wider range of data was collected through repeated interviews in a panel study, the roles of different groups were considered (such as labor unions and political parties), and the analysis was more explicitly political. But the orientation of the study was similar, and the thrust of its findings was a corroboration of the conclusions of the earlier work. For example, the analysis confirmed that the formal political activities of labor unions and parties were less important than individual interaction in shaping attitudes. Since interpersonal association occurs most frequently within broad class and ethnic lines, the political allegiances of and cleavages between groups are rather stable.

The conclusions of the Columbia studies were shaped, inevitably, by the expectations of the researchers. As virtual pioneers in the analysis of individual voting behavior, the authors initially had little in the way of direct evidence to belie the popular wisdom. However, Lazarsfeld had worked with econometric models of consumer preference that projected both rationality and high levels of information on economic decisions; he may well have presumed that these qualities would (or should) characterize vote decisions as well. Berelson, who had a larger hand in the Elmira study, attributes his expectations to his reading of classical democratic theory. Whatever the sources, these a priori standards of rational voter behavior intrude upon the analysis throughout. The voters consistently fail to meet the expectations of the researchers, and the researchers fail to examine the rational elements of the observed behavior of the voters.

The image of American voters in these works is sharply at odds with the popular ideal. These voters do not determine the shape of their political universe; instead, they react rather passively to events and decisions made outside of their experience. Rather than carefully evaluating and weighing issues, these voters actually may delude themselves as to the positions of the candidates. Rather than seeking more information when faced with a difficult choice, they may withdraw from political activity. They vote the way their friends and associates do. In general, they show greater concern for the short-run social consequences of their political positions than for the longer-run policy implications.

The Columbia researchers do not hide their disappointment with their subjects. In *The People's Choice*, in the context of a discussion of "doubters," they offer this analysis:

> . . . there was a small number of conversion cases—very small—who were greatly interested in the election, who felt that there was something important to be said for each side, who tried more or less conscientiously to resolve their doubts one way or the other during the campaign. They,

and only they, conformed to the standard stereotype of the dispassionate, rational democratic voter.

For the most part, such persons had "weak" predispositions, i.e., they tended to fall at or near the center of the [index of political predispositions] score. In other words, their social position was such that they could "afford" conversion through thought. . . .

The real doubters—the open-minded voters who make a sincere attempt to weigh the issues and the candidates dispassionately for the good of the country as a whole—exist mainly in deferential campaign propaganda, in textbooks on civics, in the movies, and in the minds of some political idealists. In real life, they are few indeed.[23]

The implications of their findings are amplified in the concluding pages of *Voting*:

Perhaps the main impact of realistic research on contemporary politics has been to temper some of the requirements set by our traditional normative theory for the typical citizen. . . .

The ordinary voter, bewildered by the complexity of modern political problems, unable to determine clearly what the consequences are of alternative lines of action, remote from the arena, and incapable of bringing information to bear on principle, votes the way the trusted people around him are voting. . . .

. . . the usual analogy between the voting "decision" and the more or less carefully calculated decisions of consumers . . . may be quite incorrect. For many voters political preferences may better be considered analogous to cultural tastes. . . . Both have their origin in ethnic, sectional, class, and family traditions. . . . Both seem to be matters of sentiment and disposition rather than "reasoned preferences" . . . they are relatively invulnerable to direct argumentation and vulnerable to indirect social influences. Both are characterized more by faith than by conviction and by wishful expectation rather than careful prediction of consequences.[24]

Contributions of the Survey Research Center

The Truman-Dewey contest was being evaluated from another quarter as well. The Survey Research Center (SRC), a subsidiary of the Institute for Social Research of the University of Michigan, undertook the first national study of the presidential vote using probability sampling in 1948.[25] The SRC survey, involving pre- and postelection interviews of a large sample of eligible voters, has been conducted for every national election since that time, expanding in scope with each successive administration. A great many articles, books, and research papers have resulted from the study of the responses to these surveys. By 1960 the SRC was firmly established at the leading edge of voting research.

No single model or theory of voting behavior can be attributed to the Michigan researchers. In the first place, they have never claimed a particular theoretical position, although they have made frequent statements of a theoretical nature. Further, the Michigan school incorporates the work of a number of researchers with different personal research interests, produced over the course of more than two decades. Thus any attempt to ascribe a particular theory to this diverse literature is bound to be frustrated by contradictions from one course or another and to do injustice to the richness of their collective output. Nevertheless, there are certain elements that can be identified, justifiably, as constituting cornerstones of the SRC approach.[26]

Although the SRC's research began without any clearly specified model of voting behavior, there was a commitment to a research strategy. Specifically, the SRC researchers set out to explore the role of psychological variables in voting:

> In unraveling the causal threads leading to the vote we begin with the immediate psychological influences on the voting act. By casting a vote the individual acts toward a political world whose objects he perceives and evaluates in some fashion.[27]

The orientation of the SRC analysts thus involves a deliberate shift in emphasis away from the sociological approach of earlier studies to what are believed to be more proximate causal forces in voting than simple social characteristics.

Three categories of political objects have commanded the attention of Michigan researchers with great consistency from the outset: the major political parties, the major party candidates, and the issues. Over the course of their experience, the SRC authors have put forward a number of distinct approaches to elections, but each has reflected this tripartite division of voter concerns. Thus, in *The Voter Decides*, voter orientations toward parties, issues, and candidates were treated as motivational factors influencing both the individual's decision to vote and candidate preference in proportion to the strength and partisan consistency of these orientations.[28] Two subsequent models—the six-factor model and the normal vote—were products of initial observation and further thought about the relationships between such attitudes.

The six-factor model employs multiple regression techniques to generate various measures of the relative importance of components of vote decisions.[29] The six factors are attitude scale scores reflecting comments about the two major party candidates, general performance of the parties, group benefits, and foreign and domestic issues. The combination of these scores in a linear regression model, with vote choice as the dependent variable, produces a set of coefficients that may be interpreted as the weight of each factor in the outcome of the election. Evidence from the application of this model has provided support for many of the SRC's conclusions about voters.

The consistency with which respondents to the SRC survey vote according to their party identification led directly to the concept of the normal vote.[30] According to this formulation, the total vote in an election may be split analytically into two components: first, the normal vote division to be expected as a consequence of long-term partisan forces (party identification), and second, the deviation from that norm that occurs as a function of the immediate circumstances of the specific election, that is, candidates and issues. This view is further supported by data that indicate that responsiveness to short-term forces varies inversely with strength of party identification. Normal vote analysis is most frequently employed to measure the importance of a particular issue in an election. The long-term component indicates the extent to which attitudes on the issue correspond to party identification; the short-term component is a measure of the proportion of the electorate who voted according to issue position rather than party identification.

These models represent the most explicit formulations of the relationships between the principal objects of politics that the Michigan researchers have advocated. Of course, the considerable body of literature that has emanated from the principle authors over the years contains many statements about particular relationships that are not captured in these models. Given this diversity, the most practical approach to the SRC work is to examine the character and role of each of the principle objects.

Political Parties

The major political parties have always loomed large in the SRC's analysis of voters and elections. The central position of the parties is based largely on three sets of empirical observations and a crucial set of assumptions about the relationship between voters and parties. First, it is clear that parties are highly salient for voters. In the 1952 survey, for example, 74 percent of the respondents indicated that they generally thought of themselves as Democrats or Republicans, and an additional 17 percent indicated that they were closer to one of the major parties.[31] Furthermore, this distribution of party identification also evidenced a great deal of stability over time, even in the face of the intense political activity of election campaigns.[32] Finally, party identification seemed to have implications for voting behavior in its relatively high degree of association with consistent (party) voting over elections, straight ticket voting, and vote choice for president.

The impact of these empirical observations was bolstered by certain assumptions, made at a very early stage of the SRC work, about the role of parties. Lazarsfeld's pioneering work had analyzed voting behavior in terms of the social-psychological dynamics of groups. The Michigan researchers followed his lead, as well as their own interests, in characterizing parties as groups:

> We propose to consider the parties as social groups. . . . The present analysis of party identification is based on the assumption that the two parties serve as standard-setting groups for a significant proportion of the people of this country. In other words, it is assumed that many people associate themselves psychologically with one or the other of the parties, and that this identification has predictable relationships with their perceptions, evaluations, and actions. . . . We would expect high party identification to be associated with conformity to perceived party standards and support of perceived party goals.[33]

For the SRC, party identification represents a long-term psychological commitment based on an affective attachment to a particular group, the roots of which lie largely beyond the influence of the electoral process. Affiliation with a party is seen as a consequence of political socialization:

> It is apparent . . . that an orientation toward political affairs typically begins before the individual attains voting age and that this orientation strongly reflects his immediate social milieu, in particular his family.[34]

This view is supported by evidence from the surveys that indicates a high degree of correspondence between the party affiliations of children and their parents, a relationship much like that observed in the matter of religious affiliations.

The major significance for voting behavior of party identification is its psychological effect on voter attitudes. The "group conformance character of this postulated force on the voter" is a consequence of "the importance of the parties as points of psychological anchoring."[35] In effect, party identification is conceived to have causal priority over short-term political attitudes toward other political entities:

> Apparently party has a profound influence across the full range of political objects to which the individual voter responds. The strength of relationship between party identification and the dimensions of partisan attitude suggests that responses to each element of national politics are deeply affected by the individual's enduring party attachments. . . .
>
> If party identification deeply influences the partisan character of a field of psychological forces, it also will have marked effects on the internal

consistency of the field. Our conception of the role of partisan loyalties leads us to expect this result. Identification with a party raises a perceptual screen through which the individual tends to see what is favorable to his partisan orientation. The stronger the party bond, the more exaggerated the process of selection and perceptual distortion will be.[36]

The central role of the major parties is affirmed in a summary comment in *The American Voter*:

Evidently no single datum can tell us more about the attitude and behavior of the individual as presidential elector than his location on a dimension of psychological identification extending between the two great parties.[37]

Issues

When the SRC undertook the evaluation of the electorate's involvement with issues, they brought to the task certain a priori standards of what might be called issue rationality. In part, these standards derived from their reading of democratic theory and the feeling that "classical assumptions about voting behavior have attributed overweening weight to the issue factor. . . ."[38] Thus, the SRC researchers employed their own version of the naive model of the democratic citizen, which became quite sophisticated and detailed (see below). Their research on the issue involvement of voters lends support to the advocates of elitist notions of democracy who argue that voters are incapable of sophisticated policy determination through elections. For example, after the 1968 election they concluded that "pushing beyond the expression of narrow and superficial attitudes in the mass public to the cognitive texture which underlies the attitudes is a rather disillusioning experience."[39]

The SRC's examination of the role of issues in elections began by laying out the conditions for an issue-oriented citizen. In general, such a citizen is one for whom questions of governmental policy are of paramount importance:

He will not "vote for the man" nor will he "vote his party" except as the man or party represents governmental policies which he himself wishes to see enacted or protected.[40]

In order to test for issue orientation, three criteria were specified as conditions to be fulfilled if an issue is to bear upon a person's decision:

(1) The issue must be cognized in some form.
(2) It must arouse some minimal intensity of feeling.

(3) It must be accompanied by some perception that one party represents the person's own position better than do the other parties.[41]

These criteria are simple, reasonable, and, in fact, pose quite minimal barriers to the classification of individuals as issue-oriented voters. That very few voters ultimately did qualify should not be attributed to the rigorousness of the standards in their initial formulation, nor to any predilection on the part of SRC researchers to demean the quality of the electorate. Rather, the disillusionment of these researchers should be attributed to the subsequent application of a quite different set of standards to voter attitudes, standards that demand more of the voter but that have no necessary connection to issue concern.

These more stringent standards are reflected in the SRC's misgivings about the quality of the public's response to issues, which fall broadly into two categories encompassing the content and the structure of attitudes related to issues. With regard to content, there was observed a definite lack of richness in voters' articulations of their concern with policy. For example, Campbell, writing about "the relative insignificance of policy issues in the minds of the voters" in the 1952 election, observed that:

> There were no great questions of policy which the public saw as dividing the two parties. Instead the voters were thinking about "the mess in Washington," the stalemate in Korea, and General Eisenhower's heroic image.[42]

It is clear from the context of this comment, and the general discussion in *The American Voter* and other sources, that issues are to be confined to particular pieces of pending or past legislation or to concerns that are capable of being expressed in terms of particular policies. Thus voters who express their political concerns in terms of the expected responsiveness of candidates or parties to the interests of particular groups are criticized because:

> ... there is little comprehension of "long-range plans for social better-ment" or of basic philosophies rooted in postures toward change or abstract conceptions of social and economic structure of causation. The party or candidate is simply endorsed as being "for" a group with which the subject is identified or as being above the selfish demands of groups within the population. Exactly *how* the candidate or party might see fit to implement or avoid group interests is a moot point, left unrelated to broader ideological concerns. But the party or candidate is "located" in some affective relationship toward a group or groups, and the individual metes out trust on this basis.[43]

Similarly, voters who respond to the promises of parties or candidates "to bring about a certain product or state, such as more jobs, peace, or higher farm prices" are behaving inappropriately:

> The tendency to focus upon these pledges as the issue core of politics seems to token narrow time perspectives, concrete modes of thought, and a tremendously oversimplified view of causality in social, economic, and political process.[44]

Finally, many voters who otherwise exhibit issue content in their attitudes are unable to perceive any advantage in their issue area that might accrue from the election of one or the other party's candidate:

> It cannot be denied that actual ambiguities in the positions of the parties must have some effect on views of party differentiation. But we feel that a large measure of the observed failure to perceive party differences by people holding opinions on an issue can be traced to the same personal limitations that keep many others from recognizing the issue at all. . . .
>
> Although some small portion of the electorate is continually sensitive to party stands even on transient and discrete policy issues, it may take controversy of such breadth, depth and duration [as the more than 20-year debate on the New Deal] to create a sense of party policy differences across as much as one-third or one-half of the adult population.[45]

Beyond these concerns about the content of the electorate's issue attitudes, doubts were expressed about the extent to which voters understand politics, based on evidence about the structure of issue attitudes. The SRC researchers brought to their examination of attitude structure a set of expectations that constitute a substantial extension of the naive model of the democratic citizen over previous formulations. Simply stated, the expectation was that the educated, attentive, and informed citizen eventually would come to understand political conflict as occurring along a single dimension defined by two opposed value clusters:

> For the truly involved citizen, the development of political sophistication means the absorption of contextual information that makes clear to him the connections of the policy area of his initial interest with policy differences in other areas; and that these broader configurations of policy positions are describable quite economically in the basic abstractions of ideology. . . .
>
> We define a *belief system* as a configuration of ideas and attitudes in which the elements are bound together by some form of constraint or functional interdependence. . . .
>
> One judgmental dimension or "yardstick" that has been highly serviceable for simplifying and organizing events in most Western politics

for the past century has been the liberal-conservative continuum, on which parties, political leaders, legislation, court decisions, and a number of other primary objects of politics could be more—or less—adequately located.[46]

The search for attitude structure takes a variety of forms ranging from the content analysis of attitudes to the examination of correlations between attitudes (issue positions) across the electorate, the latter taken to be evidence of the extent of opinion constraints, on the assumption that the higher the correlation between issue positions, the more likely that a single dimension of evaluation underlies the issues.[47] Each method yields evidence taken to indicate the absence of structure in voter attitudes. Yet there are several reasons to question this entire approach, as well as to suppose that some structure may exist in spite of this sort of evidence.

First, no single dimension, including the liberal/moderate/conservative continuum, is capable of providing the basis for a consistent ordering of all the issues an informed citizen may encounter.[48] To the extent that American politics is characterized by pluralism, one ought to expect this to be the case. Nor can the preference orderings of a set of individuals on a single issue necessarily be represented on a single dimension.

Second, the liberal/moderate/conservative continuum is a sociocultural phenomenon and not the revealed battleground of good and evil; it has an empirical, not a logical, base.[49] Thus its employment by a large number of people represents the influence of various institutions of socialization or the arbitrary grouping of issue positions by parties or individual politicians. Further, it is subject to shifting meanings over time or population subgroups, that is, the same descriptive terms may apply to different dimensions of evaluation.[50]

Third, even if every voter had perfectly structured issue positions, there is no reason to suppose that these would aggregate to a unique social ordering. What is actually tested through the examination of constraint is the extent to which the society agrees on a single dimension of evaluation and not the extent to which individuals may use such dimensions.

Fourth, if the liberal/moderate/conservative continuum, or any other dimension of evaluation, did order political events in such a way as to provide a useful guide to political events, then one should expect political leaders—who are generally well educated, attentive, and informed—to exhibit consistency in their attitudes. Yet the SRC's own analysis of attitudes among elites (a sample of 1958 congressional candidates) does not yield impressive evidence of such constraint. If elite behavior is one of the principal agents of social transmission of this organization of political affairs, it is not surprising that elite confusion is reflected in the attitudes of the masses.[51]

Finally, although a moderate ideological position appears to be acceptable according to the verbal analysis, it is not clear what consistent moderates look like operationally. If moderates balance their positions, they will appear, by these criteria, nonideological.[52]

It is no doubt true that the extent to which the SRC has characterized the voter as incompetent has been overstated by many of their critics. For example, Converse quite accurately laid the lack of wide ranging, specific information on issues and the absence of structure in part to information costs and the fragmentation of the electorate into "issue publics." But this empathy for the voter's plight is inconsistent; in other places the same deficiencies in the area of issues are laid to the voter's lack of education, lack of interest in political affairs, and the corrupting influence of party predispositions. Because of the central role that the SRC research has played in both the debate about voter rationality and the empirical justification of elitist models democracy, it is worthwhile to quote extensively from the SRC's summary of findings:

> Our detailed inquiry into public attitudes regarding what we took to be the most prominent political issues of the time revealed a substantial lack of familiarity with these policy questions. . . .
>
> Neither do we find much evidence of the kind of structured political thinking that we might expect to characterize a well-informed electorate. We have been able to identify a pattern of attitudes regarding certain questions of welfare legislation and a similar cluster of attitudes toward internationalist foreign policies. These express rather gross dimensions of opinion, however; they do not relate to each other or to other political attitudes with which one might expect to find them associated in a larger attitudinal structure. When we examine the attitudes and beliefs of the electorate as a whole over a broad range of policy questions—welfare legislation, foreign policy, federal economic programs, minority rights, civil liberties—we do not find coherent patterns of belief. The common tendency to characterize large blocs of the electorate in such terms as "liberal" or "conservative" greatly exaggerates the actual amount of consistent patterning one finds. Our failure to locate more than a trace of "ideological" thinking in the protocols of our surveys emphasizes the general impoverishment of political thought in a large proportion of the electorate.
>
> It is also apparent from these protocols that there is a great deal of uncertainty and confusion in the public mind as to what specific policies the election of one party over the other would imply. Very few of our respondents have shown a sensitive understanding of the positions of the parties on current policy issues. Even among those people who are relatively familiar with the issues presented in our surveys—and our test of familiarity has been an easy one—there is little agreement as to where the two parties stand. This fact reflects the similarity of party positions on

many issues, as well as the range of opinion within parties. But it also reflects how little attention even the relatively informed part of the electorate gives the specifics of public policy formation.

We have, then, the portrait of an electorate almost wholly without detailed information about decision making in government. A substantial portion of the public is able to respond in a discrete manner to issues that *might* be the subject of legislative or administrative action. Yet it knows little about what government has done on these issues or what the parties propose to do. It is almost completely unable to judge the rationality of government actions; knowing little of particular policies and what had led to them, the mass electorate is not able to appraise either its goals or the appropriateness of the means chosen to serve these goals.[53]

Candidates

The SRC analysis of the role of candidates in elections is best understood in the context of an ideal model of elections that seems to underlie their treatment of the candidate factor. This ideal model places parties at the center of electoral conflict: parties present coherent, consistent packages of issue positions to the voters; the issue packages of the major parties define the boundaries, range, and dimension of political debate; the parties choose candidates to *represent* the parties' issue packages. The ideal candidate, then, is a mere personification of the party platform—an intrusion on elections necessitated by the formal requirement that individuals be elected to occupy various offices.*

The idealization of the candidate's role carries implications for the model voter as well. Specifically, the voter ought to be concerned with candidates, as with parties, only in terms of the package of issue positions that each represents. Of course, candidates may provide a convenient focus, or "psychological anchoring," for an evaluation of issue positions; such cases are to be distinguished from the nonpolitical concern with the personal attraction of candidates. Thus the boundaries are clearly drawn in the initial major analysis of the role of candidates:

> *Candidate orientation* may be broadly defined as the structuring of political events in terms of a personal attraction to the major personalities involved. . . . Limitation of the concept of candidate orientation in this manner is consistent with most other general theorizing in this area.

---

*Of course this model is nowhere explicit in the SRC's works, and there are instances of greater sensitivity to the role of candidates outlined in the following chapter. Nevertheless, the model can be identified in various arguments and evaluative comments. Perhaps it is more recognizable as a parliamentary model. Aside from the evidence cited later, there is support for this interpretation in the SRC's survey instrument. Through 1968, all questions dealing with issue preference asked which *party*, not which candidate, was preferable.

Conceptualizations of reactions to public figures evidenced in such terms as "identifiacation," "father figure," "charismatic leader," "authoritarian follower," all imply a personal attraction to these figures, and not a response to such things as their "liberalism," or "governmental experience," or "Republicanism." Restriction of the concept of candidate orientation is also dictated by the demands of the theoretical framework of the study. Since we are concerned, in the analysis, with differentiating "party identification," "issue orientation," and "candidate orientation," it is important to exclude from the concept (and measures) of the candidate variable, reactions to the candidates in "party" or "issue" terms.[54]

The Eisenhower-Stevenson contests of 1952 and 1956 provide much of the empirical basis for the SRC conclusions about the roles of candidates, but the lessons of this experience are ambiguous. For example, the 1952 data suggest that:

... it is not unlikely that most new Presidents take office without their stance toward issues or groups having had much impact on popular attitude. What perceptions the public has are likely to be highly derivative carry-overs from perceptions of the President's party.[55]

By 1956, however, the electorate was more familiar with the candidates so that "the tendency to evaluate the candidates in terms of party was less pronounced in the second of these elections."[56] On the other hand, the additional exposure did not enrich the bases of candidate perception in the direction of greater political relevance: "A full classification of references to Eisenhower suggests that his appeal, already strongly personal in 1952, became overwhelmingly so in 1956. . . . These frequencies leave the strong impression that in 1956 Eisenhower was honored not so much for his performance as President as for the quality of his person."[57] The SRC authors, in their own summary, point to a diverse set of considerations comprising candidate image:

A good deal of the public response to these political actors simply expresses feeling or affect. Many people see this party or that candidate as "honest," "dependable," "capable," or more generally, as just "good." In a similar way, a large proportion of the electorate sees the parties or candidates as good or bad for this or that segment of the public, often referring to the group with which they themselves identify. But our examination of public attitude shows that certain generalized goals of government action enter the image of the parties and candidates and that these goals play a major role in electoral change.[58]

A more developed statement about candidates appears in Stokes's analysis of the shifting impact of various political objects as measured by the six-factor model over a series of elections.[59] A study of the weights of the components having to do with "popular reactions to the personal attributes of the candidates" attests to "General Eisenhower's personal hold on the electorate" and "shows Johnson to have been an asset to his own candidacy in 1964." Although the candidates "bring to a campaign certain 'real' properties as stimulus objects," there are many corrupting influences intervening between the stimulus and the perceivers, such as the mediation of candidates by the mass media. The major distortions arise from the response dispositions of the perceivers themselves, that is, from the tendency of individuals to make similar evaluations of associated stimuli. The most important source of bias is:

> . . . the profound influence which partisan loyalties may have on the voter's perceptions of the men seeking office. The stronger the voter's party bias, the more likely he is to see the candidate of his own party as hero, the candidate of the other party as villain.[60]

Candidates have not commanded a great deal of attention from the SRC researchers compared to parties and issues. The reason is perhaps most eloquently expressed in the conclusion of the first motivational analysis of the 1952 vote: "Of the three factors we have considered, candidate appeal would appear to be the most susceptible to the vagaries of public sentiment."[61]

Summary

Although there is no SRC commitment to a single explanation of voting behavior, the normal vote model comes closest to the theory implied throughout their work. Briefly, the normal vote makes an analytic distinction between the portion of the electoral outcome reflecting the long-term impact of party identification and the portion accounted for by the issues and candidates peculiar to a particular election. The separation of long-term partisan effects at the first stage preserves the central, primary, predisposing role of party identification in understanding both elections and the underlying stability of the political system:

> Few factors are of greater importance for our national elections than the lasting attachment of tens of millions of Americans to one of the parties. These loyalties establish a basic division of electoral strength within which the competition of particular campaigns takes place.[62]

The centrality of party identification leads to a picture of the voter which, again, is a vivid contrast to "[t]he ideal of the Independent citizen, attentive to politics, concerned with the course of government, who weighs the rival appeals of a campaign and reaches a judgment that is unswayed by partisan prejudice. . . ."[63] Instead of these ideal citizens, the American electorate is composed of, on the one hand, a group of voters who are attentive, involved, and informed, but whose identification with a party betrays a willingness to conform to party positions; and, on the other hand, a group of voters free of party ties but otherwise inattentive, uninvolved, and misinformed.

The salvation of the voter, and the distinguishing characteristic of good voters, is advanced education. In a tract appropriately subtitled "Education and the Upgrading of the Electorate," Converse asks:

> What political difference, if any, does this great advance in the educational composition of the electorate make? By most normative theories of democracy . . . it should have some degree of ameliorative effect with regard to the quality of electoral response.[64]

In fact, education has been found to be correlated with measures of information, ideological constraint, involvement, interest in the campaign, and participation. However, the relationships are not as simple and clearcut as Converse's summary: "The higher the education, the greater the 'good' values of the variable. The educated citizen is attentive, knowledgeable, and participatory, and the uneducated citizen is not."[65] An example of the benefits of education is its effectiveness in breaking down the party identifier's "willingness to conform":

> . . . advanced education may tend to free the individual from the restraints of party voting, make him better informed and more selective regarding the individual candidates, and give him greater confidence in his ability to manipulate a split rather than a straight ticket.[66]

The thrust of the consistent emphasis on the association of appropriate voting behavior with education is that, to the extent that the American voter falls short of the ideal voter, the blame is attached to the voter and not to the political system. Voters are simply incapable, on the whole, of making sound judgments about questions of policy. Consider, for example, Converse's analysis of the survey item that asks respondents whether they agree that "Sometimes politics is too complicated for a person like me to understand." Since 1952 respondents have expressed agreement with this statement by margins of two or three to one. Converse concludes that:

> . . . the item suggesting that politics is too complicated to understand is the most purely cognitive of the efficacy items and reflects more on the person agreeing with it than it does upon flaws in the political system.[67]

Similarly, of those who feel that the political system is unresponsive to them, *The American Voter* concludes that "we may suppose that the people we have described as feeling 'politically ineffective' are virtually beyond the reach of political stimulation."[68]

Finally, it should be noted that the great body of SRC research is well integrated with the elitist theories of democracy. The final chapter of *The American Voter*, devoted to drawing out the implications of their work for the political system, depends heavily upon the electorate's focus upon candidates and parties rather than issues:

> The segment of the electorate most likely to alter its image of these political actors is not the part that is best informed about government but the part that is least involved in politics, psychologically speaking, and whose information about details of policy is most impoverished. Change is not limited entirely to people of low information and involvement, but they are more likely than others to respond to the wars or economic recessions or other gross changes in the political environment that may generate substantial shifts at the polls.[69]

The implications of this flightiness on the part of the voters give both the empirical and the normative *raison d'être* of elite dominance of the political system:

> The quality of the electorate's review of public policy formation has two closely related consequences for those who must frame the actions of government. First, it implies that the electoral decision typically will be ambiguous as to the specific acts government should take. . . .
> The second consequence of the quality of the public's review of policy formation is that the electoral decision gives great freedom to those who must frame the policies of government. . . . [T]he fact that the wider public has so little to say on specific policies strengthens the position of special publics and particular "interests" in making their demands on government. Yet in important respects the latitude of government decision makers in framing public policies is enlarged by the fact that the details of these policies will be very largely unknown to the general electorate.[70]

Thus, because of the poor quality of their review of public policy, voters cannot and should not exercise direct control over the formulation of policy. Instead the job of policy formulation is, of necessity, and ought to be, left to government decision makers and to the active, informed, involved representatives of particular interests.

CONCLUSION

The empirical study of voting behavior began without a clearly specified model of rational voting behavior in the American political system. Instead, the naive model of the democratic citizen, in one form or another, provided the standards for the evaluation of voter behavior. But in every case these standards were articulated apart from any analysis of the particular cultural setting and institutional structure of American politics.

In some instances, as in the expectation that politically enlightened individuals will identify the single, underlying dimension of political conflict, the standards that define the naive model of the democratic citizen are simply arbitrary. In others the standards are derived from an understanding of classical democratic theory, as in the examples of the interest and information requirements. The application of arbitrary standards is without justification; the appraisal of the second case is more complex.

Standards of good citizenship derived from classical democratic theory constitute ideals that may be considered to be rational behavior in a particular, ideal context. It is not inappropriate to employ such standards in order to make normative evaluations of modern American voters; as norms, they transcend context. But the applications reviewed in this chapter exceed these bounds. In each of these cases, the naive model of the democratic citizen serves as a description of rational behavior.

Rational behavior, as the concept is employed in this work, is specific to a particular context. Thus the application to American voters of standards of rational behavior that are unaccompanied by—let alone derived from—an analysis of the context of American elections is at least arbitrary. It follows that it was wrong for Schumpeter to base the need for a new democratic theory on the failure of the American voter to match the naive model of the democratic citizen. Similarly, it was mistaken for voting analysts to employ arbitrary standards of rationality to evaluate the quality of voters' responses to elections.

The particular nonrational account of voting behavior embodied in the social-psychological model is a product of the roots of voting research in demographic analysis and certain assumptions of the researchers outlined above, for example, the assumption in *The American Voter* that political parties are social groups. But equally important is the failure of the researchers to examine their evidence for rationality of a character other than that contained in the naive model. Instead, they remained within the Schumpeterian framework, with rational content denied to behavior that did not conform to a priori standards. The revision of democratic theory to modify the dependence of policy on the will of the people was clearly compatible with the evidence that that will was apparently without rational quality. The argument in the remainder of this work that voters do behave rationally in the context of American presidential elections suggests that that compatiability is at least problematic.

NOTES

1. Joseph A. Schumpeter, *Capitalism, Socialism, and Democracy* (New York: Harper & Row, 1950). The relevant text is Part IV: "Socialism and Democracy," pp. 233–302.

2. Ibid., pp. 289–96.

3. Carole Pateman has criticized Schumpeter's work on the grounds that no single classical doctrine of democracy exists and that Schumpeter fails to specify, and thus misrepresents, the arguments of earlier democratic theorists; cf. Carole Pateman, *Participation and Democratic Theory* (Cambridge: Cambridge University Press, 1970), esp. pp. 3–6, 16–20. Pateman's argument offers sufficient grounds for describing the standards of good citizenship in Schumpeter's work as naive. However, in the present case, "naive" refers to the application of such standards to American voters on an a priori basis, that is, without due regard for the structuring of political participation by our political system (see Chapter 4).

4. Schumpeter, *Capitalism, Socialism, and Democracy*, pp. 253–54.

5. Ibid., p. 283.

6. Ibid., p. 269.

7. Ibid., p. 290.

8. I do not propose to add to the debate about whether it is appropriate to label such formulations elitist. I mean by the use of that term those theories that advocate or describe a minor, indirect, and restricted role for the average citizen in democratic government, generally on the ground that the average citizen is inadequate for a larger voice. The argument for grouping a number of somewhat distinct theories under the title "elitist theories of democracy" is made well by Jack Lively, *Democracy* (New York: G. P. Putman's Sons, 1977), pp. 78–80.

9. The conditions for success of the democratic method are contained in Schumpeter, *Capitalism, Socialism, and Democracy*, pp. 290–96.

10. Schumpeter further notes that "this principle clashes with the classical doctrine of democracy and really spells its abandonment." Ibid., p. 295.

11. Pateman applies the same criticisms to Berelson's analysis as to Schumpeter's in *Participation and Democratic Theory*, pp. 5–8.

12. Bernard R. Berelson, Paul F. Lazarsfeld, and William N. McPhee, *Voting* (Chicago: University of Chicago Press, 1954). The particular text described below is contained in Chapter 14, "Democratic Practice and Democratic Theory," pp. 305–23. See also an earlier work along the same lines: Berelson, "Democratic Theory and Public Opinion," *Public Opinion Quarterly* 16 (Fall 1952): 313–30.

13. Berelson et al., *Voting*, p. 306.

14. Ibid., pp. 307–9. Berelson admits to being unable to specify exactly what constitutes rationality in the matter of voting, however, ibid., p. 310.

15. Ibid., p. 312.

16. Ibid., pp. 313–16. Another excerpt from this work, cited in Chapter 1, cites the dangers of excessive participation.

17. There are, of course, some exceptions. One example is Eugene Burdick, "Political Theory and the Voting Studies," in Eugene Burdick and Arthur J. Brodbeck, eds., *American Voting Behavior* (Glencoe, Ill.: Free Press, 1959), 136–49. In addition, the discovery of the new issue voter seems to have generated some recent thought along these lines (see Chapter 3).

18. A useful exposition of the history of voting research that traces a somewhat different course of development than that outlined below is Peter H. Rossi, "Four Landmarks in Voting Research," in *American Voting Behavior*, pp. 5–54.

19. Ecological correlations are essentially measures of the statistical relationships between characteristics of groups, as, for example, a correlation between percent Catholic and percent Democratic votes for a set of wards. The difficulty with such an approach is that

ecological correlations have no necessary implications for the individuals in each group. However, the data for ecological studies can be readily obtained from government publications. It is perhaps significant that Rossi chose a work employing this technique as his first landmark in ibid.

20. Paul F. Lazarsfeld, Bernard Berelson, and Hazel Gaudet, *The People's Choice* (New York: Columbia University Press, 1944). This is Rossi's second landmark; cf. Rossi, op. cit.

21. Lazarsfeld et al., *The People's Choice*, p. 27.

22. Berelson et al., *Voting*. This is Rossi's third landmark; cf. Rossi, op. cit.

23. Lazarsfeld et al., *The People's Choice*, pp. 99–100.

24. Berelson et al., *Voting*, pp. 306, 309, 312–13.

25. The SRC study of the 1948 election is reported in Angus T. Campbell and R. L. Kahn, *The People Elect A President* (Ann Arbor: Institute for Social Research, 1952).

26. A number of review articles have attempted to systematize the SRC research to some extent. The following have proved helpful in the discussion that follows: Peter B. Natchez, "Images of Voting: The Social Psychologists," *Public Policy* 18 (Summer 1970): 553–88; Rossi, "Four Landmarks"; Walter Dean Burnham, "Contributions of the SRC to the Development of Voting Theory," paper presented at the annual convention of the American Political Science Association, September 1976; Kenneth Prewitt and Norman Nie, "Review Article: Election Studies of the Survey Research Center," *British Journal of Political Science* 1 (October 1971): 479–502.

27. Campbell et al., *The American Voter*, p. 13.

28. Angus T. Campbell, Gerald Gurin, and Warren E. Miller, *The Voter Decides* (Evanston, Ill.: Row, Peterson and Co., 1954), esp. pp. 165–77.

29. Donald E. Stokes, Angus T. Campbell, and Warren E. Miller, "Components of Electoral Decision," *American Political Science Review* 52 (June 1958): 367–87; Campbell and Stokes, "Partisan Attitudes and the Presidential Vote," in *American Voting Behavior*, pp. 353–71; Stokes, "Some Dynamic Elements of Contests for the Presidency," *American Political Science Review* 60 (March 1966), pp. 19–28; and Campbell et al., *The American Voter*, pp. 524–31.

30. Philip E. Converse, "The Concept of a Normal Vote," in Angus T. Campbell, Philip E. Converse, Warren E. Miller, and Donald E. Stokes, *Elections and the Political Order* (New York: John Wiley & Sons, 1966) pp. 9–39. An extended discussion of the normal vote, with additional references, appears in Chapter 7.

31. Campbell et al., *The Voter Decides*, p. 93.

32. Ibid., pp. 93–94; Campbell et al., *The American Voter*, p. 124. This conclusion was based on changes in the marginals, that is, on a stable pattern of party identification. More recent evidence, from the SRC's own 1956-58-60 panel data, indicates that party identifications for individuals are not nearly so stable; cf. John C. Pierce and Douglas D. Rose, "Nonattitudes and American Public Opinion: The Examination of a Thesis," *American Political Science Review* 68 (June 1974): 626–49, esp. pp. 631–32.

33. Campbell et al., *The Voter Decides*, pp. 88, 90.

34. Campbell et al., *The American Voter*, pp. 146–47.

35. Campbell et al., *The Voter Decides*, pp. 147, 107.

36. Campbell et al., *The American Voter*, pp. 128, 132.

37. Ibid., pp. 142–43.

38. Philip E. Converse, Warren E. Miller, Jerrold Rusk, and Arthur Wolfe, "Continuity and Change in American Politics: Parties and Issues in the 1968 Election," *American Political Science Review* 63 (December 1969): 1,096.

39. Ibid. The implications of voter attitudes for leadership and the two-party system are treated in Chapter 20, "Electoral Behavior and the Political System," in Campbell et al., *The American Voter*, pp. 539–58.

40. Campbell et al., *The Voter Decides*, p. 112.

41. Campbell et al., *The American Voter*, p. 170.

42. Angus T. Campbell, "Voters and Elections: Past and Present," *Journal of Politics* 26 (November 1964): 752.

43. Campbell et al., *The American Voter*, pp. 234–35.

44. Ibid., p. 237. See also comments regarding "nature of the times" voters who base decisions on the products of the political system in ibid., p. 261; and comments on the insignificance of opinions on issues when the respondent is unfamiliar with current government policy in the issue area, ibid., p. 173.

45. Ibid., p. 181.

46. Philip E. Converse, "The Nature of Belief Systems in Mass Publics," in David Apter, ed., *Ideology and Discontent* (Glencoe, Ill.: Free Press, 1964), pp. 207, 214, 246.

47. The most extensive analyses of attitude structure appear in ibid., pp. 206–61; and Campbell et al., *The American Voter*, pp. 188–265. The same methodological tools are employed in a substantial body of related work by the Michigan authors, their supporters, and their critics.

48. Converse in fact notes that there is less constraint evidenced between than within broad areas of domestic and foreign policy and suggests that "Such lowered values [of constraint] signify boundaries between belief systems that are relatively independent." Converse, "The Nature of Belief Systems in Mass Publics," p. 229. However, he does not carry the implication of such independence beyond the broad foreign/domestic distinction.

49. Ibid., pp. 211–13.

50. Again, the SRC authors observed as much in ibid., p. 220, and Campbell et al., *The American Voter*, pp. 193–94.

51. Elites exhibit greater constraint than do masses (average correlation coefficients of .53 and .23, respectively), but the absolute level of constraint is not so high as to justify the attention directed to liberal/moderate/conservative labels; Converse, "The Nature of Belief Systems in Mass Publics," pp. 227–31.

52. An extensive criticism of the search for ideology, incorporating much of the above with examples, is Samuel Popkin, John W. Gorman, Charles Phillips, and Jeffrey A. Smith, "Comment: What Have You Done for Me Lately?: Toward an Investment Theory of Voting," *American Political Science Review* 70 (September 1976): 795–99. The multidimensionality of the issue space was noted in an early article by one of the principal SRC authors, although the implications were not brought to bear on the analysis of "ideology," in Donald E. Stokes, "Spatial Models of Party Competition," in *Elections and the Political Order*, pp. 161–79.

53. Campbell et al., *The American Voter*, pp. 542–43. This passage is part of a larger section outlining the implications of their findings for political leaders, pp. 541–48.

54. Campbell et al., *The Voter Decides*, p. 136. It could be argued that this treatment of candidate orientation is merely methodological; however, the analytical treatment of candidates has a theoretical underpinning, as noted in the passage cited, and it is this theoretical orientation that is the present concern.

55. Campbell et al., *The American Voter*, p. 61.

56. Ibid., p. 54.

57. Ibid., p. 56.

58. Ibid., p. 546.

59. Stokes, "Some Dynamic Elements of Contests for the Presidency," pp. 19–28.

60. Ibid., p. 23.

61. Campbell et al., *The Voter Decides*, p. 177.

62. Campbell et al., *The American Voter*, p. 121.

63. Ibid., p. 143.

64. Philip E. Converse, "Change in the American Electorate," in Angus T. Campbell and

Philip Converse, eds., *The Human Meaning of Social Change* (New York: Russell Sage Foundation, 1972), p. 323.

65. Ibid., p. 324. A summary of the association between education and participation can be found in Campbell et al., *The American Voter*, pp. 475–81.

66. Campbell et al., *The Voter Decides*, p. 96, fn. 5.

67. Converse, "Change in the American Electorate," p. 329.

68. Campbell et al., *The American Voter*, p. 543.

69. Ibid., p. 547.

70. Ibid., p. 544. There follows an example of "how well the decision makers of American government appreciate the diffuse character of the electorate's judgement" by ignoring any apparent policy implications of the electoral decision; ibid., pp. 544–45.

3

THE VOTER AS CONSUMER: THE RATIONAL VOTER MODEL AND THE NEW ISSUE VOTER

As the attention of social scientists turned to the analysis of voting behavior, the social-psychological model emerged as the most widely accepted—or at least most widely published—account of the American voter. The voter of this model was a pale reflection of the ideal voter. The political views of this voter had no political content, but were instead products of early socialization and subsequent social milieus, nurtured by nonrational psychological mechanisms. The evidence gathered in support of this image was impressive, but it was not the only account available. Those who held a more generous view of human nature and were willing to grant a modicum of rationality and autonomy to voters, while discounting the apparent evidence to the contrary, could turn to a variety of alternative models that emphasized voter rationality.

A faith in the rationality of human activity is not the only reason to turn elsewhere. Beyond this there is an unsatisfying incompleteness to the social-psychological model; the account that it offers is too static, the voters are too passive. The social-psychologists offer an explanation of the mechanisms by which certain attitudes are transmitted, maintained, and balanced, but they do not explain the origins of those attitudes. For example, the demonstrable tendency for certain groups to exhibit consistent patterns of partisanship can be understood in terms of psychological mechanisms and group dynamics, but the particular pattern of identification of groups with parties is something that needs a different sort of explanation.[1]

As the analysis of elections extended into the 1960s, voters began to exhibit patterns of behavior that seemed to partake of greater rationality than that ascribed to them in the social-psychological model. These anomalies, combined with the continuing development of the rational alternative, eventually led a number of writers to propose a new model. The new issue voter emerged in the 1970s as a synthesis of elements from rational and nonrational models.

This chapter is devoted to a review of the major contributions to the rational voter model and the new issue voter. The works covered here are a diverse lot with numerous implications for the specific actions of voters. All of these works share the assumption that voters occasionally exhibit the same sort of rationality attributed to homo economicus. Each also carries the implication that, to some extent, voters may be understood as political consumers in the electoral marketplace.

THE RATIONAL VOTER MODEL

The Contribution of Anthony Downs

The review of rational models of voting behavior must begin with Anthony Downs's milestone, *An Economic Theory of Democracy*.[2] Downs's work differs from most efforts to explain voter behavior in that it is a complete, formal theory of voting and elections, rather than an attempt to develop a body of theoretical propositions inductively from empirical observations. More importantly, Downs's theory is the antithesis, on the level of motiviation and content, of the social-psychological model.

The Downsian model of voting behavior is built upon the assumption that voters behave rationally. Rationality has a very precise and narrow meaning in Downs's work. A rational individual is one who, when faced with a range of alternatives, is capable of perceiving differences between them and consistently rank-ordering alternatives transitively, and always selects the most preferred alternative.[3] In other words, people are expected to be goal oriented in their behavior.

It is important to note, because it is so often misunderstood, that the assumption of rationality applies only to the means employed to attain a given goal, and not to the selection of goals. It assumes something about behavior, and not about ends. Thus it is not the case that rationality implies that voters will vote their pocketbooks, nor does it imply any particular goal; a politically rational individual may wish to see starving children fed, even though such a policy would reduce personal income. Similarly, it does not follow that a rational individual will always be right. On the contrary, voters may be misled or misinformed as to their own objectively determined best interests, or as to the most efficient way to achieve these ends. In fact, ignorance plays an important role in the Downsian model.

The assumption of rationality in Downs's model is accompanied by a sharp distinction between the political sphere and other realms of human activity:

> The political function of elections in a democracy, we assume, is to select a government. Therefore rational behavior in connection with elections is behavior oriented toward this end and no other. . . . Thus, we do not take into consideration the whole personality of each individual when we discuss what behavior is rational for him.[4]

It follows that instances of behavior that may be personally rational as, for example, the case of voters who sell or trade their votes in exchange for a nonpolitical return, may be classified as politically irrational in the context of the model. This qualification leads to another, specifically, that Downs intends his model to be descriptive of rational political behavior, but not to be descriptive in the general sense:

> . . . the model is not an attempt to describe reality accurately. Like all theoretical constructs in the social sciences, it treats a few variables as crucial and ignores others which actually have some influence. Our model in particular ignores all forms of irrationality and subconscious behavior even though they play a vital role in real-world politics.[5]

The model political world that Downs describes is composed primarily of two distinct sets of actors: voters and political parties. The behavior of parties is determined by a set of assumptions corresponding to and derived from the assumption of voter rationality. Downs's parties are coalitions of rational actors of a particular type. First, they are a team of actors whose members agree on all of their political goals; thus, parties are assumed to exhibit the same rationality as individuals.[6] Second, parties are assumed to be self-interested.[7] From the self-interest assumption, the motivation of parties springs:

> We assume that they act solely in order to attain the income, prestige, and power which come from being in office. . . . Upon this reasoning rests the fundamental hypothesis of our model: parties formulate policies in order to win elections, rather than win elections in order to formulate policies.[8]

It follows that parties will manipulate their policies and behavior in any way that they expect to maximize votes in the next election, within the limits of the Constitution and taking into consideration the actions of opposition parties.

Downs's stated purpose in developing his model is to integrate government with private decision makers in a general equilibrium theory. Thus it is

not surprising that he borrows heavily from economic theory, or that the
political system that he describes bears a great resemblance to the welfare
economists' model of the competitive market. For example:

> . . . we borrow from traditional economic theory the idea of the rational
> consumer. Corresponding to the infamous *homo economicus* . . . our
> *homo politicus* is the "average man" in the electorate, the "rational
> citizen" of our model democracy.[9]

Similarly, parties are the analog of producers, competing for the votes of the
electorate.

The market analogy is more than an interesting perspective on
Downs's model; it is essential to it. The market analogy embodies Downs's
conception of democracy and makes clear the direct links to Schumpeter's
revised democratic theory. Downs's enthusiasm for the market is un-
disguised:

> The model of perfect competition drawn up by welfare economists is a
> triumph of selfishness. It demonstrates how, under certain conditions,
> society actually gains when men attempt to maximize profits and utility.[10]

The economic theory of democracy is merely an extension of the economic
model to the political sphere, following the ground broken by Schumpeter:

> . . . the social meaning or function of parliamentary activity is no doubt to
> turn out legislation, and in part, administrative measures. But in order to
> understand how democratic politics serve this social end, we must start
> from the competitive struggle for power and office and realize that the
> social function is fulfilled, as it were, incidentally—in the same sense as
> production is incidental to the making of profits.[11]

Downs's invocation of the market analogy underscores the ethical
dimensions of his theory. First, the democratic political system, like the
market, is a mechanism for social decision making through the registration
of individual preferences, albeit one where all have the same purchasing
power in their vote. As with Schumpeter, democracy is defined in terms of
institutions and the social conditions for their operation, and bears no
implications for the goals of society beyond the preservation of democracy.[12] At the same time, however, certain standards of good citizenship are
implied in the model.

The free market model is fueled by the utility-maximizing behavior of
individual consumers and the profit-maximizing behavior of firms. The
economic model of democracy employs the political counterparts of these
actors, namely, utility-maximizing voters and vote-maximizing parties, with

votes replacing dollars as the medium of exchange. The market model optimizes the production and distribution of goods and services subject to an ethical principle.* Downs's democracy has parties in the business of discovering and implementing optimal policies in terms of votes:

> Our model attempts to forge a positive relationship between individual and social end structures by means of political device. Because each adult citizen has one vote, his welfare preferences are weighted in the eyes of the government, which is interested only in his vote, not his welfare. Thus . . . we admit openly that we are adopting an ethical principle— equality of franchise.[13]

Just as the efficient operation of the market depends upon the rationality of economic actors, the efficient operation of government in Downs's theory depends upon the rationality of political actors. Because government decision makers choose policies according to their effects on vote intentions, irrational voting will produce suboptimal (in the context of the model) sets of policies. The proper social policy depends upon voters accurately representing their interests.† It follows that good citizenship entails individual rationality. Individual rationality, in turn, has specific implications for voting behavior that lead to a different set of standards than those expressed in the naive model of the democratic citizen.

Downs's rational voter faces a restricted choice set, namely, the platforms of the opposing parties. The voter must decide: how much information to gather to inform any subsequent actions, which party or candidate to prefer, and whether to support that preference by voting. Although these questions are interrelated in the model, they may be separated analytically.

---

*Two broad qualifications to this statement are necessary, but do not affect the larger argument. First, there are a number of phenomena that produce suboptima in the market model, for example, externalities, monopolies, and collective goods, which in fact create needs for government activities. Second, the ethical principle is expressed in the notion of Pareto optimality, that is, the market model optimizes by maximizing social welfare subject to a particular distribution of wealth in money terms. The beginning distribution may or may not satisfy other ethical criteria.

†This is generally the case. However, under certain conditions voters may benefit by misrepresenting their preference, for example, in multiparty systems. Also, the introduction of government into the general equilibrium model may disturb individual marginal equilibria (cf. Downs, pp. 164–204) so that, overall, policy is not optimal, even with rational voting. This possibility arises because economic and political actors employ different criteria (money and votes) for optimizing, and policies that are optimal in terms of one criterion may not be optimal in terms of the other. The economic and political spheres could be reconciled only by their total isolation from each other or their integration in terms of a common medium of exchange, as in a marketplace where votes could be bought and sold.

Downs explicitly considers the cost of information as a factor in the first decision. While a great deal of information is made available without charge during the course of a political campaign, there are almost always opportunity costs associated with the time used in analysis and evaluation of it. Other information entails more tangible costs. Two important consequences follow from the costliness of information. One is that the voter will try, where possible, to economize by relying on information shortcuts such as party labels or expert opinions. The other is that the voter will only continue to collect information as long as the expected value of the next bit of information exceeds the cost of obtaining it. Thus Downs introduces a concept unique in democratic theory, the somewhat Orwellian notion of rational ignorance.

The Downsian voter's decision as to which party or candidate to support is reflected in the voter's differential. This reflects the differential value of the election for the individual if one's most preferred party wins, based on the consideration of strictly political benefits and costs, that is, on the expected value of changes in one's utility stream resulting from the policies, programs, and positions of the competing parties. Intensity is reflected in the weighting of the various issues.

Party differential is composed of issue-specific and generalized components. The issue-specific component includes the individual's evaluation of the differences between the parties that are related to the parties' positions on specific issues of concern to the individual. The generalized component, on the other hand, contains surrogates, or information shortcuts substituted for specific issue positions. The relative importance of these two components depends upon the amount of information the individual has and the degree of uncertainty characterizing the election. In general, the less information the voter has, the greater reliance will be placed on the generalized component as a method of reducing costs of information; the more information the voter has about specific issues, the less need there will be to fall back on surrogates.

The turnout decision is based upon the individual's vote value. In addition to being an expression of preference, the vote has, for Downs, another political purpose that is a function of the occurrence of elections per se. Each individual's vote has value as a unit of support for the political system, that is, the existence of elections is a collective good to which the individual contributes by voting. This is the long-run participation value. Thus there are two distinct sources of benefits to the voter, represented by party differential and long-run participation value. But because each voter is only one of many contributing to the collective outcome of the election, each of the benefits must be discounted by the probability of an individual's vote affecting the outcome. Finally, these benefits, appropriately discounted, must be compared to the costs associated with voting to determine the net vote value. Those for whom the net vote value is positive have an incentive to vote; others abstain.

The role of political parties in the vote decision illustrates the contrasting standards of rational voting behavior (or good citizenship) implied in the Downsian model and the naive model of the democratic citizen. For Schumpeter and the social-psychologists, a voter using party as a criterion in vote choice is expressing a nonrational, nonpolitical, psychological commitment to a political object. For Downs, though, party identification is a product of political experience, a sort of moving average of party performance over a series of elections. Voters employ party as a relevant variable in their calculus only as an information shortcut—a cost-saving device—and only to the extent that they are uninformed on the issues. This is not to suggest that all Downsian voters are well informed, but rather that the influence of party is part of a rational decision-making process.

In general, however, Downsian voters are not subject to the rigorous information requirements of the naive model of the democratic citizen. Because, ceteris paribus, information about their most important issues is more valuable to them than information about peripheral concerns, it is likely—and quite rational—that their information will be limited to a narrow range of issues at most. They may choose any number of a wide range of information cues, including party labels, ideology, demographic characteristics, and the "nature of the times" as substitutes for information. Finally, because Downsian voters' issue concerns are weighted in their calculus by the contribution of the issue concerns to their utility stream, they likely will be more informed and concerned about issues that affect them personally than about issues that have widespread but less personally significant repercussions.

The Downsian innovation that has had greatest impact on voting studies of all sorts is the notion of ideology, defined as "a verbal image of the good society and of the chief means of constructing such a society."[14] Downsian voters adopt ideologies as substitutes for specific information:

> ... many a voter finds party ideologies useful because they remove the necessity of his relating every issue to his own philosophy. Ideologies help him focus attention on the differences between parties; therefore they can be used as samples of all the differentiating stands. With this short cut a voter can save himself the cost of being informed upon a wider range of issues.[15]

Downsian ideologies lead to rankings of the major parties and issue positions on a single dimension of evaluation that:

> ... consists of a linear scale running from zero to 100 in the usual left-to-right fashion. To make this politically meaningful, we assume that political

> preferences can be ordered from left to right in a manner agreed upon by
> all voters. They need not agree on which point they personally prefer, only
> on the ordering of parties from one extreme to the other.[16]

This conceptualization of ideology is the basis of an elegant theoretical treatment of spatial competition of political parties that is rich in conclusions about the need for ideological consensus as a condition of stability in democratic political systems.[17]

Despite obvious problems with applying Downs's notion of ideology to American voters, his analysis, or one like it, led to the adoption of ideology as a standard for evaluating the issue rationality of the electorate. Evidence of the presence or absence of ideological constraint or the use of a liberal/moderate/conservative dimension is repeatedly cited in the debate about the importance of issues in spite of the fact that these criteria are irrelevant to the question. As noted in Chapter 2, even if every voter employed a single political dimension, there is no reason to suppose that these would aggregate to a single dimension for the entire electorate. Downs circumvented this problem by assuming that the parties would articulate their own ideologies (and implicitly assuming that the parties would agree on a single dimension). The voters merely adopt a party ideology. He further assumed that ideology would serve, in the stead of issue-specific information, only for so long as and to the extent that the positions of the parties on various issues conformed to their ideological claims. Yet, despite the ideological impurity of American political parties, despite the evidence that American political elites are not ideologically constrained, despite the difficulty that voting researchers have had in defining the ideologies to which they ask voters to conform, and despite the irrelevance of the criterion to the questions to which it is most often applied, the SRC and others, including critics of their conclusions, have employed ideological constraint as a criterion of sophisticated voting.

Downs's work has played a major role in setting the terms of the debate over the issue rationality of the American voter. Thus it is important to note that the set of assumptions upon which his theory is built bears little resemblance to the American political system. In particular, for present purposes it should be noted that candidates have no role in the Downsian democracy; instead, parties of the parliamentary type exercise such strong control over their members that they become mere agents. On the other hand, in pushing issues to the fore, Downs offers a political interpretation of such principle components of the social-psychological model as party identification and citizen duty. Perhaps Downs's most original and important contributions to the analysis of voting behavior are his treatment of uncertainty and the introduction of information costs as relevant considerations. The latter have a key role in the investor-voter model described in the following chapter.

Unfortunately, Downs left the tasks of operationalizing and testing his theory to others. Only a few empirical tests of Downsian models have been published, and these generally involve incomplete or partial models.[18] Still, Downs's work provides the starting point for most modern analyses of the rationality of the American electorate.

The Contribution of V. O. Key

Downs's approach to rational voting behavior was to develop an explicit theoretical model of the voter's calculus that enabled him to deduce the characteristics of rational decisions. Not all of the work of those who embrace the rationality of the electorate is so formal, however. Probably the most important of the softer treatments of this issue is V. O. Key's *The Responsible Electorate*. Subtitled "Rationality in Presidential Voting, 1936-1960," the book explicitly addresses the rationality debate:

> The perverse and unorthodox argument of this little book is that voters are not fools. To be sure, many individual voters act in odd ways indeed; yet in the large the electorate behaves about as rationally and responsibly as we should expect, given the clarity of the alternatives presented to it and the character of the information available to it. In American presidential campaigns of recent decades the portrait of the American electorate that develops from the data is not one of an electorate straitjacketed by social determinants or moved by subconscious urges triggered by devilishly skillful propagandists. It is rather one of an electorate moved by subconscious urges triggered by devilishly skillful propagandists. It is rather one of an electorate moved by concern about central and relevant questions of public policy of governmental performance, and of executive personality.[19]

Key analyzes shifts in the popular vote over the course of seven national elections. He divides the electorate into standpatters, switchers, and new voters, according to whether the individual has stayed with a party choice from the previous election, switched party preference, or is voting for the first time. Analyzing data from a variety of sources, he is able to find justification for the positions of standpatters and switchers in terms of the correspondence between their objective interests and party preferences. Key concludes that there is a kind of rationality pervasive in the electorate—an absence of false consciousness, in a manner of speaking. This in turn suggests a political interpretation of party affiliation that is evidenced by the rationality underlying the shifting party allegiances of the switchers. Overall, Key is encouraged by his findings:

> From our analyses the voter emerges as a person who appraises the actions of government, who has policy preferences, and who relates his vote to those appraisals and preferences.[20]

The impact of the Key study on the rationality debate is limited in two ways. The first is in his perception of the backward focus of issue concern:

> The patterns of flow of the major streams of shifting voters graphically reflect the electorate in its great, and perhaps principal, role as an appraiser of past events, past performance, and past actions. It judges retrospectively.[21]

Voters are restricted by this claim to a sort of passive-aggressive, monitoring function in democracies. The second limitation is closely related to the first and is captured in the SRC's critical response to Key's work: "Key was quite explicit in his desire to explain movement and change in the electorate, rather than voting behavior in a more general sense."[22] Thus, the bulk of the voters may serve a stabilizing function, for better or for worse, for the political system.

Finally, Key's study shares with others in the quality-of-the-electorate debate (with the notable exception of Downs) the identification of rationality with issue concern. The emphasis in such work is on the demonstration that issues do or do not occupy a central role in the voter's calculus. The criteria for issue rationality range from simple tests of correspondence between objective interests and vote, to more sophisticated analyses of the richness and consistency of voter attitudes. Whatever the standards, however, the focus of the debate has been on the issues, with the candidates placed firmly in the background.

THE NEW ISSUE VOTER

During the 1950s and 1960s the SRC dominated voting research for a variety of reasons. The published output of their critics did not seriously dent their reputation and was easily matched in terms of volume by their own. However, events in the real world of American presidential elections conspired to present psephologists with a number of what can only be called, from the perspective of the social-psychological model, anomalies. By the 1972 election it had become apparent that these anomalies were of such sufficient scope and duration that they could no longer be ignored, and that the account developed during the Eisenhower era was in need of revision. This revision took the form of adopting various aspects of the rational approach and combining these with the existing model to produce the image of what is called here the new issue voter.

The most serious problems for the social-psychological model lay with the assumption that "the influence of party identification on perceptions of political objects is so great that only rarely will the individual develop a set of attitude forces that conflicts with this allegiance."[23] In spite of the predisposing effects of party identification, voters in the Solid South who considered themselves to be Democrats carried their states for Republican Barry Goldwater in 1964, for American party candidate George Wallace in 1968, and for Republican Richard Nixon in 1972. The great vote shift between the Democratic landslide of 1964 and the Republican avalanche of 1972 incorporates many such cases of violation of party standards, including the record abandonment of their candidate by Democrats in 1972. Dissension within the Democratic party in 1968 forced an incumbent president to step down, and in 1972 led to a sizable "Democrats for Nixon" organization.

The Wallace candidacy was particularly disturbing for the old model. The SRC has argued that "The conserving influence of party identification makes it extremely difficult for a third party to rise suddenly and with enough popular support to challenge the existing parties."[24] Yet Wallace did just that, and the analysis of the 1968 election took on an unfamiliar tone:

> In point of fact, the Wallace candidacy was reacted to by the public as an issue candidacy . . . about half of the reasons volunteered by our respondents for favorable feelings toward Wallace had to do with positions he was taking on current issues.[25]

This analysis did not occasion a rethinking of the assumptions of the model, but its impact was felt in the addition of some important qualifications to the earlier discussion of party:

> It seems clear from the 1968 data that one of the cardinal limiting conditions is the "drag" or inertia represented by habitual party loyalties: as soon as features of the situation limit or neutralize the relevance of such a factor, issue evaluations play a more vital role. . . . But in the moment of truth in the polling booth, party allegiance seems the most relevant cue for many voters *if conditions permit it to be used.*[26]

These electoral outcomes do not exhaust the anomalies that have accumulated against the social-psychological model. For example, the distribution of party identification itself has changed to reflect a greater proportion of the electorate considering themselves independents, a fact that cannot be accounted for within the framework of the old model at the same time that it results in a narrower scope of application of the old model. Similarly, recent trends in participation run counter to the expectations of the education-driven account of turnout advanced by the SRC. First, blacks overcame their "relatively low motivational levels,"[27] increasing their participation rate as a group in response to the removal of legal restrictions and the increased attention of the political system. Furthermore, the overall participation rate, as well as various indicators of interest and concern, have declined consistently since 1960 despite increases in the educational achievement of the electorate.

These and other discrepancies eventually led to a revised model of voting behavior, with the SRC/CPS* again leading the way. The new issue voter models generally share two characteristics. Advocates of the new models find a much greater concern with issues on the part of the erstwhile party-oriented electorate. But the applicability of the social-psychological model to the voters of the past is not seriously questioned; rather, the new voter arises as a consequence of new issues, changes in the political context, or increased education.

The arrival of the issue-oriented electorate on the American political scene was formally announced by the SRC/CPS analysts in "A Majority Party in Disarray: Policy Polarization in the 1972 Election."[28] More than anything else, that election was characterized by "a new issue politics," which "exposed the pervasive consequences that follow from dislodging party loyalty and candidate appeal from positions of dominance in mass electoral politics. . . ."[29] This new issue politics resulted from the happy conjunction of "leadership behavior that brings the substance of issue politics into the public domain," with "a spectacular change in the quality of mass attitudes toward questions of public policy."[30]

The evidence that sets the 1972 election apart from those that went before is the apparent "increased importance of issues as predictors of the vote decision." In particular, it was found that McGovern voters differed substantially from Nixon voters and Democrats not supporting McGovern on a set of issues that were not weighted for the degree of concern that voters had about each and did not include traditional economic issues. It also was observed that the mean placement of Nixon on seven-point Vietnam policy and other issue scales was closer to the mean position of voters than the mean McGovern position, which suggested that McGovern had been perceived as too far left for most voters. Finally, a normal vote

---

*By the 1972 election the SRC had been absorbed by the Center for Political Studies, hence SRC/CPS. Because the change coincides with the articulation of a new theory as well as the departure of many of the principal authors of the earlier work, the new designation will be used where appropriate.

analysis of several issues demonstrated "the importance of issues as short term factors in the 1972 election."

Complementing these findings is the analysis of "a new policy-oriented style of elite leadership." Much of the credit for the new issue politics is given to the candidates of the major parties in the elections since the "issueless fifties" whose focus on national problems and policy alternatives reshaped the electorate.[31] The trend toward differentiation on the part of candidates culminated in 1972 with the aforementioned clear distinction between the Nixon and McGovern positions on issues: "Such sharp differentiation between the candidates clearly facilitates the translation of issue demands into a vote decision."[32] However, a contributing factor was that "McGovern was not a personally appealing candidate—a very important factor under conditions of issue polarization, for it allowed issue differences to gain maximal importance."[33]

Coinciding with "the upgrading in the quality of political rhetoric and debate" is "the increase in the ideological nature of public opinion":

> The universe of policy questions came to be reasonably well ordered by the electorate with apparently sophisticated structuring.[34]

The evidence for this is the familiar interitem correlation matrix or index of attitude constraint. For 1972, however, the analysis involved different standards. First, a factor analysis of candidate proximity scores for 12 issues produced four general issue dimensions defined by positions on the war and economic, social, and cultural issues. Then correlations between issues were examined within dimensions for ideological constraint. The evidence that issues within dimensions were more-or-less correlated with each other, and that each dimension is similarly associated with the respondent's self-placement on the liberal/moderate/conservative scale "suggests a degree of consistency in issue attitudes that has traditionally been associated with an ideological interpretation of politics."[35] Finally, much of the credit for the structured thinking of the electorate is given to education:

> Given their generally higher level of formal education, the population of actual voters in 1972 was better prepared to respond to the candidates in terms of policy preferences than were the voters in 1964.[36]

Somewhat different conclusions are reached in recent SRC/CPS work by Miller and Levitin.* These authors analyze the 1972 election in terms of

---

*Warren E. Miller and Teresa E. Levitin, *Leadership and Change: The New Politics and the American Electorate,* © 1976. Reprinted by permission of Winthrop Publishers, Inc., Cambridge, Massachusetts.

New Politics, which is described as a "new version of the liberal-conservative continuum."[37] The New Politics is defined by a particular consistency in attitudes toward the events of the 1960s. Specifically, a group of "new liberals" is identified by their positive attitudes toward all four:

> ... separable but interrelated types of concerns [that] defined the rise of the New Politics: (1) the evolution of a counterculture; (2) the growth of support for protest against national political and social policies and against established institutions; (3) the growth in the belief that emphasis on law and order was becoming repressive; and (4) the development of reactions against agents of social control charged with containing protest and maintaining law and order.[38]

Those who evidence negative attitudes toward all four concerns constitute the "silent minority"; the rest of the population compose the "center." The concept of the New Politics resembles the earlier Scammon and Wattenberg notion of "the social issue,"[39] except that the later work finds that over two-thirds of the electorate are inconsistent, rather than opposed, in their attitudes toward the changing society.

The agents of change that brought about the New Politics operated throughout the 1960s, but only converged with significant consequences in the 1972 election:

> The first change, that of the quality of political life, was a change from the quietude and conformity of the 1950's to the New Politics of the 1960's. . . .
> The second change was that political leaders began to articulate opposing positions on the issues of the day through sustained debate and disagreement. . . .
> The third element was the growing concern of the electorate with issues, a concern that was ultimately translated into issue voting.[40]

Except that the earlier paper placed greater emphasis on the effects of education, the two SRC/CPS analyses identify essentially the same agents of change in the electorate. However, the meanings associated with issue leadership and increased constraint are quite different.

The initial SRC/CPS analysis laid the Democratic defeat largely to the fact that "McGovern was perceived as so far left on the issues that Nixon was generally closer to the electorate's average issue position."[41] It was the "sharp differentiation" between the candidates that made issue voting possible in the election. Similarly, Miller and Levitin identify McGovern's issue positions as catalysts in producing issue voting:

McGovern made some New Politics themes part of his campaign, appealed to New Politics supporters and took positions on the issues of the day which were different from those of Nixon. The electorate responded with an unprecedented proportion of issue voters, and issues, indeed, contributed more to the election than at any time in the previous twenty-five years.[42]

However, McGovern's extremist positions did not render the election outcome a foregone conclusion:

Each separate factor of party strength, issue preferences, and New Politics sentiments favored the Democrats; taken together these factors pointed to a Democratic victory.[43]

If voters were issue oriented, and McGovern was closer on the issues, it would seem that voters would support him. However:

. . . McGovern's issue positions were closer to those of the electorate than that electorate perceived them to be. Our explanation of the discrepancy is that McGovern somehow failed to convince many of those who already shared his positions that they indeed did so.[44]

Now it appears that the positions that McGovern took were not nearly so destructive to his candidacy as the way that he took them, and that sharp differentiation between the candidates may be a function of something more than their issue positions.

There are discrepancies in the analyses of ideology as well. The initial paper spoke of the upgrading of the quality of political thinking in general terms and as occurring across "a broad segment of the population." Miller and Levitin, by contrast, argue that "Only within the New Politics ideologues are the qualities that have been assumed to have changed across the entire electorate to be found."[45] This conclusion is consistent with their description of the New Politics themes as a new liberal-conservative dimension and their admission that "By definition, the New Politics themes are structured, coherent, and important to the ideologues, but not to the Center."[46] But one is not told how many of those in the center continue to employ the old liberal-conservative continuum, or both together, in their understanding of politics; in fact, indexes of constraint or consistency cannot address this question.

On the other hand, Miller and Levitin do attempt to justify the persistent search for a single, underlying dimension of conflict on which all political events can be ordered with yet another democratic theory:

If a representative democracy is to reflect some general mandate of the people, then individuals must be able to establish and make their mandate known. The people cannot vote a mandate on the basis of their preferences on single issues alone. There will be no mandate unless and until an issue voting electorate links policies into more general, shared, relatively coherent political preferences. There must also be some consensus among the represented and their representatives about the nature of those linkages.[47]

The authors are concerned that the aggregation of issues, not to mention multiple dimensions of evaluation of a single issue, prohibits analysts from assigning a clear and precise meaning to the outcome of an election. But the solution offered is, in fact, no solution at all, and invokes a curious notion of democracy.

Those who cheer evidence of increased constraint in voter attitudes or the use of ideological labels as guides to vote choice have always assumed that ideology indicates enlightenment and that ideologues share a common understanding of politics. Now that the new issue voter has arrived, with a heightened ideological consciousness, a number of authors suggest that democracy has been enhanced. Because the public understands politics, one may substitute for the vague meanings attached to elections in the past a more exact reading of the public pulse from which specific policy implications flow. But even if everyone agreed on a particular dimension, no such mandate could be assumed. At best one would know which of the two alternative issue position sets the majority of voters was "closer to." Even if a voting method were devised so that, with an equal weighting of individual preferences, a uniquely preferred point on a single dimension of conflict could be identified, one could still read no mandate because there would be no way of weighting the various issues that contributed to the outcome. The nature of a mandate is itself ambiguous. If the 1972 election had pitted a hawk on Vietnam against a dove, and the hawk amassed 51 percent of the vote, would that imply a policy of massive escalation, moderate escalation, or the status quo?

Beyond the technical deficiencies of this position, it is quite ambiguous as a democratic theory. If it is desirable to transform representatives into instructed delegates, why not poll constituents on separate issues? It is not clear what the representative's function is in this scheme, but it is implicitly assumed that the character of the representative should not enter the voter's decision, that is, that all candidates are equally competent and reliable representatives of their issue positions. Another aspect of this scheme worthy of more consideration is that it proposes to enhance communication by constraining it. While it may be easier for election analysts and public officials to interpret vote totals, the cost of imposing a one-dimensional interpretation on politics is the systematic distortion or discarding of incompatible information or issue positions. Finally, this notion of democracy ignores not only all classical democratic theory, but also the pluralist tradition that dominates American political science today. This tradition not only leads one not to expect a single dimension of conflict, but also further identifies the absence of such a single dimension as one of the stabilizing influences on democratic systems. The notion that all members of society should be pitted against each other in ideological conflict is certainly unique in democratic theory.

Yet another analysis of the new issue voter is Nie, Verba, and Petrocik's *The Changing American Voter*. Again, as the title suggests, the application of the social-psychological model to earlier elections is not challenged and the need for a new theory is ascribed to changes in the external environment:

> For the public of the late fifties, party was the guide to political behavior. It no longer is. . . . In the fifties, citizens thought of political issues in the crudest of terms; they had inconsistent sets of issue positions, and their issue positions were relatively unrelated to the vote.
>
> As party has declined, issues have become important to the voter. The reasons are simple: new issues have appeared and the meaning of old issues has changed. This in turn has affected the ways citizens think about politics—not what issue positions individuals hold, but the way in which they conceptualize such issues, the coherence of their issue positions, and the extent to which they are guided in their vote by their issue positions.[48]

The major party candidates play a key role in the Nie et al. account by their articulation of issue positions that enrich or impoverish the political content of voter attitudes. However, they explicitly reject, and offer convincing evidence to refute, the SRC/CPS claim that the enrichment of public attitudes is due to the increased educational level of the electorate.[49] By far the greatest weight as a catalyst for change is given to the new issues:

> . . . the issues that emerge in the 1960's foster coherence in citizen attitudes and a greater use of issue positions as criteria for political evaluations. The characteristics of the new issues are: (1) they are issues that catch the attention of the public; (2) they are issues that penetrate into the personal lives of citizens; (3) they are issues that cluster together.[50]

Unfortunately, the evidence that is cited on behalf of the idea that the new issues are "new" in these characteristics provides no substantial support for such a conclusion. For example, the authors cite a breakdown by categories of the issues that the public has identified as most important in 48

Gallup polls between 1949 and 1972. In 47 of the polls the most important issue was the current foreign policy crisis (Korea, Sputnik, the Bay of Pigs invasion, the Cuban missile crisis, Vietnam), the economy, or civil rights/ integration. These three categories account in every case for the preponderance of responses and only once are as many as 38 percent of the responses in other categories. On the matters of attitude consistency, ideology, and constraint, Nie et al. employ the familiar tools, again noting an increase in each area. They depart from tradition, however, in identifying the clustering of attitudes as an empirical phenomenon not related to a transcendant dimension of truth.

Gerald Pomper's contribution to the picture of the new issue voter in his recent book *Voter's Choice*, which contrasts the old image of the dependent voter (namely, the social-psychological model) with the new image of the responsive voter:* "The character of this voter, and the influences upon his choices, are not permanent, but change with the circumstances of the times and with political events."[51] Pomper departs from the pattern set by other advocates of the new issue voter by suggesting that the quality of voter response is not permanent but may change again, although he expects continually greater emphasis on issues (see below). He returns to the fold by citing changes in the voter, rather then any shortcomings of the dependent voter model, as the reason for a new model:

> The evidence of recent political history is that the American electorate has significantly changed in character. The dependent voter has been supplanted by the responsive voter. With a different electorate, a new American politics becomes likely.[52]

Pomper attributes the new American politics in large measure to national integration, which facilitates the homogenization of American politics, and to changes in the issues, both of which bring about the familiar increase in ideological politics:

> The political map of America increasingly is the same for all Americans. They agree on the policy directions and ideological positions of the parties, and they react to the same issues. . . .
> A more ideological politics is also seen among individual voters. Citizens have clearer perceptions of differences between the parties on a series of policy questions. . . . Given these clearer perceptions, their ballot

---

*Specified excerpts from *Voter's Choice: Varieties of American Electoral Behavior* by Gerald M. Pomper Copyright © 1975 by Harper & Row, Publishers, Inc., New York, N.Y. Reprinted by permission of the publisher.

choices show a greater effect of issue preferences. As the importance of traditional partisanship, candidate personality, and sociological influences has declined, the impact of issue preferences on the vote has increased. . . .

The character of salient issues has been transformed, with an emerging new emphasis on such basic matters as war and race. These questions are not ones that can be bargained out and eventually compromised. . . .

Issue preferences have also become more coherent. Voters grasp the connections between different policy questions, rather than reacting to each matter separately. Their outlook on politics is more integrated, as they can more readily place preferences on individual issues into a general ideological framework. . . .

American politics is likely to become even more ideological. The increasing numbers and influence of the young and the educated point in this direction.[53]

Pomper concludes his analysis with a proposal that American politics be made still more responsive by strengthening the major parties in order to impose ideological coherence on elections.

Historical Perspectives on the New Issue Voter

When the new issue voter is placed alongside the image developed in *The American Voter* and other sources, certain unresolved conflicts become apparent. First, it is clear that the standards for issue voting have changed, while it is not at all clear that issue voting is, or was in 1972, any more prominent than in the 1950s. Second, if the social-psychological model had been an accurate portrayal, the new issue voter never could have evolved, and the efforts that have been made to account for the discontinuity between the two models do not suffice. Third, with respect to the theoretical roles of parties and candidates, the lessons of the 1972 election have been lost in the excitement about issues.

The standards of issue orientation by which the voters of the 1950s were judged are set out in some detail above. Beginning with the 1968 election survey, respondents were asked to place themselves, the major parties, and the major candidates on seven-point issue scales, making possible for the first time comparison of positions. This, in turn, gave birth to the new proximity standard of issue orientation:

> . . . the policy voter is the individual who casts his ballot for the candidate most proximate to him on those issues about which he holds an attitude before the election.[54]

The proximity standard is neither better nor worse than its predecessors. While stringent information requirements of the earlier standards are relaxed so that it is more likely that issue orientation per se is measured, there are other serious issues to be considered. The very notion of proximity implies that issue positions can be compared spatially, an assumption that is less than intuitively obvious. Beyond this, there are the problems of weighting issues, testing for salience, and treating sets of issues that may incorporate multidimensionality. Because there are no standards of richness involved, it is impossible to distinguish informed estimates of candidate positions from those based on rationalization, projection, or sheer guesswork. Finally, there is no reason to suppose that the standard is correct; voters certainly may be concerned with the final product of the political process rather than the president's position per se.[55]

Whatever the respective merits of the two standards, it is clear that the finding of new issue concern is based on different criteria than were employed in the earlier studies, and that the limitations of the earlier survey instruments prevent the application of the same standards retroactively. On the matter of the increased correlation between positions on a number of issues, there is an impressive body of evidence that some greater degree of constraint occurred during the 1960s, which, however, did not extend into the following decade. But because the idea of constraint has never been incorporated into the notion of issue voting in any theoretically meaningful way, this evidence hardly supports the contention that issue voting has increased.[56]

There is, however, another model that is relevant to the question at hand and can be applied uniformly to each of the elections from 1952 through 1976. The SRC six-factor model, although it has been dropped from their repertoire, is based upon a series of open-ended questions that has appeared in each of the major election surveys. This method employs multiple regression techniques to generate various measures of the importance of the major parties, the issues, and the candidates in an election. The six-factor model was an important anchoring for the social-psychological model and surely should reflect changes in the roles of the various factors of the scope that give rise to the new issue voter.

In a previously published comment on the SRC/CPS analysis of the 1972 election, a version of the SRC's six-factor model was replicated for elections between 1952 and 1972. The claims that new high levels of issue concern were reached in 1972 are contradicted by the evidence of that test. In fact, the weights and other measures of importance associated with issues in 1972 are not impressive relative to those associated with issues in the "issueless fifties," while the measures associated with the two candidates indicate that the candidates in the 1972 election were both more important than any of the other factors for 1972 and more important than any previous candidates since 1952.[57]

The results of a six-factor model for 1972 and 1976 are reported in Tables 3.1, 3.2 and 3.3. The unstandardized regression coefficients (b) reported in Table 3.1 are measures of the unit clout or weight associated with each factor in accounting statistically for the distribution of votes in each election. The product of the unstandardized regression coefficient and the mean for each factor ($b_i \bar{x}_i$) can be interpreted as the net contribution (that is, weight times size) of a factor to the overall outcome of the election. The product of the same coefficient and the standard deviation ($b_i s_i$) reported in Table 3.3 is a measure of the difference in the probability of a Republican vote attributable to a particular factor, or weight times the degree of conflict, and is an indicator of vote-related polarization.[58]

The six-factor model results are valuable for placing the new issue voter in perspective. Based upon these statistical estimates, the two candidates dominated both the 1972 and 1976 elections. In terms of the importance attached to particular factors, the candidate weights in both elections are approximately equal to the weights of the other four factors combined. In terms of net contribution, the McGovern candidacy was of substantial benefit to Republicans in 1972. The lower candidate effects in 1976 reflect generally mixed reviews of Carter and also less enthusiasm for Ford than Nixon. In terms of vote-related polarization, it is again the candidates who are the major focus of division, albeit more so in 1976 than in 1972. In effect, McGovern was the least controversial of the candidates by these measures, only because there was a general agreement across the electorate about his presidential qualities. The six-factor model is complex and quite rich in statistical evidence about the election; a more thorough analysis, however, lies beyond the scope of this book. The evidence is sufficient to establish that, in both elections, voters looked beyond issues to the candidates in weighting their vote choices.

There are other notable discontinuities between the two SRC models besides the changing standards of issue orientation. For example, there is the identification of the "spectacular change in the quality of mass attitudes toward questions of public policy" in 1972. While this change was attributed largely to education, such a conclusion seems to contradict the conclusions of *The American Voter*:

> We presume that any cognitive limitations affecting the modes of political thinking would have a rather constant effect over time, although a rising level of education might permit a slow upgrading in the level of conceptualization.
>   . . . we would never expect this change to be of sweeping magnitude,

TABLE 3.1: Regression Equations for SRC Six-factor Model

	b	Democratic Candidate b (t)	Republican Candidate b (t)	General Management b (t)	Groups b (t)	Foreign Issues b (t)	Domestic Issues b (t)	N	r / r²
1972	.4443	.0803 (*)	.1060 (*)	.0101 (*)	.0663 (*)	.0738 (*)	.0493 (*)	827	.696 / .485
1976	.4851	.0735 (12.7)	.0755 (12.7)	.0396 (6.16)	.0544 (8.18)	.0330 (3.25)	.0530 (9.46)	1631	.687 / .472

t—scores not available in original.

Sources: All 1972 figures from Michael R. Kagay and Greg A. Caldeira, "I Like the Look of His Face: Elements of Electoral Choice, 1952–1972," paper delivered at the annual meeting of the American Political Science Association, San Francisco, September 2–5, 1975. All 1976 figures produced by the author, based upon the Kagay-Caldeira coding scheme.

TABLE 3.2: Net Importance as Measured by $b_i \bar{x}_i$.

		Democratic Candidate	Republican Candidate	General Management	Groups	Foreign Issues	Domestic Issues
1972	x	-.512	-.406	-.191	.715	-.455	-.287
	b x	-.0411	-.0430	-.0019	.0474	-.0336	-.0142
1976	x	.057	-.272	-.264	.800	-.116	.255
	b x	.0042	-.0205	-.0104	.0435	-.0038	.0135

Note: - means pro-Republican.
+ means pro-Democratic.

Sources: All 1972 figures from Michael R. Kagay and Greg A. Caldeira, "I Like the Look of His Face: Elements of Electoral Choice, 1952–1972," paper delivered at the annual meeting of the American Political Science Association, San Francisco, September 2–5, 1975. All 1976 figures produced by the author, based upon the Kagay-Caldeira coding schemes.

TABLE 3.3: Polarization as Measured by $b_i s_i$

		Democratic Candidate	Republican Candidate	General Management	Groups	Foreign Issues	Domestic Issues
1972	s	1.186	1.313	1.112	1.461	1.377	2.003
	b s	.0952	.1392	.0112	.0969	.1016	.0987
1976	s	1.780	1.793	1.557	1.461	.913	1.758
	b s	.1309	.1354	.0617	.0794	.0301	.0932

Sources: All 1972 figures from Michael R. Kagay and Greg A. Caldeira, "I Like the Look of His Face: Elements of Electoral Choice, 1952-1972," paper delivered at the annual meeting of the American Political Science Association, San Francisco, September 2-5, 1975. All 1976 figures produced by the author, based upon the Kagay-Caldeira coding scheme.

and there is still less reason to believe that the picture of the voting public presented previously was captured at an abnormal moment.[59]

The most serious discrepancy between the two models is their differing treatment of the roles of issues and parties, matters that are at the very core of each model. Here is how the SRC/CPS analysts account for the change:

> During a period of issue consensus or strong alignment between issue orientation and traditional partisan divisions, party ties can be expected to have a significant impact, both direct and as a predisposing agent, on the vote decision. However, during periods when questions of policy attain new levels of public salience and divide the population in a fashion that is orthogonal to traditional partisan differences, other political stimuli, such as new candidates and especially candidates associated with the new issues, may become relatively more important in explaining voting behavior.[60]

In other words, when the positions of major parties reflect the division of the electorate on the central issues of the day, voters lose sight of issues and become conformists to party standards. But when issue positions and party identification are not consistent across the population, issues assume greater importance. In fact, if the old theory were correct, such orthogonality between issues and party could not have developed in the first place.

Despite the apparent problems in this attempt to reconcile the two theories, the SRC/CPS analysis of the 1976 election adopts the same line. The problem the analysts faced for the 1976 election was that while many of the conditions that had been regarded as crucial to understanding the 1972 election (such as education and ideological thinking among the electorate) remained undisturbed, the vote choices of the electorate corresponded to their party identifications to a greater degree in the latter election:*

> Even more important for our attempt to explicate the rise in party voting and the decline in issue voting between 1972 and 1976, it is apparent . . . [that] the renewed impact of party identification on the vote in 1976 clearly was not the result of a decay in ideological structuring of attitudes.
>
> Apparently, during the four-year period between elections economic attitudes and ideological orientation among partisans were either shifting

---

*Arthur H. Miller and Warren E. Miller, "Partisanship and Performance: 'Rational' Choice in the 1976 Presidential Election," paper delivered at the 1977 annual meeting of the American Political Science Association, Washington, D.C., September 1–4, 1977. This and all following quotes from Miller and Miller reprinted by permission of the American Political Science Association, Washington, D.C.

to come more into alignment with party identification, or party attachment was changing to conform with issue and policy preferences . . . the net result of the change was to increase slightly the correlation of certain attitudes with party identification, thereby decreasing somewhat the independent effect of these issue attitudes on the vote.[61]

Notice that issues are assumed to have no independent effects when issue position is consistent with party identification.

In general, the SRC/CPS analysis of the 1976 election retreats from the hard issue line adopted for 1972 and does not identify a single, overriding characteristic of the 1976 contest. Instead, the report touches all bases, describing the resurgence of party voting, the decline of issue voting, the constancy of ideological voting, the importance of economic issues and the events of the campaign, the decline of trust in political institutions, and the multifaceted nature of candidate evaluations. Perhaps it is the analysts, and not the voters, who are shifting.

Finally, consider this account of the links between the old and new models, from the 1972 rejoinder:

The elements of a behavioral model linking candidates, issues and the vote choice have . . . been specified by *The American Voter*; . . . and they have been operationalized with the proximity measures used in "Majority Party." Briefly stated, the model specifies that voters have various issue preferences, that candidates are perceived to take differing policy positions, and that voters cast their ballot in accordance with some function that describes the relationship between the perception of the candidate positions and their own issue preferences.[62]

This novel interpretation of *The American Voter* emphasizes the gulf that actually exists between the two models and the reluctance of contemporary analysts to account for it.

Failure to confront these apparent conflicts has obscured the lessons of recent elections. The willingness of large numbers of voters to vote contrary to their party identification in 1968 and 1972 should have resulted in a tempering of the psychological impact of party identification and reinterpretation of party attachments in political terms; instead, one is told that sometimes party identification has a predisposing effect and sometimes it does not. Similarly, the 1972 election clearly demonstrated the impact of a candidate, which is relatively independent of issue positions, in the collapse of the McGovern campaign. Instead, one is told that: "It is apparently far easier for college-educated individuals to translate issue attitudes into a vote decision than for the relatively less well educated who use the candidate as an intervening focus for their ideology."[63] In general, the only progress that candidates made in moving up the ladder of politically respectable voting criteria during the era of the new issue voter was in terms of their role in articulating issue positions.

Overall, the evidence is not at all impressive that voters have entered a new era of heightened issue orientation. Instead, this interpretation is best understood as an overreaction by analysts, a projection made possible by the weak theoretical underpinning of the extant model. On the other hand, the defensive reaction toward *The American Voter* and the vast SRC legacy is unwarranted; it is on weak ground in its attempt to reconcile the old and new and, at the same time, it does a disservice to the real pioneers in voting analysis. The work of Campbell, Converse, and Stokes needs no such defense; it is, naturally and inevitably, flawed by its time-boundedness, the limitations of early surveys, and the necessity for the authors to innovate virtually every test, measure, and model they used. But the work is both imaginative and valuable, even if it is not timeless.

CONCLUSION

The emergence of the social-psychological model as the most authoritative account of voting behavior and the articulation of an alternative conceptualization of voter participation in elections in the rational voter model prompted a debate in the voting literature of the 1960s over the rational quality of the electorate. The polar positions in the debate were largely defined by the work of the SRC, however, as the more important contributions of the rational school, concerning information costs, were displaced by the central role accorded to issues in rational models. Specifically, the debate has focused upon the impact of issues, narrowly defined, and the arguments have revolved around the alternative positions that voters are either issue oriented or party oriented, with candidate orientation falling by the wayside.

The voter-rationality debate has called attention to weaknesses in each of the competitors. Evidence mounted against the party-based interpretation during the most recent elections when voters exhibited elements of issue rationality and an independence of party uncharacteristic of the voters it had described. Thus the social-psychological model was supplanted in the early 1970s by the model of the new issue voter.

The appearance of the new issue voter signals the liberation of the dependent voter of earlier work. Due to qualitative changes in American politics and increased education, this voter is occasionally able to exhibit independence of the bonds of party and a rational consideration of issues. But the account of the new issue voter is inconsistent in its appraisal of voter rationality, combining issue rationality with the nonrational elements of the earlier model. It depends upon a dramatic change in voters, issues, and politics to reconcile it with the earlier model, which denied the possibility of such change. There are serious questions about the empirical evidence for the changes, particularly for the sharp increase in issue voting. The new model, as did its predecessors, ignores crucial elements of context in its account of voter behavior.

The rationality debate did not produce convincing evidence for either side because the models of voting identified with each position were flawed. The social-psychological model ignored the rational elements of voter behavior; the rational voter model assumed an idealized parliamentary system. Both underplayed the role of the candidates in American elections and the personal responsibilities of the president.

NOTES

1. Strictly speaking, the SRC does offer an account of the broad patterns of partisanship that recur over a series of elections in their analysis of realigning elections, cf. Campbell, et al. *The American Voter,* pp. 531–38. But this account is quite ambiguous. At times the argument appears to be that during realigning elections voters exhibit an uncharacteristic, rational concern for issues and party performance; at other points the argument depends on the familiar psychological mechanisms, but these must either affect groups in random patterns or exhibit some rational basis.

2. Anthony Downs, *An Economic Theory of Democracy* (New York: Harper & Row, 1957).

3. Ibid., pp. 4-11, esp. p. 6.

4. Ibid., p. 7.

5. Ibid., p. 34.

6. This assumption is essential to the subsequent development of the model because it cannot be assumed that the preferences of rational individuals will aggregate to a rational preference for a group; cf. Kenneth J. Arrow, *Social Choice and Individual Values* (New York: John Wiley & Sons, 1951).

7. Contrary to Downs's claim, only parties are assumed to be self-interested. If self-interest here referred to independence of individual utility functions, then he would not be able to derive the conclusions that follow. Instead Downs means to assume more than this—a narrow-minded selfishness on the part of parties that is explicitly denied to individuals; cf. ibid., pp. 27–28, p. 37.

8. Ibid., p. 28.

9. Ibid., p. 7.

10. Ibid., p. 283.

11. Joseph A. Schumpeter, *Capitalism, Socialism, and Democracy,* (New York: Harper & Row, 1950), p. 282; quoted in Downs, *An Economic Theory,* p. 29. This does not exhaust the links between the two works, the scope of which is reflected in a footnote to these remarks: "Schumpeter's profound analysis of democracy forms the inspiration and foundation for our whole thesis, and our debt and gratitude to him are great indeed." *An Economic Theory,* p. 29, fn. 11.

12. Ibid., pp. 23–24.

13. Ibid., p. 18.

14. Ibid., p. 96.

15. Ibid., p. 98.

16. Ibid., p. 115.

17. Unfortunately, the assumptions of this theory are of dubious empirical relevance and there are problems in the derivation of Downs's conclusions as well; see the criticism of this theory in Samuel Popkin, John W. Gorman, Charles Phillips, and Jeffrey A. Smith, "Comment: What Have You Done for Me Lately?: Toward an Investment Theory of Voting," *American Political Science Review* 70 (September 1976): 795–99.

18. One attempt to operationalize and test the full Downsian model, which is quite successful in predicting turnout and preference decisions in a simulation of one election, is reported in Norman Frohlich, Joe A. Oppenheimer, Jeffrey A. Smith, and Oran R. Young, "A Test of Downsian Voter Rationality: 1964 Presidential Voting," *American Political Science Review* 72 (March 1978): 178–97.

19. V. O. Key, Jr., *The Responsible Electorate* (Cambridge, Mass: Harvard University Press, 1966), pp. 7–8.

20. Ibid., pp. 58–59.

21. Ibid., p. 61.

22. Philip E. Converse, Warren E. Miller, Jerrold Rusk, and Arthur Wolfe, "Continuity and Change in American Politics: Parties and Issues in the 1968 Election," *American Political Science Review* 63 (December 1969): 1,096.

23. Angus T. Campbell, Philip E. Converse, Warren E. Miller, and Donald E. Stokes, *The American Voter* (New York: John Wiley & Sons, 1960), p. 141.

24. Ibid., p. 553.

25. Converse et al., "Continuity and Change in American Politics," 1,097.

26. Ibid., p. 1,099, emphasis in original.

27. Angus T. Campbell, Philip E. Converse, Warren E. Miller, and Donald E. Stokes, *The American Voter* (New York: John Wiley & Sons, 1960).

28. Arthur H. Miller, Warren E. Miller, Alden S. Raine, and Thad A. Brown, "A Majority Party in Disarray: Policy Polarization in the 1972 Election," *American Political Science Review* 70 (September 1976): 753–78. Although this article was not ultimately published until 1976, it appeared in the form of a paper presented at the American Political Science Association convention three years earlier, and thus antedates the works cited below.

29. Ibid., p. 753.

30. Ibid., p. 754.

31. Ibid., pp. 753–54.

32. Ibid., p. 761.

33. Ibid., p. 773.

34. Ibid., p. 754.

35. Ibid., p. 766.

36. Ibid., p. 771.

37. Warren E. Miller and Teresa E. Levitin, *Leadership and Change: The New Politics and the American Electorate* (Cambridge, Mass.: Winthrop, 1976), p. 1.

38. Ibid., p. 63.

39. Richard Scammon and Benjamin Wattenberg, *The Real Majority* (New York: Coward McCann Geoghegan, 1970).

40. Miller and Levitin, *Leadership and Change*, pp. 60–61.

41. Miller et al., "Majority Party," p. 760.

42. Miller and Levitin, *Leadership and Change*, pp. 61–62.

43. Ibid., p. 165.

44. Ibid., p. 145.

45. Ibid., p. 174.

46. Ibid.

47. Ibid., p. 171. The message appears throughout, esp. pp. 16–17, 46–47. See also the discussion of responsible party systems in Chapter 8 of this work.

48. Norman H. Nie, Sidney Verba, and John R. Petrocik, *The Changing American Voter* (Cambridge, Mass.: Harvard University Press, 1976), p. 96.

49. Ibid., pp. 119–21 and pp. 148–50. The evidence shows that ideological thinking has increased across the spectrum of educational achievement. The education hypothesis is also refuted in Popkin et al., "What Have You Done for Me Lately?," p. 783.

50. Nie et al., *The Changing American Voter*, p. 97.

51. Gerald M. Pomper, *Voter's Choice: Varieties of American Electoral Behavior* (New York: Dodd, Mead, 1975), p. 8.

52. Ibid., pp. 210–11.

53. Ibid., pp. 213–14.

54. Miller et al., "Majority Party," p. 765.

55. These are important elements in the development of the investor-voter model in the following chapter. The notion that voters are concerned with output rather than position is introduced in Popkin et al., "What Have You Done for Me Lately?"

56. For another treatment of changing standards that also casts doubt on the conclusion that issue voting has increased, see Michael Margolis, "From Confusion to Confusion: Issues and the American Voter (1956–1972)," *American Political Science Review* 71 (March 1977): 31–43.

57. The analysis of the six-factor model appears in Popkin et al., "What Have You Done For Me Lately?," pp. 780–86. Similar analyses reporting similar results are cited in fn. 15, p. 784. The six-factor model results, using a somewhat different coding scheme, are replicated in Michael R. Kagay and Greg A. Caldeira, "I Like the Looks of His Face: Elements of Electoral Choice, 1952–1972," paper delivered at the annual meeting of the American Political Science Association, San Francisco, September 2–5, 1975. Although the SRC/CPS authors seem to prefer the Kagay version, his results are largely consistent with the Popkin, et al. analysis and certainly do not support the SRC/CPS analysis. However, the figures cited in the tables in this chapter are based on the Kagay-Caldeira version of the six-factor model coding scheme obtained in private correspondence.

58. Each of these measures is developed and justified in greater detail in Popkin et al., "What Have You Done for Me Lately?," pp. 782–85.

59. Campbell et al., *The American Voter*, pp. 255–56.

60. Miller et al., "Majority Party.," p. 770.

61. Arthur H. Miller and Warren E. Miller, "Partisanship and Performance: 'Rational' Choice in the 1976 Presidential Election," paper delivered at the 1977 annual meeting of the American Political Science Association, Washington, D.C., September 1–4, ms. pp. 38, 45.

62. Arthur H. Miller and Warren E. Miller, "Ideology in the 1972 Election: Myth or Reality—A Rejoinder," *American Political Science Review* 70 (September 1976): 839.

63. Miller et al., "Majority Party," p. 770.

4

THE VOTER AS INVESTOR: CONTEXTUAL RATIONALLY IN AMERICAN PRESIDENTIAL ELECTIONS

*T*he efforts of voting analysts to develop a consistent explanation for the vicissitudes of voter behavior in American presidential contests have been frustrated by failure to take into account crucial aspects of the contexts of those elections. The consequent misapplications of arbitrary standards of good citizenship to the American electorate have generated predominantly pessimistic appraisals of voters' capacities for rational decision making. The investor-voter model described in this chapter is a revision of the theory of the American voter that explicitly incorporates elements of the electoral context. Including these elements leads to rather different expectations of rational voter behavior than those implied in the naive model of the democratic citizen. The outcome of this revision is a more optimistic appraisal of voter rationality that at the same time raises serious questions about political system performance.

Much of the development of the investor-voter model involves the direct adaptation of the earlier efforts of Anthony Downs to the American context.[1] In the process, the outline for a formal theory of rational voting behavior in American presidential elections is presented. Although the derivation is rarely explicit, a Downsian analysis of the voter's calculus, with the modifications specified in each instance, underlies the arguments in this work. Naturally, the results should be subjected to the same rigorous standards of logical entailment that one would apply to Downs's own theory.

THE RATIONALITY ASSUMPTION

In order to derive propositions about behavior from an institutional context, it is necessary to adopt some assumptions about the nature of behavior. Throughout the following, it is assumed that individuals are rational, both in their personal lives with respect to the decision to participate in elections, and as political actors. By rationality is intended the same assumptions that Downs made, namely, that faced with a set of alternatives, individuals perceive differences, rank order alternatives in terms of preferences consistently and transitively, and pursue the most preferred alternative.[2] In other words, given a set of perceived alternatives and an individual's preference ordering among them, one can deduce that the most preferred alternative is the rational choice, and if the individual is rational, one can predict—or explain—a choice from among the alternatives. It is important to note, once again, that the assumption that individuals are rational by itself does not restrict in any way the ultimate ends that they may pursue; rather, it implies that given an individual's values and state of knowledge, an account can be given of that individual's behavior.

The specification of a set of standards of rational behavior is not a moral prescription, except to the extent that rationality is itself prescribed. In other words, if one wishes to be efficient in the allocation of one's resources in this particular political context, one ought to follow these standards, insofar as they are correctly derived. Instead, this is a descriptive model of a particular type: it describes the behavior of rational individuals. It is not presumed that all individuals behave rationally at all times; clearly this is not the case. But it is presumed that the model has empirical content, that enough people behave rationally enough of the time that a rational model can account for their behavior.

A consequence of specifying rational behavior within a particular context is that this approach is conservative with respect to the values of the individuals who are its subjects, and, indeed, the values that characterize the entire system. That this is appropriate might be argued in terms of the desirability of a value-free social science, but this position is not taken here. Instead, this approach reflects the important influence of institutions in shaping behavior. Even those institutions that are nothing more than mere codifications of repeated behavior (such as some rules of etiquette) begin to exert an independent influence on behavior from the moment that they become institutionalized. Thus the purpose of this approach is to identify and account for behavior that is endemic to the American political system. If people are found to be behaving rationally with respect to the institutional structure, and if this behavior is found wanting based on some set of moral criteria, then approbation ought to be addressed to the institutional context of their behavior. One implication of the analysis below is that one reason for the failure of American voters to meet the standards of model democratic citizenship is that the American political system falls short of being a model democracy.

The distinction between personal and political rationality is an important part of the investor-voter model. The personally rational individual is one for whom participation in the various spheres of activity is rationally ordered, that is, one who decides when and on what terms to engage in which activities, subject to the demands of the environment and available resources. A politically rational individual is one whose political activity has political ends. Specifically, it is assumed that voters vote the way they do in order to affect the output of the political system; the decision whether or not to vote, on the other hand, involves personal rationality. Consequently, the first task is to specify the place of political activity for the personally rational individual.

THE PERSONAL CONTEXT OF VOTING BEHAVIOR

The artificial status of the analytical isolation of voting behavior from all other aspects of the individual's life experience is reflected in the myriad personal meanings attached to political activity. For the purpose of analyzing voting behavior, politically irrational, personal considerations must be ignored, with one major exception. It is possible to make a general statement about the place of political activity in the lives of American citizens that is empirically defensible and has important implications for behavior in the political sphere.

The most important aspect of American attitudes toward politics is that political activities are, to a significant extent, isolated from other aspects of life. As pointed out in Chapter 1, liberal culture fosters this distinction, investing it with a positive moral status and obscuring the impact of avowedly political events on other important areas of personal and social life. Occasionally, such as in the cases of the military draft and school integration decisions, the integration of one's private life with public policies is demonstrated with unmistakable force, but these are exceptions to the rule. In general, people cannot be expected to undertake political activity as if politics were central to their lives. Instead, in the American context, the decision to participate in elections is a marginal one for the individual.

The personally rational citizen faces an assortment of potential activities to which are attached various reward structures and that require the investment of various amounts and combinations of resources. Time and energy, for example, are inherently scarce commodities that the rational citizen will allocate among activities in such a way as to attempt to maximize total personal utility from all activities, subject to environmental constraints. If one assumes that every activity bears decreasing marginal returns after some level, then one would not expect people to specialize in a single activity, but rather to invest some resources in work, some in leisure, some in entertainment, and so on. Obviously, the rewards and costs associated with various activities vary with individuals.

If political activity were costless, it would be reasonable to expect that citizens who perceived their environment to be affected by the outcome of political contests would take action to see that such contests were resolved according to their values. However, voting requires a certain amount of time and effort, at a minimum, for casting a ballot and informing that activity; more active forms of political participation may entail correspondingly greater demands on resources. Because some resources must be applied, political participation inevitably entails opportunity costs. Opportunity costs are the returns foregone from the investment of resources in one activity rather than another. The potential voter, then, weighs both the cost of the required investment against the expected returns, and the returns from voting against the potential returns from the investment of the same resources in other activities.

The returns to individuals from voting may be internal or external. In the first category are included the psychic gratifications associated with participating in a community event, making a contribution to the collective outcome of the election, and supporting an appropriate political or moral position. External rewards from voting depend upon the effects of the election on the output of the political process, in terms of its impact on both specific policies and more general concerns, for example, the responsiveness of the system to various groups. It is the external impact of the election (its effect on political outputs) that defines the value of the internal rewards (see Chapter 1). For this reason and because they are more tangible, it is these external rewards that play the greater role in the voter's calculus, particularly with regard to candidate preference.

There are two important implications of this brief analysis. First, because the election is not an end in itself, voters will base their evaluations of competing alternatives on the expected returns from each rather than upon consideration of policy positions per se. It is in part because they apply their resources (voting costs) to the expected returns from future activities of the political system, rather than to present policy positions, that investor-voters are distinguished from consumer-voters of the rational voter model. Second, citizens' incentives to vote increase with the expected returns from voting, which in turn increase as a function of their perception of the stakes in the election (the differences between the expected returns from each alternative), and the extent to which their vote will affect policy outputs. It cannot be assumed that all citizens will find voting to be profitable and will vote; instead, the level of turnout in elections may vary with contextual determinants of the importance of voting. Finally, the consideration of costs of participation opens the possibility of understanding much voting behavior as involving efforts to conserve on costs.

INFORMATION COSTS

The accumulation of political information requires the investment of scarce resources. At the minimum, some time must be allocated for gathering and digesting new information. Of course, the costs and returns associated with different bits of information are intrinsic to individuals, but, informing oneself on the qualifications and positions of competing candidates is generally a costly process. Thus one can expect rational voters to try to conserve on information costs wherever feasible.[3] The implications of costly information are summarized in the three general points immediately below, with more detailed implications reserved until the discussion of context is completed.

(1) Voters will take advantage of free information. Free information is that information gathered for purposes other than the candidate preference choice to which it may be applied; in other words, it is information the costs of which are absorbed by other activities of the voter. Typically, free information will be that gathered by individuals for application in their daily lives, such as farmers who follow farm price supports and import quotas for use in their own planning.

Another source of free information is what might be called fun information: information that is accumulated because the possession of it is satisfying in itself, or because it is incidental to a pleasurable activity. Many citizens watched the Watergate hearings or the presidential debates on television not because they wanted to be better informed, but because they enjoyed the spectacle of the confrontations. Much information gathered from television news shows, political rallies, and so on undoubtedly would fall into this category. Unfortunately, this analysis does not suggest anything about the distribution of fun information across the population. It does suggest that the information in the possession of the electorate may be biased toward the spectacular or the entertaining, however. This may have important implications of its own.

(2) Voters will use information shortcuts. An information shortcut is a piece of information that either summarizes a more complex set of

information or bears a fairly strong observable association with certain relevant attitudes and is in some sense cheaper or more accessible than the information for which it is substituted. Thus one might reasonably suppose that a black candidate would be more sensitive to black issues than a white candidate, based only on blackness, ceteris paribus, and without knowing anything about the candidate's political history. Such an assumption might be wrong, but it clearly will be right more often than it is wrong, and the alternative information (issue positions, past voting records, campaign statements) necessary to make a sophisticated choice on this question is considerably more costly and often without much greater guarantee of reliability.

(3) Voters generally will have limited information. The bases for their candidate preference decisions generally will exhibit two limitations. First, voters will have information only about a narrow range of issues, in particular those issues where they can apply free information and those where they are directly and personally affected. Second, each voter's information will be limited in the sense that much of it will be composed of generalized criteria of the type that constitute most information shortcuts. The particular kinds of information voters will employ is discussed below.

A further limitation on voters' information arises from the limited choice set facing them in an American presidential election. Because most voters recognize only two alternatives, they need only gather enough information to choose between the two. The expenditure of additional resources for information is irrational unless that information has a high probability of changing the voter's preference. Once a voter has determined a preference, new information will be limited to incidental information that is essentially costless (for example, those who watch the news regularly will inevitably add to their stocks of information), the odd startling revelation that threatens to upset a previous choice, and whatever additional information the voter may find necessary to support a preference publicly.

THE INSTITUTIONAL CONTEXT OF VOTING BEHAVIOR

The cultural settings of elections establish certain parameters for the behavior of voters. Consideration of the place of political activity in American liberalism led to the hypothesis that voting is a marginal activity for citizens, with the participation decision based on an implicit comparison of expected returns and costs. Among the most significant costs are those associated with gathering information about the alternatives; voters economize on information costs where feasible and thus are less than fully informed. The institutional structure of the American political system also influences voters' stocks of information, both limiting the amount of information they will gather and shaping their requirements for certain kinds of information. Several aspects of the institutional context of elections that have implications for voter behavior are identified below.

A Presidential Election Is a Collective Decision-Making Activity

Each voter in a national election is only one member of a much larger group of citizens who will share the outcome of the election, whatever it is. Voters may safely assume that an outcome will be provided without their contribution, and that the system of elections will survive at least through the next election period, so that it is only the quality of the outcome that can be affected by personal participation. But each individual (potential) voter bears only a very small (for all practical purposes, invisible) portion of the responsibility for the quality of the outcome. In other words, elections are collective goods, and the electorate is subject to the same incentive structure as are other large groups attempting to provide themselves with collective goods.[4] Each potential voter has an incentive (namely, the conserving of private resources) to try to shift the burden of determining the qualifications of the candidates, probing them for weaknesses, analyzing their issue positions, and even voting, to other members of the electorate. This is true even though the voter may realize that every other member of the electorate shares the same incentives, and that if everyone behaved accordingly, the outcome would not be the best for the group (that is, it would not exhibit group rationality). Voters may rest somewhat assured that other elements of the society—such as the media and the opposition— because of their private incentives, are doing some candidate testing for the voters. Any outrageous or criminal behavior, prejudicial remarks, and so on by the candidates surely will be brought to their attention. Thus they need only gather enough information to assure themselves that they are probably voting for the candidate for whom they would vote if they were fully informed, that is, that their contribution is a positive one.

Voters Face a Limited Choice Set

For most voters in most presidential elections, there are only two alternatives: the candidates of the Republican and Democratic parties. With few exceptions, a vote for any other than the major party candidates can have symbolic value only, unless directed to a short-term goal like guaranteeing enough votes to secure a ballot position in the next election or indicating support within a third party for a particular individual. (A larger view of the electoral process incorporating primary elections substantially increases the number of viable candidates and the opportunities for strategic voting, requiring correspondingly more sophisticated information.)

Ceteris paribus, the limitation of the number of candidates facilitates the use of relatively crude approximations of candidate positions with reasonable confidence. Voters in the 1976 election who wished primarily to see defense spending reduced needed to know only that Jimmy Carter threatened to reduce the budget, while Jerry Ford insisted on the importance of maintaining the current level of expenditures. They could have voted rationally on this basis, without any more details about the candidates' positions. The addition of a third viable candidate who wished to reduce defense spending would require additional information (about positions on defense spending or secondary issues) if voters wished to maintain the same confidence in their decision.

Because information is costly and the value of the election places an upper limit on the amount they are willing to spend, it does not follow that voters will add information in proportion to the number of alternatives. Voters may either find it worthwhile to evaluate all the candidates on all the issues, thus making finer distinctions and increasing their "informedness," or economize on candidate evaluation by reducing the number of issue dimensions or increasing the confidence interval around candidate placement on those dimensions (in other words, using less reliable information) or both, thus reducing their "informedness."

In general, when elections are limited to two candidates, voters can be expected to employ relatively crude measures on even the most important issues, unless they are able to apply free information.

The Relevant Alternatives in American Presidential Elections Are the Candidates, Not the Parties

No single indication of the extent to which structural characteristics have been ignored in voting studies is more impressive than the repeated failure to distinguish between candidate and party in the construction of questionnaires and the analysis of data. The examination of party "positions" and party "ideologies" often is carried on as if the United States had the equivalent of a disciplined parliamentary party system, where party platforms take precedence over individual candidates and provide reliable guides to policy orientation. But parties, policy positions, and candidates clearly are not interchangeable in American politics.

The American president is not a creature of his party in the legislature. He is elected on his own and, if anything, the members of his party in the legislature owe their elections to him rather than the opposite. The United States does not have a responsible party system, a fact frequently bemoaned by political scientists.[5] Several contemporary examples point to the relative independence of candidate from party. Consider, for example, that the party of Jimmy Carter is also the party of John Stennis, Bella Abzug, and Fred Harris. Richard Nixon's 1972 election campaign was led by the Committee to Re-elect the President, an organization entirely separate from the Republican party, and there was considerable discussion in the 1976 campaign about the extent to which the Democratic party platform bound, or even represented the views of, the Democratic candidate. Finally, Popkin et al. report a 1972 McGovern survey that indicates that voters clearly separate candidates and parties; no more than 65 percent of the voters surveyed named the same party and party candidate when asked which party and which candidate could do the better job on their most important issues.[6] Evidence abounds that it is the positions, ideology, and characteristics of the candidates, not those the parties, that are the relevant concerns of voters. The use of party criteria, by contrast, may serve as an economical, albeit imperfect, estimate of a candidate's positions.

The Nature of the President's Job Shapes the Concerns of Voters

Because of his prominent role in the American political system, the positions of the president on various issues are extremely important. In most cases, though, the president's positions have no value in and of themselves because they are not directly translatable into policies. Rather, they are important only because his articulation of particular positions is expected to have some impact on the policymaking process. It is argued above that voters who view their participation in elections as an investment are concerned with the products of the political process. Thus they must focus not only on the candidate's positions, but also upon those factors that intervene in the formulation of policy—leadership, political acumen, trustworthiness, competence—in general, those talents that affect the candidate's ability to deliver on his promises.

This concern for performance as well as promise is reinforced by additional features of the president's job. Because he is at the center of the political system, the president is responsible for the general management of the system at the top, the personal negotiation with leaders of various interest groups as well as the leaders of foreign states, the articulation of national concerns and the building of public support, along with any number of other tasks where his success will be measured in terms at least somewhat independent of the particular outcome he prefers. Indeed, many of the president's tasks involve administrative skills almost exclusively.*

---

*One interesting implication of this argument that voters "interview" candidates according to job-related criteria is that presidential and congressional candidates would be rewarded for different qualities. The most important (visible) aspect of a representative's job is presenting the views of constituents in Congress, and the administrative demands are minimal. Thus Bella Abzug, Adam Clayton Powell, and George McGovern could be very good representatives, even though each might be a poor choice for president.

Finally, the president is the person most responsible for seeing the political system through the unanticipated issues, crises, and circumstances of the future. In such cases, old issue positions provide at best an indirect guide to the president's ability to deal with new problems. This virtually guarantees that personal characteristics of the candidates will be a factor in every voter's preference decision, although they may be outweighed by more pressing policy concerns.

In the performance of all of these tasks, the president is invested with more power than resides with any other single individual in the American political system. He not only exercises a determinant influence on substantial areas of policy, but he also does so with no effective oversight by other public agents in many cases. All of these considerations force the rational electorate to evaluate the trustworthiness of the person granted such status. The centrality of trustworthiness evaluations in the voter's preference decision is a principal theme in the remainder of this work.

Voting Is Decision Making Under Conditions of Uncertainty

Adding to the cost of information is the generally poor quality of the information that even the most enthusiastic campaign followers have available to them. Voters must wade through candidates' statements that are vague, self-serving, often contradictory, and otherwise conditioned by the pressures of the campaign. They must assess the credibility and accuracy of everything they hear before they can add it to their stock of information, then they must weigh it with their existing stock. In some areas, they will have no reliable data at all.

To the obstacles to utilizing the available information must be added the uncertainties of the future. The president, in the course of his term, will be exposed to many problems that have not, at the time of his election, been anticipated or generally recognized, and with which he will have to deal nonetheless. But even with regard to current issues, there remains the difficulty of anticipating the effects of the political process and future circumstances on the president's positions.

For these reasons and others, voters are inevitably in a condition of uncertainty regarding the aftermath of the election. This has two implications for present concerns. First, voters will be satisfied with less than complete information, knowing that they can never be certain and that efforts to improve their state of knowledge will be increasingly frustrating and costly. Second, where there are gaps in his information about important areas of concern, they will project from available information to predict behavior in those areas. Uncertainties about the future make this necessary, although of varying importance, for everyone.

Issue-Based Conflict Is Institutionally Managed by the Political System

When voters are called upon to interpret the information available to them and to anticipate the future, uncertainty is inevitable. But there is another source of uncertainty that is of greater relevance to the state of democracy and the behavior of voters. Uncertainty also is inevitable when information about issues is not available to voters in any meaningful sense. The ability of voters to address certain concerns through elections is limited by two broad characteristics of American politics: the institutionalization of political processes and the two-party system, with consequent implications for voter participation and information.

The Institutionalization of Political Processes

The most spectacular developments in the American political system during this century have centered in the executive branch. By any measure of expenditures, personnel, or functions, the federal bureaucracy has grown immensely. Concomitant with bureaucratic expansion has been the inexorable accumulation of power in the executive branch under the nominal control of the president. While writers from Jurgen Habermas to Samuel Huntington to George Orwell have dealt with the issues raised by these developments, their implications for voters have not been incorporated into the voting literature.

The most important implication of these developments for citizens is a loss of control over various aspects of their lives. With each new government agency, jurisdiction over some function shifts to a locus that is inevitably remote from the citizenry, not only in terms of physical interaction in decision-making processes, but also in terms of the political control that elections might provide. The shift in power embodied in these developments may be said to occur, in general, on three dimensions.

(1) An executive agency assumes exclusive authority in a particular functional area, thus removing the function from the potential control of the legislature and/or the personal control of individuals, and placing it instead in the hands of agents who are at best only indirectly subject to popular control.

(2) The sphere of politics is reduced as solutions to erstwhile political questions are institutionalized in bureaucratic procedures, effectively removing the qualitative aspect of problem solving from electoral contests and focusing debate on quantitative questions.

(3) Bureaucratic processes become increasingly technologized, rendering the information necessary to monitor them inaccessible to the nonexpert citizen through complexity or secrecy.

A more complete development of these propositions unfortunately lies beyond the central concern of the present work. However, a few examples should suffice to establish the importance of such developments. Virtually every aspect of foreign relations, for instance, partakes of these trends. The conduct of the Vietnam war made it clear that despite the intentions of the framers of the Constitution to provide otherwise, decisions about the use of troops are the almost exclusive province of the office of the president. Much of that exclusive control in turn derived from an apparent monopoly of expertise in the conduct of war that facilitated the manipulation of public support. As an ongoing process, the determination of national defense policy is an appropriate example. The question of whether national defense ought to be pursued by the maintenence of quantitative and technological superiority in weapons sytems does not enter electoral politics; the answer to this question has been institutionalized in the relations among congress, the military, and weapons producers. Instead, the public debate takes the form of questions such as whether the B-1 bomber is an efficient way to pursue the given policy, or whether the military budget should shrink or expand—questions to which members of the general public cannot be expected to give informed responses within the context of a highly technical, given policy. On the domestic front, various government and private regulatory agencies routinely determine public policy with little political control or publicity.

Although these developments may occur to different degrees with respect to particular policy processes, they adequately summarize trends that characterize broad segments of American politics and have profound implications for the political process:

> In advanced industrial society, information has become a crucial prerequisite for both political control and opposition politics, a necessity which is due to factors such as the complexity of society, the growth of governmental bureaucracies, and the tremendous distance between those who make the decision and the individual citizen. Even though the mass media and the growing literacy of the population create the preconditions for an informed public, it could be argued that the political information the individual possesses decreases in proportion to the total information that exists, much of which is reposited with governmental agencies. The limited knowledge of contemporary society that can be acquired through educational institutions in addition to governmental constraints on communication leave most of the public ignorant of the mechanisms of the decision-making process and the forces influencing it. Unfamiliarity with the facts and arguments considered in political decisions and policy formation results in a reluctance to evaluate governmental actions, especially if they do not seem to have a bearing on everyday life.[7]

Along with the loss of control, the remoteness of the decision-making process, and the inaccessibility of information goes an almost inevitable loss of perceived responsibility for institutionalized processes. This is exactly the phenomenon that Schumpeter identified in his indictment of the rationality of the American electorate. He noted that rationality commonly characterizes the behavior of people with regard to matters that personally concern them, but that:

> . . . when we move still farther away from the private concerns of the family and the business office into those regions of national and international affairs that lack a direct and unmistakable link with those private concerns, individual volition, command of facts and method of inference soon cease to fulfill the requirements of the classical doctrine . . . the sense of reality is so completely lost.
>
> This reduced sense of reality accounts not only for a reduced sense of responsibility but also for the absence of effective volition. . . .
>
> The reduced sense of responsibility and the absence of effective volition in turn explain the ordinary citizen's ignorance and lack of judgment in matters of domestic and foreign policy. . . .
>
> All of this goes to show that without the initiative that comes from immediate responsibility, ignorance will persist in the face of masses of information.[8]

Schumpeter took the behavior of citizens as given and fixed in his reformulation of democracy ("People cannot be carried up the ladder"[9]), thus effectively blaming the people for their display of narrow-minded irrationality in their failure to meet the standards of the classical doctrine. Instead, according to this argument as well as his own, he should have attributed these results to, among other things, remote political institutions and a political culture that fosters such behavior by advocating the partition between private and public concerns (to which he refers in the quotation above) and divorces the individual from public responsibility.

Apart from the voting literature, there is empirical evidence that individuals are capable of rational action and do exhibit volition, information, and generally rational behavior on matters that concern them and over which they are able to exert some control. To cite but a single example, a Survey Research Center study (unrelated to the voting studies) of public attitudes toward government activities offered "direct evidence that the lower classes are not disproportionately uninformed as to their stake in the social security program; self-interest operates to overcome educational limitations."[10] These observations on the effects of personal contact with government agencies are amplified in the general statement:

A national election demands that an individual commit himself on alternatives that involve remote decisions. The operations of metropolitan-based administrative agencies are diffuse and without the drama of partisan politics, to be sure. But these operations are direct extensions of personal and household reality for each citizen. They are activities of immediate involvement and concern about which he can have more realistic judgments than about the more remote issues of national politics. Understandably, public perspectives toward these administrative processes, although hardly well informed, are relatively articulate and strikingly reflective.[11]

The implications of all this are quite clear. First, citizens will be increasingly frustrated in their attempts to control, by voting, political processes that are effectively sheltered from political control, and this in turn will have an adverse affect on their evaluations of voting as a form of political participation. Second, the lack of control over and responsibility for, and the inaccessibility of information about, remote political processes will result quite naturally in a citizenry generally uninformed about those processes. Consequently, the electorate will fail to meet the standards of the naive model of the democratic citizen by failing to participate or by being well informed only on those matters that affect them personally.

The Two-party System

Political parties have been analyzed by a host of writers. Rather than review this extensive literature here, a relatively simple argument will be made about the operation of the parties in the American system that is consistent with the extant theory and relevant empirical data, although by no means comprehensive.

One should begin by identifying the Republican and Democratic parties, however loosely organized, as entities providing institutionalized access to public office. That is to say that the parties have as one of their functions the facilitating of the election of various individuals to political office by providing an organizational base generating manpower and financial support, linking various candidates (with spillover effects), conferring legitimacy upon individual candidates, guaranteeing access to a place on the ballot, and other forms of campaign aid. It is safe to say, in most cases and in particular with respect to the presidency, that the major parties exercise a virtual monopoly on access to office. One implication—that voters generally need consider only two candidates—is noted above.

Another noteworthy aspect of the American two-party system is its remarkable stability over time. Not only do the same two parties dominate election after election, but, since the last major realignment, there has been more continuity than discontinuity in the internal leadership structure of the parties, the ties of the parties to various private interest groups or segments of society, and the broad appeals of each to various groups. Such consistency is essential to the strength of each major party in that it provides some assurance that the long-term investment of political capital of various leaders and organizations (for example, those working their way up the party infrastructure as well as labor leaders, the NAACP, and so on) ultimately will be rewarded. The other side of the consistency argument is that significant costs are attached to most deviations from past policy in terms of the alienation of former members and the set-up costs for a new organization, as well as the costs of losing credibility.

The combination of their monopoly of access to office and their stability places the major parties in a unique position within the political system to manage the electoral manifestations of issues and social conflict in general. The major parties being competitors, however, such management must either be generally recognized to be in their mutual interest and/or be a consequence of institutional imperatives. Similarly, the parties are not tightly knit organizations that can enforce restraints on competition on their membership. Nor can the parties restrain the larger population from any political activity it may undertake. Nevertheless, and regardless of intentions, the two-party system occasionally operates so as to limit the scope of political conflict in at least the following ways.

(1) Excluding options: Although the parties cannot legally prevent third parties from challenging their dominance, nor prohibit any candidates from independent challenges, nor even tightly control the intraparty nominating process, there are any number of opportunities for exercising a de facto exclusion of alternative positions or candidates. All of the institutional arrangements, formal and informal, by which campaign support is allocated on the basis of past performance tend to exclude third choices. These include arrangements for financing, media access, and all of those instances where the label of a major party confers legitimacy, as in attaining a place on ballots. These various mechanisms were seen at their most effective in the 1976 McCarthy campaign, and their limitations in the 1968 Wallace campaign.

(2) Incorporating conflict: Since there are only two major parties, it is possible for political conflict to be absorbed into the competition between parties through an asymmetric appeal to one of the participants. In this way conflict can be channeled into safe outlets. Perhaps the best example is the appeal of the parties to blacks. Because the Republican party attitude toward blacks has been one of benign neglect for the past 20 years, it has been possible for the Democratic party to win the support of black voters quite cheaply. Because black voters have nowhere else to go, Democrats can count on a substantial block of black votes simply by offering enough to make it worthwhile for blacks to turn out. Thus instead of the spectacle of two parties attempting to outdo each other to win black voters, or

alternatively, the threat posed by a militant, neglected black population, racial conflict is integrated into electoral politics and political energy is harmlessly released. While this example is quite simplified, it is not without substance.

(3) Setting the terms of debate: Again, because of their monopoly on the means of election, the parties are not only able to exclude alternatives, but their candidates also define the issues that do enter public debate. Thus when Ford and Carter agreed to debate the issues of national defense in terms of the size of the military budget, they had in effect excluded any other approach to national defense from a public hearing while setting the outer limits of acceptable defense budgets. Voters, then, insofar as they wished to express an opinion about national defense with their votes, were limited to supporting positions within the range and along the dimensions agreed upon by Ford and Carter.

The 1968 presidential election provides some interesting examples of these effects of the two-party system. Social scientists and casual observers agree that, except for parts of the black population, the most important issue in 1968 was the Vietnam War. One might suppose, then, that the sharp divisions within the society would be reflected in the positions of the major party candidates. Instead, a recent study by William Schneider presents evidence that: "Neither of the two major-party candidates was widely perceived to hold any specific position on the Vietnam issue."[12] On the other hand, Wallace in 1968 and McGovern in 1972 were perceived to hold quite clear positions on Vietnam. Schneider concludes that his data show "a striking tendency for voters to perceive clarity where there is clarity and to perceive confusion where there is confusion. . . . One major source of 'issue distortion,' then, is a purely objective one—the candidate does not come across clearly because he does not choose to make himself clear."[13]

The SRC analysis of the 1968 election suggests that voters frustrated with Nixon's "secret plan" to end the war and the general failure of the major party candidates to address their concerns gave the Wallace candidacy the large measure of success it obtained. It was noted in the previous chapter that the Wallace candidacy seemed to be based to a greater degree on issue positions than did those of the major party candidates. His campaign slogan that "There's not a dime's worth of difference" between the major parties seems to have tapped a general frustration with two-party domination:

> Within the South, white attitudes toward Wallace are quite sharply associated with our scales of political efficacy and cynicism about government. People drawn to Wallace tend to feel they had little capacity to influence government, and expressed distrust of the morality and efficiency of political leadership. . . . All told, then, a sense of political

alienation was a rather visible correlate of the sorting of the citizenry away from the conventional candidates toward Wallace.[14]

It is worthy of note that this alienation was expressed through a vote for a maverick candidate, rather than through abstention.

(4) Adopting ambiguous platforms: Anthony Downs, in his spatial model of party competition, argued that: "In a two-party system, party policies are (a) more vague, (b) more similar to those of other parties and (c) less directly linked to an ideology than in a multiparty system."[15] Downs based this position on the problematic assumptions of a unimodal distribution of voters on a left-right continuum and a party strategy of maximizing potential appeal by avoiding specific stands that alienate voters:

> Ambiguity thus increases the number of voters to whom a party may appeal. This fact encourages parties in a two-party system to be as equivocal as possible about their stands on each controversial issue. And since both parties find it rational to be ambiguous, neither is forced by the other's clarity to take a more precise stand.[16]

Alternatively, one might argue that parties adopt ambiguous positions because: party leaders are uncertain about the distribution of public opinion on an issue or the impact of a more specific position; party leaders wish to hedge their bets against future shifts in public opinion that may leave them in a specific, unpopular position; party platforms must be acceptable to a number of different candidates with different constituencies, all running under the same party banner; or specific promises are more difficult to keep than ambiguous promises.

The extent to which the major parties confound rational, issue-based voting by adopting ambiguous positions, avoiding issues, and making empty promises is unsettled. Certainly there is some justification for complaint on this score and some evidence of meaningful party differences, and little likelihood that the balance can be definitively resolved.

One interesting attempt to address this question is Gerald Pomper's analysis of party platforms in the 1944–64 presidential elections. His study suggests that winning strategies for parties may conflict with the specific representation of political conflict:

> In choosing their issues, parties act rationally, emphasizing the policy areas of their strength and neglecting the strong points of their opponents. They tend to be specific on these issues of direct, distributive benefit to the voters and to resort to rhetoric or vagueness where the voters are unclear, uninterested, or divided. . . . Where opposing minorities exist, the party rationally evades a policy choice. The parties do not often

disregard majority preferences in an appeal to "passionate minorities." When they do make such appeals, as in civil rights, the parties are likely to imitate one another in the specificity and direction of pledges. These responses probably contribute to political stability by de-emphasizing the most intense social conflicts.[17]

Nevertheless, the evidence of platform pledges and party performance is sufficient for Pomper's conclusion that Democrats and Republicans are no more Tweedledee and Tweedledum than they are practitioners of party government. Instead, platforms generally reflect the divergent appeals of the parties to the groups composing their electoral coalition.

In any case, there is some empirical evidence that the American parties are more ambiguous than their multiparty system counterparts. For example, Campbell and Valen found this to be the case in their comparative study of attitudes toward political parties in the United States and Norway. Norway has a parliamentary government with a multiparty system (six major parties at the time of the study) and proportional representation, and the authors conclude that:

> . . . (1) differences between parties in stands on issues are both greater and clearer in Norway than in the United States; (2) Norwegian parties are more specific than American parties in appealing to various groups and sections of the electorate; (3) differences on policies between the parties are more effectively brought to the attention of the public in Norway than in the United States.[18]

Further analysis of survey data from the two countries suggests some implications of these structural dissimilarities. First, the constituencies of the Norwegian parties are considerably more distinctive in socioeconomic background and class identification than are those of the American parties. The Norwegians perceive greater policy differences between parties than do Americans. Corresponding to the greater perceived differences between the parties, and conforming to the ideological positions of party leadership, there are greater differences between the issue positions of adherents of Norwegian parties than between the positions of American party identifiers. Finally, the reported level of voting was higher in Norway than in the United States.

This evidence suggests that, in the United States, the domination of electoral politics by two major parties has operated on occasion so as to limit the capacity of voters to address issues in presidential elections. Among the many implications for rational voters are: greater information costs involved in interpreting ambiguous party or candidate positions; projection from clear issue positions to ambiguous ones and greater use of information shortcuts; greater incidence of error or confusion in identifying issue positions; and lower perceived stakes in the election (as a function of the differences between alternatives) with consequently lower levels of information and turnout.

Finally, this analysis prompts a reinterpretation of one element in the SRC analysis of the political system, wherein it is argued that voters define "broad goals of governmental action," rather than concrete policy positions:

> In gauging popular attitudes, political leaders develop a strong sense of what the permissible bounds of policy are. Large areas of public policy do not enter into public discussion because there is broad consensus that they lie outside the range of tolerance. These largely unspoken but widely accepted injunctions may have far greater significance in the electoral mandate than such issues as may become the subject of partisan controversy. They set the limits within which the parties offer policy alternatives.[19]

The infrequency with which political leaders tread beyond the range of tolerance in election campaigns and the rapidity with which the electorate can come to tolerate such "unthinkable" events as Nixon's trip to China suggests, in the light of the foregoing analysis, that the restraints on the issue positions taken by presidential candidates in elections may be as frequently accounted for by internal incentives as by the boundaries of public tolerance.

The Stakes Are Limited in American Presidential Elections

It is impossible to be precise about the importance of the questions that are in some sense settled in any presidential election. Clearly though, a very substantial portion of the electorate perceives the stakes to be quite small. From many perspectives, it is not unreasonable to compare the election of a president to the election of a board of directors for a corporation. That is, one assumes that the board of directors will continue to focus on the profitability of the enterprise, applying a greater or lesser degree of skill, talent, and imagination to the task. Similarly, the president rarely changes the direction of the society in a fundamental sense through his own efforts, but instead manages the system in the face of constant change.

There are always more substantial areas of agreement than disagreement between the Democratic and Republican candidates. Major candidates for the American presidency simply do not challenge the institutional structure of the political system, the basically capitalist orientation of the economic system, the assumptions of foreign policy, or the thrust of the positive state in the areas of welfare, regulation of the economy, and the like.

It is neither naive nor evidence of a lack of personal development to conclude that electoral politics in the United States does not have a great impact on one's personal life. One may reach this perspective from a sophisticated ideological argument that sees the basic class structure in the United States as fixed relative to electoral politics, or from a relatively simple application of experience. For example, the needs of migrant farm workers have been ignored by a long succession of presidents of both major parties.

The implications for voters are many. First, the presumed benefits of victory in electoral politics are themselves problematic for many people. Indeed, participation in elections may even be valued negatively by some groups because it drains political energy that might otherwise be channeled into more effective political activity and is thus counterproductive. Second, nonissue concerns may be promoted to primary importance by voters who view themselves as bound to lose on their most important issues regardless of the outcome of the election. Finally, the incentives to be fully informed and to vote are reduced when the correct choice is not likely to avail much more than an incorrect choice would cost.

The broad implication of this analysis of the context of American presidential elections is that it is unreasonable to expect voters in American elections to meet the standards applied in many voting studies, namely, to be fully informed on a wide range of issues and the candidates' positions on those issues. On the contrary, voters have many incentives to limit the amount of information they gather to apply to candidate preferences; to use general, nonissue criteria; and even to ignore the whole process. At this point it is possible to specify several decision rules for the rational voter that are both falsifiable and testable, and that add significantly to an understanding of elections in the United States.

INVESTOR-VOTER DECISION RULES

The investor-voter has been defined in an earlier work as one whose vote represents "an investment in one or more collective goods under conditions of uncertainty with costly and imperfect information."[20] The decision rules described below constitute a framework for rational voters' evaluation of their "investments."

The Turnout Decision*

The first, and for many the last, decision point in a given election is the resolution of the participation question. Each potential voter must weigh the

---

*This analysis of the turnout decision is an extension of, but in no way supersedes or affects the arguments of, the analysis of turnout in Chapter 1.

expected returns of personal activities against the estimated costs—to determine whether it is worthwhile to participate—and then against the opportunity costs. Obviously such calculations cannot be carried out with great precision, especially with regard to returns and costs that will be realized only in the future. Thus, one would expect potential voters to be guided largely by their experiences of the past, where these are available. Unless there is an exceptional consideration in the forthcoming election, for example, one of the candidates promises to bring a new group into full participation in the political process, the experiences of the past should prove a reasonable and efficient indicator of the responsiveness of the political system to a particular voter's needs in the immediate future.

While some citizens doubtless alternately drop in and out of electoral politics as their estimates of the potential returns vary, most probably operate according to standing decisions. Although such decisions may be periodically reevaluated. One implication of this argument is that the participation decisions of a large number of voters are made before the campaign begins. One should not be surprised, then, that numerous studies indicate that chronic nonparticipants do not possess much information about the candidates and issues or exhibit great interest in the campaign.

It should be clear that participation is being used here in the broad sense of following the campaign with attention to the candidate preference question and with the presumption that participation will culminate in voting. For most voters, extraordinary forms of participation, such as contributing money or volunteer work, will depend on the expected candidate differential, that is, the difference to the voter of the election of a preferred candidate rather than that candidate's opponent. The expected candidate differential in these cases may well include nonpolicy returns such as future access to the candidate or local prestige in the party. Finally, a tentative decision to vote may change by the end of the campaign if no positive candidate differential has emerged or if the costs of voting per se, generally not evident until on or near election day, are extraordinarily high. Still, most voters may be expected to follow through on their initial participation decisions.

There are two broad categories of exceptions to this analysis of turnout. One is the case of the voter whose vote is motivated by nonpolitical rewards, for example, the person who votes at another's insistence, or the person who votes in order to conform with public notions of good citizenship. The other is the case of alienated voters, those citizens who reason that their votes are meaningless and yet cannot bring themselves to abstain for quite nonrational reasons, including those motivated solely by a sense of citizen duty. It is argued in Chapter 1 that citizen duty cannot stand alone as a motivating force for voting, that it must be accompanied by the expectation that voting will have consequences that will give it meaning. Nevertheless, in the short run there may be voters who cling to citizen duty in the face of their belief that the vote is meaningless for much the same reasons as one may refuse to accept that one's love is unrequited. The first case belongs to the set of cases where personal rationality intrudes upon political rationality because political activity has acquired nonpolitical meaning. The second case, while it may be explained by the need to maintain some psychic balance through a transition period, is by its very nature irrational.

The Candidate Differential

The rational voter bases a vote decision on an estimate of the personal returns from the election of each candidate, naturally voting for the candidate from whom the greater returns are expected.* The difference in expected returns from the election of the preferred candidate is the voter's candidate differential. The value of the election to the individual increases with the size of the candidate differential.

The voter approaches the candidate preference decision by evaluating the candidates across a set of concerns of varying degrees of specificity. This evaluation is based on the expected benefits that will be realized in each area from the election of each candidate. The areas of concern are weighted according to their relative importance for the voter, and the candidate differential is the difference in the weighted sums of expected returns across the range of voter concerns.

The field of concerns of each voter is not fixed for any length of time, although it may exhibit great stability over time. The most important universal criterion for inclusion of a policy area in the voter's field of concerns is that performance in the area is perceived to be the responsibility of the president. Beyond this, each concern must represent an area where some policy response, including continuation of existing policies, matters in the sense that it will have some noticeable effect on the voter's personal utility stream.

Several important implications follow from this identification of the voter's concerns. First, the range of legitimate concerns is limited only by the requirement that the concern be something that the president can do something about. Concerns such as "the mess in Washington" do not become illegitimate by virtue of their vagueness of definition or the absence of supporting information. On the other hand, some more highly regarded issues like crime and drug abuse may be irrelevant to the outcome of an election if the electorate generally perceives these to be areas where the

---

*In an election with more than two alternatives, rational voters may misrepresent their preferences; that is they may vote for a candidate other than their most preferred in an attempt to maximize their returns from the election. This exception does not affect the analysis that follows.

president is powerless. It is not for political scientists to judge whether voters exhibit issue rationality or not on the basis of the richness of their information, the range of their concerns, or the consistency of their positions on a set of independent issues. The sole criterion for rational voting is the association between a vote and a set of desirable political outcomes. Beyond this one has only value judgments about what voters ought to regard as important or the way they ought to order their thinking; these are very important issues, but they are irrelevant to the question of whether or not citizens are politically rational.

Second, the range of voter concerns and the relative weights of various concerns are capable of being altered by the voter's experience. Voters learn, and the principal agents of the learning process are the political system and the behavior of the candidates. Thus the set of voter concerns will change as the political system addresses its efforts to new problems, with greater or lesser degrees of success, or institutionalizes established patterns of response. It might be argued, for example, that the degree of government intervention in economic affairs established during the New Deal era has been neutralized as a political issue by the experience of a succession of admistrations of both parties that have not challenged but have extended such intervention. The candidates themselves play an important role in inserting issue content into the campaign when they choose to do so. In 1968, for example, Richard Nixon's campaign stressed the law and order issue by suggesting that the president could do something about crime; by 1976 voters apparently had learned that crime could not be eliminated by dollars from Washington.

The weighting of concerns is doubtless an imprecise exercise, but the difficulty of arriving at actual relative weights does not bear on the argument that there is a weighting process. For example, it is clear that many voters have single concerns of such overriding importance that their most important concern outweighs all others; blacks who voted for Johnson in 1964 are a good example.[21] A group of voters with a common overriding concern in a particular issue comprise an "issue public." Such groups are the primary units that candidates attempt to sway into their coalitions of supporters through appeals to their central concerns. The fragmentation of the electorate into issue publics also has implications for voter information. Those individuals who comprise the issue public for a certain policy area are likely to have more information about the policy area simply because it is more important to them than to the electorate at large. Furthermore, one should expect "inconsistencies" in voter attitudes—for example, a black voter who likes Nixon on law and order, but votes for LBJ—because issue positions are not packaged with any logical consistency.

The importance of any particular area of concern in determining the voter's ultimate preference depends not only upon the weight associated with the concern, but also upon the expected candidate differential in each area. Thus a high expected candidate differential in one area of concern may promote that area to a position of greater importance in determining the voter's preference than another area with greater weight but lower expected candidate differential. A low expected candidate differential on important issues will lower the overall expected candidate differential and contribute to low levels of information and diminished turnout due to lack of incentive.

Another factor affecting the weights attached to policy areas and the larger composition of candidate differential is the time frame employed by the voter. While Downs restricted voters to consideration of the next interelection period, there is no necessary reason to do so. It is not irrational to look beyond the next election period and to use one's vote in the hope of influencing policy in the longer run. This would be the case, for example, of a member of some political bargaining unit (such as the NAACP or a labor union) whose vote represents a unit of political capital donated to the group in order to improve that group's negotiating position for the next round of elections.* The familiar postelection scene of various groups claiming credit for the election of the winner and demanding compensation is evidence of such calculations. An even longer-range view may animate voters for Socialist or Vegetarian party candidates. In general, however, most voters will limit their calculations to the shorter run because future returns must be appropriately discounted.[22] With the exceptions noted above, the remainder of the discussion is as if voters considered only the next election period in their calculations.

Trust and Ability to Deliver

The expected policy returns in an issue area are a function of both the candidate's positions on the issue and the voter's estimate of each candidate's ability to deliver their positions. This reflects the investor-voter's concern with the output of the political system rather than personal compatibility with the candidates. Machine candidates always held an advantage over their opponents in one respect: they could make good on their promises (and threats) with a high probability, while the deliverability of the opposition was problematic.[23]

In modern American presidential elections, the ability to deliver may be based on a diverse set of criteria including political standing, relations with Congress, experience, political acumen, and general competence. There

---

*Thanks to Joe Oppenheimer for this example. These voters may have zero candidate differential for the next election period, or a very small or even negative one.

may be an interaction effect between position and ability to deliver as well, in the sense that the position that a candidate articulates may reflect more or less understanding of the political climate. Thus the expected returns from voting for a candidate with the voter's same positions on the issues may, if those positions are utopian in the present political climate, be lower than those associated with a candidate with more moderate positions but a greater probability of implementing the program. On the other hand, when the effects of the vote on the policy process are expected to be indirect, that is, when a voter casts a symbolic vote for an obviously hopeless candidate in order to send a message, criteria bearing on ability to deliver are irrelevant.

A related consideration in the evaluation of issue positions is the extent to which the candidate can be trusted. The investor-voter must consider not only what candidates say their positions are, but also their sincerity (whether candidates are accurately representing their positions) and the strength of their commitments to those positions (that is, the likelihood that sincere candidates may bargain away their positions). A more detailed theoretical and empirical treatment of trust and ability to deliver as elements of candidate trustworthiness is reserved for the chapters following.

Components of Candidate Differential

The field of concerns of a voter will include areas capable of definition to varying degrees of specificity. Specific concerns generally will include those that are most important and/or those that affect the voter personally. These are the areas where a voter is most likely to exhibit a richness of information because of a personal incentive and/or a supply of free information to apply. As concerns become less salient, there is a greater incentive to conserve on information costs, with a corresponding reduction in the richness of information.

At the opposite end of the specificity spectrum lie two broad categories of evaluation that may be called general policy and general management. The general policy category includes those issues on which voters are unable to define specifically their own positions or to identify the positions of the candidates in any detail without incurring unjustifiable costs. The absence of detailed information carries no implication that the general policy category is relatively less important to voters or that they do not have the capacity to deal with specific policies without becoming confused. The only implication is that voters find policies within this category to be adequately dealt with in general terms. Indeed, the general policy area may reflect the voters' commitments to rich visions of some future America or an elaborate systems of social justice that lie outside the scope of normal politics. On the other hand, voters may perceive their fortunes to be tied rather directly to the fortunes of a particular social group (such as labor) or social concept (such as the extension of civil rights to blacks) that can quite adequately be summarized for them on a single dimension. As long as no anomalous information reaches them, summaries of a broad range of policies in general terms may suffice in the face of the costs and low expected returns from the accumulation of additional information.

The general management category captures all of the elements of the presidency that are not directly related to policy positions, but may include aspects of the candidate's ability to deliver. Among these outputs of the presidency is a major influence on the political climate: the level of internal conflict, the sense of purpose activating the people, the quality of leadership, the symbols that animate the political consciousness, the degree of respect of the people for political processes and institutions, and so on. Political philosophers often have held such concerns to be of far greater importance than the mere details of public policy. The president exerts a shaping influence on the political climate by virtue of his position at the center of the policymaking process, as the primary media link between the government and the people, and in general as the symbol of "what America stands for."

Beyond his responsibility for the top-level management of the political system, the president's job demands certain general management talents for dealing with particular issues. Because his term of office lies in the future, voters cannot possibly interview each candidate on every situation and combination of circumstances with which he will be confronted. It is possible, however, to specify certain characteristics that the president ought to bring to his treatment of these unforeseen events, characteristics that encompass the talents and personality of the chief executive. A partial list of such qualifications might include trustworthiness, competence, fairness, an even temper, leadership ability, foresight, and certain technical skills.

Inasmuch as these aspects of the political climate are collective goods for the society, it is expected that virtually every voter will form an opinion of the candidates' abilities to manage the political system. On the other hand, the importance of the general management category will vary as a function of the presence of important issues in the voter's field of concerns and the apparent state of the political climate at the time of the election. In addition, such concerns can be promoted to importance by the events of the campaign, as appears to have been the case in the 1976 elections.

In summary, the elements of the voter's field of concern fall into three categories: specific concerns, general policy, and general management. The returns to the voter within each category are weighted by their relative importance and summed to produce the voter's expected returns from each candidate, and the difference between returns is the expected candidate differential. Concerns within each category call for different responses from the voter in terms of the kind of information appropriate for each. In the remainder of this chapter, the voter's calculus is considered for each category separately.

INFORMATION CONDITIONS IN CANDIDATE DIFFERENTIAL COMPONENTS

The components of candidate differential have been defined thus far by a combination of the voter's approach to different aspects of the election and the types of information that are expected to be employed. While these two criteria are expected to exhibit substantial covariance, there will be certain exceptions, such as occur when a voter is richly informed on a trivial concern by serendipity. In general, however, such exceptions do not evidence a fundamental theoretical weakness in the model and are ignored below.

Specific Concerns

Specific concerns are most likely to arise from two sources. First, the political system occasionally is the arena for grappling with a major social problem; the Depression, the Vietnam war, and Watergate are modern examples. These present challenges of the type that must be understood in order to understand one's social context, which reach into many different aspects of people's lives, which engage the "hearts and minds" of the populace, and which in general transcend electoral politics. Voters have a variety of incentives to be informed and to form opinions about these issues. Second, the effects of actions taken within the political system are most salient when they affect the voter personally. Issues such as the busing of school children, the military draft, civil rights laws, and purely economic questions confront citizens in their daily lives. Consequently, they are likely to be informed about these quite apart from the electoral process.

While each of these types of issues may be quite complex with regard to both definition and possible responses, it does not necessarily follow that the information required to make a correct choice of candidate positions is equally complex. The details of any policy response are subject to the vagaries of policy processes and technologies that lie beyond the immediate reach of electoral politics. Thus it may be quite sufficient to deal with complex issues in rather simple terms. For example, voters could have voted rationally and with confidence that they were doing the right thing with regard to the Vietnam war—a very complex issue—if they had known only that one candidate expressed a general commitment to disengagement while another supported some notion of victory.

Still, it is on these issues that voters most strongly resemble the naive model of the democratic citizen. They are more likely to have information about the nature of the issue and the particular positions, if any, of the candidates, as well as an opinion on the best way to deal with the issue. Also, they are likely to vote consistently for the candidate whose issue position most resembles their own, given that it is also often their most important concern. Of course, their evaluations of the candidates on such issues will be tempered by considerations of trust and ability to deliver, as outlined above.

General Policy

The general policy category encompasses all of the concerns that the voter recognizes but does not have the information—nor the incentive to obtain the information—needed to differentiate, define, and form separate opinions about each. The treatment of issues in this category is incompatible with the naive model of the democratic citizen, yet it represents the most characteristic response of American voters to the issues. In order to conserve information costs, the voter treats these policy areas through the use of information shortcuts, which are characteristics of the candidates that summarize, in a fairly reliable manner, their positions on a wide range of issues. Useful information shortcuts are listed below.

Party Labels

Despite the criticism leveled earlier against the focus on parties as the objects of choice, party labels nevertheless provide some information about candidates. In particular, party labels are a generally adequate indicator of the political groups to which the candidates are likely to be attentive. It would not be unreasonable, for example, to conclude that the Republican candidate would exhibit more probusiness attitudes than a Democratic opponent, or that the latter would be more open to the concerns of organized labor. Similarly, it would be possible to generalize about the support or opposition that the major parties have historically lent to such economic issues as spending for social programs, protective tariffs, and tax policies. The remarkable stability of the New Deal era coalitions presents little opportunity for testing how quickly such generalizations are abandoned in the face of adverse information. On the other hand, there seems little doubt that, for example, labor and blacks receive a more favorable hearing from Democrats and are thus justified in using party labels as a measure of the candidate.[24] One would not want to predict specific issue positions from party labels, nor would one expect perfect consistency with actual behavior, but the purpose of using a summary term is to save the costs of obtaining detail and perfection.

Ideological Labels

While terms like liberal, moderate, and conservative are employed in voting studies to refer to a consistent set of attitudes across a wide range of issues, they, like party labels, are often found wanting. For example, in foreign affairs these terms are practically meaningless and must be replaced by another set of terms, such as interventionist/isolationist or some other dimension. It also is important to remember that such terms reflect a pattern based on the empirical correspondence of certain attitudes and not the unveiling of a single dimension of truth. Nevertheless, ideological labels, partly because of their empirical grounding, provide an economical index to candidates' positions. The reliability of such labels may be even more impressive when voters apply them to a relatively narrowly defined range of issues, such as, government spending decisions.

Demographic Characteristics

Demographic characteristics have two advantages over other cues. First, they are readily verifiable, unlike campaign statements, the second, voters observe the correspondence between such characteristics, on the one hand, and behavior and attitudes on the other, as part of their daily experiences. In some cases the link is direct, as in the cases of sex, race, or localism. Knowing that Jimmy Carter is from the South is likely to be a reliable indication that during his administration the South will, to some extent, reenter the political mainstream and receive a larger proportion of the attention of the administration than in the past. In other cases the link may be less direct, may even be entirely symbolic, but not necessarily less reliable. Knowing whether a candidate is rich or was born in a log cabin, was a career military man or served a single tour of duty, is Catholic, Jewish, or Protestant, or has a Ph.D. or a B.A. are all likely to be adequate guides to attitudes in particular areas. Similarly, the characteristics of a candidate's supporters may prove a valid indication of the general direction of that candidate's policy statements.

Projection from Other Issues

When voters have a great deal of information in one area of concern so that they can thoroughly test the candidates in this area, they may conserve on information costs across the remainder of the issue field by projecting from the candidates' positions on the issue(s) where their own information is more complete. Obviously, this approach would be of greatest reliability where a voter's examination of the candidates on specific issues had produced a clear preference for a particular candidate. Projection does not imply that a voter does not care about other issues, but rather that the marginal cost of information is prohibitive given the low probability that additional information will affect preference.

The Nature of the Times

One very reasonable perspective on the political system would suggest that the marginal impact of most single policy decisions on the life of any individual is quite small. On the other hand, all of the policy decisions during a president's term add up to a particular political climate that forms a major part of the context of the individual's life. Thus an appropriate criterion for evaluating the performance of an incumbent is the quality of the political environment that he has produced. Modern elections have seen this phenomenon in the president's accountability for law and order and inflation.

There are limitations to this approach that qualify its use in the American context. First, the nature of the times can be used to evaluate only an incumbent running for reelection or a candidate perceived as likely to continue the policies of a past administration. Second, the use of this criterion implies the perspective noted above, which essentially equates the presidency with the directorship of a corporation. Finally, the president obviously is only partly responsible for the quality of life at the end of his term, although he is one variable affecting that quality that voters can change.

General Mangement

Certain elements of the general management category would appear to be minimum qualifications for the presidency; a candidate ought to attain a certain level of competence, trustworthiness, leadership, and other qualities in order to be considered for the job. This would hold regardless of the candidate's issue positions, unless the vote were a merely symbolic show of support for an ideological position. The voter, however, has a number of agents working to weed out totally unqualified aspirants. The media, party regulars, and the primary election system rigorously examine the potential candidates on these qualities, so that the voter may reasonably assume that any candidate who has secured the nomination of a major party is at least minimally qualified for the job.

This minimal qualification certification is important because it reduces the general management category to the position of rough parity in the voter's calculus with the specific concern and general policy categories. Every voter can be expected to check the candidates for minimum qualification, and to eliminate from consideration any candidate found wanting at that point. However, virtually every major party candidate would be found to possess the minimum qualifications, so that the general management concerns of the voter are a matter of degree of qualification—in a manner of speaking, a quantitative rather than qualitative measure of the candidates.

The set of personal qualities comprising the general management ability of a candidate will be weighted differently by individual voters and variably with the apparent needs of the political system. Nevertheless, certain qualities can be expected to appear on every voter's agenda, including competence, trustworthiness, leadership, essential skills, intelligence, and experience. In addition, personality characteristics that bear on the president's management ability and the general category of style are proper concerns of the voters.

Probably in no other area of concern do the events of the campaign period bear so directly on candidate evaluation. For many presidential candidates the campaign is the first exposure to a national constituency, or at least their first exposure as candidates. During this period the candidates are constantly in the public eye and are forced to respond to a variety of issues. While the positions articulated are likely to be shaped by campaign considerations and so are less than reliable indicators of a candidate's likely behavior, it is possible to respond to the campaign itself more or less successfully. It is clear, for example, that George McGovern's 1972 candidacy was such a dismal failure at least in part because of his handling of the campaign, quite apart from the positions he adopted. Similarly, the 1976 election campaign, and especially the debates, were more significant for the way the candidates handled themselves than for the positions they took.

An important element of campaign performance is the selection of prominent advisers, aides, and nominees for future appointments. McGovern's performance in first selecting, then rejecting, Thomas Eagleton as vice-president, and his subsequent well-publicized inability to find another running mate, contributed substantially to the demise of his candidacy. The attention paid to the selection of the vice-presidential candidates by the major contenders before the 1976 conventions is further testimony to the importance of this process.

Beyond the campaign, it is clear that voters form their opinions of the candidates' general management abilities by projecting from their performances in other related areas. For example, in 1952 Eisenhower was perceived as a man capable of dealing effectively with current problems on the basis of his performance in World War II:

> ... the Eisenhower candidacy seemed extraordinarily well suited to the demands of the time. Eisenhower's unparalleled reputation as a successful military leader gave promise of an answer to the desperate question of Korea. And his freedom from association with the seamier aspects of

party politics and his widely acknowledged personal integrity carried a special appeal to many people who were disturbed at the level of political morality in Washington.[25]

It also would be reasonable to expect some projection from issue positions to general competence, trustworthiness, and so on. A candidate who shares one's positions on a number of issues cannot be all bad, nor can a candidate who always disagrees with one be all good. At a minimum, the fact that a candidate generally agrees with one's positions on a number of issues makes that candidate a good bet to do so on the issues that come up later.

In summary, voters' evaluations of a candidate's general management abilities are based on campaign performance, credentials, and a host of other criteria ordinarily omitted from election analyses, and only indirectly on issue positions. Together, these present a picture, or at least an outline, of the person who will sit atop the political system for the next term.

CONCLUSION

The investor-voter model is consistent with the major empirical findings of voting analysts during the age of survey research, if not with their interpretations of the phenomenology of voting. By virtue of incorporating both the cultural setting and crucial elements of the institutional context of American presidential elections in a rational account of voter behavior, it is the only one of the models reviewed here that is capable of providing a consistent account of the variable attachment of voters to parties, issues, and candidates during the 1950s, 1960s, and 1970s.

The major differences between the investor-voter model and the others are their competing accounts of the principal objects of politics.

Parties

For the social-psychologists, the Democratic and Republican parties mean little more to voters than social groups that happen to engage in political activity. Thus the relationship between voters and parties is largely devoid of political content. Downs, by extreme contrast, sees the parties as the principal actors of electoral politics, articulating issue positions and selling them with ideologies. While Downs gave the parties political content, his assumptions about them bear little relationship to American parties. In the investor-voter model, the parties are part of the institutional context of elections, providing the organizational framework for election to public office and generating crude information cues for voters. The relationship between voters and parties is explicitly political and largely material.

Candidates

For the social-psychologists, candidates serve as personifications of more complex values, programs, and issue positions embodied in the parties. Voters who are incapable of abstract conceptualization look to candidates as an intervening focus for the more relevant stuff of politics. Downs excluded candidates from his analysis by assumption, and it is safe to say that others of the rational school did likewise, albeit implicitly. In the investor-voter model, however, candidates are properly placed at the center of electoral contests. It is nothing but the choice of candidates that is settled in American elections, and it is the characteristics, as well as the issue positions, of the presidential candidates that are the proper focus of rational voters.

Issues

For the social-psychologists, the issues in a campaign are a set of problems requiring policy response that are relevant by virtue of their presence in the campaign. Voters who properly understand politics ought to know something about each issue and ought to be consistent in their positions on each. Downs properly returns the designation of problems as issues to the voter, and thus expects no such consistency and complete information. It is in the analysis of information costs and uncertainty and in voters' weighting of issues in proportion to their effects on their psychic income that the investor-voter model borrows most heavily from Downs.

The investor-voter is further concerned with issues that are inherently incapable of specification, of the type contained in the general management category. These are the most disparaged and ignored of the voter's concerns in voting literature. Thus, little progress has been made in defining the dimensions of candidate evaluation within this category.

One of the major contributions of the investor-voter model is the emphasis placed on personal characteristics of the candidates, both as an intervening consideration in the evaluation of issue positions and in the general management area. In the following pages, the voter's concern with these characteristics is treated under the heading of candidate trustworthiness.

NOTES

1. The analysis in this chapter draws extensively upon both the earlier work by Anthony Downs, *An Economic Theory of Democracy* (New York: Harper & Row, 1957), and Samuel Popkin, John W. Gorman, Charles Phillips, and Jeffrey A. Smith, "Comment: What Have You Done for Me Lately?: Toward an Investment Theory of Voting," *American Political Science*

Review 70 (September 1976): 779–805. Joe A. Oppenheimer made helpful comments on an earlier draft.

2. Cf. Downs, *An Economic Theory*, pp. 4–6.

3. His analysis of the effects of information costs is Downs's most important contribution to the study of voting behavior; cf. ibid., pp. 207–59.

4. The most prominent work on collective goods problems is Mancur Olson, Jr., *The Logic of Collective Action* (Cambridge, Mass.: Harvard University Press, 1965). The substantial and diverse literature on this subject is brought to bear on the analysis in Norman Frohlich and Joe A. Oppenheimer, *Modern Political Economy* (Englewood Cliffs, N.J.: Prentice-Hall, 1978), pp. 32–65.

5. The general inadequacies of the American party system were the subject of extensive analysis after World War II; see the report of the Committee on Political Parties of the American Political Science Association, "Toward A More Responsible Two-Party System," *American Political Science Review* 44 (September 1950): supplement.

6. Popkin et al., "What Have You Done for Me Lately?," p. 793.

7. Claus Mueller, *The Politics of Communication* (New York: Oxford University Press, 1973), p. 88.

8. Joseph A. Schumpeter, *Capitalism, Socialism, and Democracy* (New York: Harper & Row, 1950), pp. 261–62.

9. Ibid., p. 262.

10. Morris Janowitz, Deil Wright, and William Delany, *Public Administration and the Public—Perspectives toward Government in a Metropolitan Community* (University of Michigan, 1958), p. 27.

11. Ibid., p. 102.

12. William Schneider, "Issues, Voting, and Cleavages: A Methodology and Some Tests," *American Behavioral Scientist* 18 (September 1974): 129–30.

13. Ibid., p. 130.

14. Philip E. Converse, Warren E. Miller, Jerrold Rusk, and Arthur Wolfe, "Continuity and Change in American Politics: Parties and Issues in the 1968 Election," *American Political Science Review* 63 (December 1969): 1,101.

15. Downs, *An Economic Theory*, p. 297; derived in ibid., pp. 114–41. Downs's pioneering work on ambiguity has prompted others to examine ambiguity as a rational campaign strategy. This literature is considered in Chapter 5.

16. Ibid., p. 136.

17. Gerald M. Pomper, *Elections In America: Control and Influence in Democratic Politics* (New York: Dodd, Mead, 1968), p. 177.

18. Angus T. Campbell and Henry Valen, "Party Identification in Norway and the United States," in Angus T. Campbell, Philip E. Converse, Warren E. Miller and Donald E. Stokes, *Elections and the Political Order* (New York: John Wiley & Sons, 1966), p. 248.

19. Campbell et al., *The American Voter*, p. 547.

20. Popkin et al., "What Have You Done for Me Lately?," p. 780.

21. The SRC identified this same example of an overriding issue concern in their analysis of the 1968 election: "Blacks stood out as the major demographic grouping most exercised about the entanglement in Vietnam. They were more likely than whites to opine that the government should never have undertaken the military commitment there. They also were more likely to feel that American troops should be brought home immediately, a position not generally associated with the Johnson administration. None the less . . . Negro enthusiasm not only for Hubert Humphrey, but for Lyndon Johnson as well, remained high to the very end. It seems quite evident that when black citizens were making decisions about their vote Vietnam attitudes paled into relative insignificance by contrast with attitudes toward progress on civil rights within the country. . . ." Converse et al., "Continuity and Change," p. 1,085.

22. See Downs's discussion of the necessity for discounting future returns in Downs, *An Economic Theory*, pp. 166–68.

23. In the 1945 Boston mayoralty election, machine candidate James Michael Curley won solidly despite being under federal indictment for mail fraud at the time (he was later convicted). A survey of voters in that election showed that many voted for Curley, because Curley would be in a position to deliver more to them than the others. Jerome S. Bruner and Sheldon J. Korchin, "The Boss and the Vote: Case Study in City Politics," *Public Opinion Quarterly* 10 (Spring 1946): 1–23. Thanks to Joe Oppenheimer for this reference.

24. The stability of partisan alignments naturally facilitates such associations and renders them quite reliable. See the discussion above as well as Downs, *An Economic Theory*, pp. 103–11, on party reliability and responsibility.

25. Campbell et al., *The American Voter*, p. 526–27.

5

THE SALIENCE OF TRUST

*T*he issue of the political significance of trust is manifestly topical. Among the many lessons of Watergate and Vietnam was a vivid verification of duplicity in the actions of the nation's highest officers. The evidence in Chapter 1 indicates that a continuation through 1976 of the long-term, overall decline of public confidence in the political system and its separate institutions has contributed to lower rates of turnout in the past two decades. Finally, virtually everyone from reporters to candidates considered the Ford presidency and the 1976 election to be largely about restoring the faith of the people in their president, their political system, and their national identity.

But the timeliness of the topic should not obscure the larger purposes of the present work. First, the analysis of trust here is set in an explicit theoretical context, the investor-voter model. Conversely, the testing of certain hypotheses regarding trust should be regarded as tests of particular aspects of the larger model. Second, the analysis is not restricted to the present political climate. Although recent events clearly have promoted concern with trust, this argument is based instead on the structure of the political system and the role of the president.

THE ROLE OF TRUST IN THE VOTER'S CALCULUS

The investor-voter model in the preceding chapter contains a schedule of specific and general issues comprising voters' fields of concerns, for which they estimate expected returns from the election of each of the competing candidates. The model of the voter's calculus is developed as if voters actually did—or could—make more or less precise calculations in arriving at a preference. Nevertheless, the thrust of the analysis is that such precision is not possible, necessary, or even desirable (from a cost-efficiency perspective). The voter's calculus, then, is a metaphor employed to facilitate the identification and organization and to describe the interaction of analytically distinguishable elements of vote choice. In the same spirit, trust is treated here as a separate element in the voter's calculus with distinct roles corresponding to the specific and general components of the model.

In its specific application, a voter's estimate of candidate trustworthiness is an estimate the candidate's reliability, or the probability that the candidate promises will be kept. In its general application, trustworthiness involves a more complete evaluation of the candidate, incorporating competence and political values (such as issue positions) in an overall estimate of the future performance of the candidate not related to specific, current issues. Thus candidates who adopted consistently offensive issue positions could nevertheless be regarded as trustworthy in the specific sense if they always delivered on their promises. On the other hand, one would not trust such candidates in the general sense because their past performances suggest that they would continue to do the wrong things. The specific sense of trustworthiness is more nearly objective, that is, one can demonstrate reliability empirically, while the general evaluation of trustworthiness is based on voters' personal criteria. In the following pages, each application of trust is developed in greater detail.

The Specific Role of Trust

The stake for voters in a presidential election is the differential performance of the political system during the following interelection period under the direction of the alternative candidates. During the campaign, candidates offer to the electorate various representations of their positions, values, capabilities, priorities, and intentions, which the voters then sift and sort in order to estimate their expected returns during the coming term. For each of the policy areas of their candidate differentials, voters estimate their expected returns based upon their internal weighting of the concern, their evaluations of the candidates' apparent positions on the issue, and any information that might bear on the processes intervening between the president's position and policy outcomes. It is in the estimation of expected returns that trust intervenes in the calculus.

There is much evidence that the voters are acutely aware of potential gaps between promise and performance by presidential candidates. The various representations of candidates by themselves and their supporters and opponents are inevitably influenced by campaign considerations, and thus may reasonably be suspected of being gratuitous, self-serving, distorted, or in some way a misrepresentation. In addition, it is much easier for candidates to escape the contradictions and consequences of their statements during a campaign than it is to observe their announced principles in subsequent political action. Thus voters must evaluate not only the sincerity of the candidate or the accuracy of their perceptions of a candidate's true position, but also the extent of the candidate's commitment or the probability that the candidate will retain a previously announced position in political bargaining. Finally, because investor-voters base their decisions on expected performance rather than on positions per se, they must estimate the influence of the candidates' positions on the political process. Such influence may vary as a function of the political competence and political resources of the new president and the general political climate. All of these factors may figure in the voter's estimate of a candidate's trustworthiness in the specific sense, that is, the degree to which the candidate may be expected to deliver on policy positions.

Although similar considerations may bear on voters' evaluations of candidate trustworthiness across the full range of issues, there is no implication in this analysis that candidates will be rated similarly on each issue. On the contrary, these evaluations may differ widely across candidates' positions, particularly when candidates adopt contradictory positions in attempts to be all things to all people. For example, a Democratic candidate's promise to support a certain bill on behalf of organized labor may be more trustworthy than a simultaneous promise to business interests to control inflation. In such cases, it is more appropriate to speak of the trust component of issue positions than of candidate trustworthiness in general. This distinction, however, does not affect the analysis in the present work.

Estimates of a candidate's specific trustworthiness enter the voter's calculus as modifiers of the expected value of the candidate's political positions. For example, a voter who wished to see a national solar energy program enacted would be pleased to hear a candidate endorse such a program. But if said voter's estimate of the candidate is that the candidate is insincere, that the solar energy program will be bargained away, or that the candidate will not command the political resources to push the program through, then the pleasure at the announcement of a compatible issue position must be discounted to take into account the decreased likelihood of the position being realized.

In general, a low estimate of trustworthiness will decrease the expected value of a candidate's election for voters who approve of that candidate's issue positions, and may have the opposite effect for disapproving voters. If the opposing candidate is rated negatively on all considerations, the effect of low trust would be to lower enthusiasm for the otherwise preferred candidate, perhaps to the point that the voter abstains. When voters are cross-pressured on the issue, that is, when they like the position of one candidate on some issues, but prefer the opponent on other issues, the trustworthiness factor alone could produce a vote switch.

The General Role of Trust

In its general sense, trustworthiness corresponds to the generalized component of expected candidate differential; it is part of the voter's estimate of the candidate's expected performance in all those functional areas that are independent of particular issue positions, including the leadership function, the national symbol function, and the general management function. As such, this component includes performance in areas that others may regard as issues, but in which some voters perceive themselves to have such small stakes personally that they do not care how the issues are resolved so long as the outcome is reached fairly, expediently, and with minimal repercussions on their own conditions. Such issues may not even be differentiated in the voters' minds from the general management of the political system. For example, most voters are indifferent to farm-price support policy unless it is so poorly handled that prices rise unreasonably or supplies dwindle.

The scope of presidential responsibility and authority is so large relative to the capacity of any single individual to observe it that it is inevitable that voters will be uninformed on a wide range of issues. Consequently, they are liable to be indifferent about a wide range of possible outcomes of such issues. But it does not follow that voters are indifferent to the handling of those issues. Rather, voters can be expected to extrapolate from certain attributes of the candidates to estimate their abilities to manage such problems as arise in an acceptable manner. The same analysis applies to the unanticipated issues of the future.

The essence of the relationship between citizens and their president as regards undifferentiated and unanticipated issues, as well as certain functions independent of issues, is trust. Trust in this sense may be formally operationalized in terms of the likelihood that the performance of the president in these areas will respect certain values that are important to the voter. This broad definition is meant to imply that the general sense of trustworthiness may reflect the application of diverse sets of standards unique to individuals.

Among the criteria of general trustworthiness that may see widespread application are such personal attributes as intelligence, technical competence, and good health, and personality characteristics like openness, coolness under pressure, and fairness, in addition to honesty, sincerity, and adherence to moral or religious principles. But, because the generalized performance of the president has a certain amount of substantive content, projection from substantive concerns is likely to contribute to the generalized estimate of trust as well. It is not unreasonable, for example, to assume that a candidate whose performance is consistently satisfactory in areas to which one is attentive is likely to be worthy of trust in areas with which one is less familiar. Similarly, the generalized trust evaluation may partake of ideological ratings or evidence of responsiveness to the interests of particular groups.

In its general application, trustworthiness enters the investor-voter's calculus as a separate element representing each candidate's expected performance in the areas not evaluated in terms of policy expectations. As the residual category of candidate differential, the relative weight of generalized trustworthiness varies inversely with the weight attached to particular policy areas. For some voters it may be the most important, or even the only, basis for the preference decision.

The Structural Basis for Concern with Candidate Trustworthiness

It is perhaps worthy of some emphasis that voters' concern with the trustworthiness of those for whom they vote is an inevitable consequence of representative government under the assumption of popular sovereignty. Inherent in the structure of government by representation is a particular set of relationships between the citizen and the state. First, the authority to make decisions binding on the whole society is alienated from the electorate, where it resides according to the doctrine of popular sovereignty, and is deposited in various representative institutions. But the legitimacy of the government's authority and the power to enforce its decisions ultimately rest on the voluntary submission of the citizens. The voluntary alienation of authority to the government by rational individuals, however, must be based at least on the expectation that compliance will yield net benefits.

It is not necessarily the case that representatives will exercise their authority in the interest of their constituents. This problem drew the attention of the architects of the American political system:

> The effect of [the delegation of the government in a republic to a small number of citizens elected by the rest] is, on the one hand, to refine and enlarge the public views by passing them through the medium of a chosen body of citizens, whose wisdom may best discern the true interest of their country, and whose patriotism and love of justice will be least likely to sacrifice it to temporary or partial considerations. Under such a regulation, it may well happen that the public voice, pronounced by the

representatives of the people, will be more consonant to the public good than if pronounced by the people themselves, convened for the purpose. On the other hand, the effect may be inverted. Men of factious tempers, of local prejudices, or of sinister designs, may, by intrigue, by corruption, or by other means, first obtain the suffrages, and then betray the interests, of the people.[1]

Indeed, the greater portion of the framers' efforts was directed toward guaranteeing the trustworthiness of those exercising the alienated sovereignty of the people:

The aim of every political constitution is, or ought to be, first to obtain for rulers men who possess most wisdom to discern, and most virtue to pursue the common good of the society; and in the next place, to take the most effectual precautions for keeping them virtuous whilst they continue to hold their public trust.[2]

Election—historically an aristocratic device—by a carefully qualified electorate was the means chosen to assure proper selection of representatives. The guarantees of their performance included almost every aspect of the structure of government (such as federalism and the separation of powers), constitutional limitations, and sociopolitical preconditions. The elaborate precautions of the Federalists underscore the extent to which the legitimacy of the government is based on the trust of its citizens.

It is interesting to note that there is a (perverse) sense in which the alienation of sovereignty imposes upon the electorate a certain communitarian sensibility in the exercise of their suffrage. In a direct democracy or any system where ultimate decisions on policy reverted to the citizenry through referenda or the instruction of delegates, voters could decide each issue entirely on the basis of a narrowly conceived self-interest. But in a system where representatives act for the electorate, with no effective mechanism for prior restraint, all voters are forced—in their own self-interest—to evaluate the character of the candidates they support. A particular individual interest may dominate, but cannot totally exclude, the interest of voters in the broader nature of their political community, or in what has been identified above as the generalized component of candidate differential. By definition, the latter cannot be evaluated entirely in terms of a particular interest, but must be weighted also by the voter qua community member, where each voter's personal interest is the same as every other member of the community. One presumes only that all voters share an interest in the competence, virtue, responsiveness, and other qualities of the president. (Everyone in the community may not agree on these generalized desiderata. In this case, the voter simply employs the same criteria all people would use if they were similarly enlightened.) Thus, without relying upon moral pedagogy, the American political system requires voters to consult the general will to some extent through each voter's own self-interest, in much the same way that Rousseau described:

> How should it be that the general will is always rightful and that all men constantly wish the happiness of each but for the fact that there is no one who does not take that word "each" to pertain to himself and in voting for all thinks of himself.[3]

Although the concern with candidate trustworthiness is a consequence of the structural characteristics identified above, and is thus expected to be of some importance to all voters in all elections, events may promote candidate trustworthiness to the status of an independent issue. This possibility is unique to the investor-voter model and arises in the following way.* Part of the output of the political system at any time is a political climate, and the nature of that climate bears directly on the returns to the voter. An era during which literally hundreds of public officials are charged with thousands of crimes and during which the president orchestrates a series of political crimes on a grand scale may lead a reasonable observer to surmise that normal political processes have been effectively perverted. In that case, the putative rationality of policy decisions becomes problematic, resistance to government increases as legitimacy declines, and ultimately both stability and progress are threatened, with obvious implications for citizens. Such situations may well promote the restoration of faith in the political system to a level of importance commensurate with or even exceeding that of other more conventional issues. This seems to have been the case for some voters who perceived the Truman administration to be heavily stocked with Communist infiltrators and saw Eisenhower in 1952 as a man uniquely capable of purifying government. In the 1976 election there is evidence to suggest that the concern with trust as an issue was quite widespread. This point is further developed below.

The Effects of Incumbency on the Role of Trustworthiness

It might be supposed that the introduction of incumbent candidates would render this analysis irrelevant, at least insofar as incumbents are concerned. After all, incumbents already have been observed in action, they

---

*Voter concern with candidate qualities is either irrational or nonrational in the social-psychological model. Both the rational voter model and the new issue voter ignore candidates. When trust is incorporated into rational models, it is only in the specific sense; see the review of such models below.

have concrete records, and the voters need not rely on their promises. This is the argument that Anthony Downs made in this regard:

> Since one of the competing parties is already in power, its performance in period t [the current term] gives [a voter] the best possible idea of what it will do in the future, assuming its policies have some continuity. But it would be irrational to compare the current performance of one party with the expected future performance of another. For a valid comparison, both performances must take place under the same conditions, i.e., in the same time period. Therefore, the voter must weigh the performance that the opposition party would have produced in period t if it had been in power.
>
> True, this performance is purely hypothetical; so he can only imagine what utility income he would have derived from it. But party B's future is hypothetical, too—as is that of party A. Thus he must either compare (1) two hypothetical future utility incomes or (2) one actual present utility income and one hypothetical present one. Without question, the latter comparison allows him to make more direct use of concrete facts than the former. . . . Therefore, we believe it is more rational for him to ground his voting decision on current events than purely on future ones.[4]

It would be absurd to ignore the current performance of an incumbent candidate in making vote choices if only simply because the available information is so reliable. But in the investor-voter model, only future performance is relevant to the choice between candidates, and a vote that is merely an expression of approval or disapproval of past performance is, by its criteria, irrational. The performance of the incumbent, then, is properly understood as the most reliable indicator of future performance, not as the immediate object of the voter's attention.[5]

In addition, such comparisons of current performance do not have the reliability in the real world of American elections that they enjoy in Downs's idealized electoral context. First, there is not an out party that presents a coherent package of alternative policies to those of the incumbent president. Even if there were a shadow administration, the independence of American presidents from party platforms would render its policies of questionable significance for such comparisons. Second, the assignment of responsibility for policy outcomes is not so straightforward in American politics as in parliamentary systems. Indeed, the vagaries of the policy-making process are such that a president may claim credit for an outcome that he actually resisted, or vice versa. Finally, the policies of an incumbent president who is eligible for reelection often take the coming election into account in such a way that the first term of a president may be a poor guide to particular policies in the second term.

On the other hand, the performance of an incumbent president is subject to empirical verification and hence is relatively reliable, particularly when applied to attributes of the candidate that are not likely to change in the face of shifting political contexts. Among the latter attributes is trustworthiness, in every sense of the word. Thus a performance rating of the incumbent, if applicable, is likely to be a major component of most voters' choices, albeit as an estimate of future performance.

Previous Analyses of Trustworthiness

On the whole, candidate characteristics as factors in vote decisions have not commanded great attention for voting analysts. In general, this neglect reflects the presumption by analysts that attitudes toward the candidates are simply reactions to Eisenhower's fatherly image or Kennedy's boyish good looks. Only recently have some authors begun to incorporate candidate characteristics into rational voting models as legitimate, relevant concerns for voters.

In the work that introduced the investor-voter model, Popkin et al. identified a dimension of candidate competence as a factor in the decisions of rational voters and attributed McGovern's 1972 defeat in large measure to "the widespread perception of his incompetence."[6] They focus on McGovern's failure to motivate those with compatible issue positions as evidence of a separate and independent ability to deliver dimension in vote decisions. Although this article laid the groundwork for the present book, their notion of competence is much narrower than trust, excluding the sincerity and commitment components of trustworthiness along with much of the generalized sense of the term.

Fiorina's formal model of vote choice includes a candidate factor much like the specific sense of trustworthiness, where the expected returns from the alternative parties are weighted by "reliability measures or uncertainty discounts":

> Candidate qualities can affect the voting decision through their effects on these weights. If a candidate is perceived to be insincere, or thought to lack integrity, the citizen will attach less weight to his evaluation of the candidate's proclaimed platform than if he perceives the candidate as sincere. If the citizen believes the candidate is a good leader and able administrator, he assigns a high [weight] to the candidate's promises, whereas if he views the candidate as an incompetent, he may discount or even ignore the candidate's promises
> . . . candidate qualities constitute a mechanism by which to discount evaluations of expected performance.[7]

Fiorina's notion of the candidate factor thus incorporates both ability to deliver and sincerity, but the general sense of candidate trustworthiness does not appear in his work.

In addition to these, there are several formal theoretical works that explore voter evaluations of issue positions from the perspective of the candidate.[8] These arguments suggest that ambiguity on issue positions in part of a rational campaign strategy, thus implicitly marking voters' evaluations of candidates' sincerity as a relevant element in a rational vote decision. Again, however, these authors treat only a narrow sense of trust and do not consider its broader (general) aspects. Thus they ignore a potential disincentive for candidate ambiguity in the possibility that the electorate may esteem specificity per se.

THE SALIENCE OF CANDIDATE TRUSTWORTHINESS

The analysis of trustworthiness as a rational basis of candidate evaluation yields two hypotheses regarding the salience of trustworthiness evaluations for the electorate.

First, the proportion of the electorate holding an opinion about the trustworthiness of the candidates in American presidential elections is substantial. The widespread employment of trust as a modifier of expected returns from specific issue positions and as a generalized criterion of candidate evaluation is a consequence of structural characteristics of the political system. Thus, regardless of the issues of the moment, most voters are forced to take account of trust in some manner.

Second, the trustworthiness of candidates is always a concern of some importance is elections, but its salience as a criterion of candidate evaluation may increase under conditions of widespread distrust of public officials. With its basis in the structure of the political system, concern with trust never goes away entirely. But the same conditions that guarantee its permanence—the alienation of public authority in a representative government—facilitate the ready promotion of trust as an issue in elections when the trustworthiness of government becomes problematic.

There is support for these salience hypotheses in scattered studies. For example, traits such as honesty and sincerity, along with general competence, often rank quite highly in polls asking for the qualities of the ideal president. One instance is a study by Roberta Sigel of a large sample of Detroit voters in the early 1960s. Given a list of personal qualities and asked which were most important in a president, her sample ranked honesty first and intelligence second among specific qualities, with the overall categories of honesty first and competence second. Of her sample, 98 percent indicated that the president's moral character should be exemplary in public life (with the remainder indicating that one cannot expect a politican to be too moral).[9] Such ideal image polls cannot deal with issues, of course.

SRC/CPS analysts, reporting on candidate evaluations in the 1976 election, also find trust and competence to be quite salient:

Competence and trust were the two most salient candidate attributes considered by the electorate in their evaluation of Ford. . . . A substantial proportion of respondents also discussed Carter's competence, making numerous references to his inexperience, but the major assessments of Carter were based upon partisan philosophies and considerations of trust. . . . Carter's personal attributes, especially his religion, southern origin and common background, formed a very salient component of his public image.[10]

A factor analysis of open-ended like/dislike responses produced a separate trustworthiness-reliability dimension of candidate evaluation.

This sort of analysis of candidate evaluations is a significant departure from earlier SRC work. Traditionally, comments about the candidates that did not reflect issues, parties, or interest groups were aggregated as responses to the personal qualities of the candidates, with no distinction made between references to Eisenhower's military record and responses to his father image. Still, such distinctions may be recovered from the available data. For example, Fiorina reviewed the references to Eisenhower from the open-ended like/dislike series in the 1952 and 1956 surveys, classifying each response as relevant or irrelevant to the job of president. He rated 82.0 percent of the 1952 responses and 68.7 percent of the 1956 responses as relevant and concluded that:

Actually, the bulk of the citizenry's impression of the candidates focuses on qualities which are of legitimate relevance to the latter's capacity to govern: experience, leadership ability, and so on. Even in the purportedly personality-dominated election of 1956 the vast majority of comments favorable to Eisenhower were comments relevant to his ability to serve as President.[11]

One may undertake the same sort of test to produce evidence of the salience of candidate trustworthiness for voters, using the same set of open-ended questions that constitute the raw material for the SRC six-factor model. The specific questions are of the form: "Is there anything in particular about (name of candidate) that might make you want to vote (for, against) him? What is that? Anything else?"* The responses are coded by the CPS staff as representing one of several hundred categories collectively incorporating a broad range of candidate attributes from issue positions to personality traits.

Three characteristics of these survey items are relevant in assessing the evidence they yield. In the first place, the series has been a standard

*Because they do not bear on the evaluation of candidates, the complementary series asking for evaluations of the parties are excluded from this analysis.

item on the SRC election surveys since 1952; thus, data are available from the beginnings of extensive survey research of voters to the present, a span of nearly three decades. Second, the questions are open-ended. Those whose responses mention the trustworthiness of the candidates have not been cued to their remarks, but instead have volunteered such an answer in a context where the designation of any issue position, aspect of political history, party label or ideology, demographic characteristic or personality trait is equally appropriate. Finally, the questions ask respondents to identify vote-related criteria, thus providing one screening for frivolous responses.

In Table 5.1, those responses directly related to the candidates' trustworthiness are reported as a proportion of all responses for elections since 1952. In the categorization of responses as trust related, the author has employed a very narrow sense of trustworthiness, selecting only those responses that seem to tap reliability/sincerity/honesty.* Given the slight notice that this factor has received in previous studies, the performance of trust in this open-ended context is surprising. The data in this table provide support for both hypotheses. First, a consistent 5 to 10 percent of all responses fall in the trust-related categories, indicating a relatively widespread concern with these qualities. By comparison, the Vietnam war, probably the most salient issue during this period, drew 13.6 percent of all responses in 1972. Of course it does not strictly follow because 10 percent mention trust that it is salient for any more than 10 percent. But the pattern on other issues, such as the war in Vietnam, is that salience is much greater than indicated by responses to the open-ended series. This is corroborated by additional evidence below. Similarly, the consistency of the overall proportion of trust-related responses, and the increased proportion in 1976, tend to corroborate the second hypothesis that trust will never disappear as a concern, although conditions may promote it to very high levels of salience.

The figures in Table 5.1 are consistent with the popular wisdom in their evaluations of candidate trustworthiness. For example, Barry Goldwater, who is widely recognized as unique among politicians for his singular devotion to his principles, clearly impressed the electorate with his honesty, if nothing else. Only Eisenhower among modern candidates approaches Goldwater's purity. Nixon, on the other hand, failed three times to achieve a

---

*The competence or ability to deliver aspects of trustworthiness are thus excluded to a large extent, although it is not possible to purge them entirely from these responses. But those responses coded as trust related are capable of relatively straightforward interpretation, while including the competence aspects of trustworthiness would force a number of questionable interpretations, diluting the significance of the evidence. Nevertheless, a substantial portion of the uncoded responses could be interpreted as relevant to competence.

TABLE 5.1: Proportion of Trust-related Candidate Attributes, 1952–76 (percent)

| | Democratic Candidate | | | Republican Candidate | | | Both |
	Likes	Dislikes	Total	Likes	Dislikes	Total	Total
1952[a]	6.1	3.2	4.9	11.3	0.9	7.0	6.0
1960[b]	8.1	2.8	5.9	4.9	6.9	5.5	5.7
1964[a]	3.5	13.0	7.0	19.2	1.7	8.0	7.5
1968[a]	6.4	3.7	5.0	3.0	5.8	4.4	4.7
1972[c]	11.3	6.4	8.1	4.9	15.4	9.0	8.6
1976[a]	15.7	17.8	16.7	20.4	7.5	14.0	15.4

[a]First responses only tabulated.
[b]Five responses tabulated.
[c]Three responses tabulated.

Responses coded as trust related:

Likes: Man of integrity, principle, high ideals, high moral purpose; means what he says, honest, won't make deals/sincere/honest, not corrupt/keeps promises/open, candid, straightforward/safe, stable/dependable, reliable, trustworthy, a man you can trust with the responsibilities of government.

Dislikes: No integrity, no principles, compromised his principles, just a politican, opportunistic, dishonest, crooked/insincere/dishonest, corrupt/undependable, unreliable, man who shouldn't be trusted with the responsibilities of government/unsafe, unstable, dictatorial, ruthless/breaks promises, doesn't mean what he says, tricky, not open, not candid, not straightforward.

Source: Data based upon Survey Research Center, Center for Political Studies of the Institute for Social Research, University of Michigan.

majority on the positive side of the ledger, and in 1972 his lack of trustworthiness was his modal dislike among voters. In fact, trustworthiness categories are not infrequently the modal response categories for candidate characteristics.

The 1976 figures clearly reflect the impact of Watergate and other instances of official deceit that were exposed in the interim since the 1972 election. The overall salience of the trust dimension nearly doubled as voters generally rewarded Ford for restoring trust in government and evidenced doubt about the unproven Carter. An examination of particular response frequencies for 1976 is revealing as well. The modal response for Carter "likes" is a comment on his honesty or sincerity. The opposite qualities are second among Carter "dislikes" to the category "weak; indecisive; vacillating; flip flops; hazy, vague on issues." Ford's incumbency is reflected in the fact that the most frequently cited positive responses, and the second most frequently cited negative responses, are references to his caretaker performance. The trust dimension follows past performance in each case, while negative references to the Nixon pardon lead the field of Ford dislikes. Direct references to Watergate were insignificant in number.

More direct evidence of the widespread salience of candidate trustworthiness is the responses to a set of questions introduced in the 1972 SRC/CPS election study and repeated in 1976. For each major candidate, respondents were asked to select a position on a seven-point scale ranging from strongly agree to strongly disagree in response to the statement "_____, as President, could be trusted." While the question has been applied to only the two most recent presidential elections, it has the distinct advantage of tapping the trust dimension directly.

The responses to this series of statements are recorded in Table 5.2. The rate of response to the series indicates that the question of candidate trustworthiness was a meaningful one to the survey subjects. For example, fewer than 3.5 percent of respondents were unable to rate either of the incumbents, Nixon in 1972 or Ford in 1976. A larger proportion of the sample were indefinite about the challengers—"don't knows" reached 7.1 percent for Carter, 10.4 percent for McGovern, and 18.5 percent for Wallace. The neutral responses (position four on the seven-point scale) follow a similar pattern, reaching a maximum of about 16 percent in the evaluation of McGovern. Neither "don't know" nor a neutral response is evidence that the respondent has not weighted the trustworthiness of the candidates, but all other responses indicate at least a claim to holding an opinion on the question. The differential response rates for incumbents and challengers lend validity to these responses, and the whole series suggests that concern with trust is of widespread salience.

The data in Table 5.2 probably tap trustworthiness in the general sense

TABLE 5.2: Candidate Trustworthiness Evaluations, 1972 and 1976 (percent)*

Candidate	Strongly Agree 1	2	3	4	5	6	Strongly Disagree 7	Don't Know
Nixon, 1972	952 35.4	336 12.5	286 10.6	381 14.2	168 6.3	142 5.3	344 12.8	78 2.9
McGovern, 1972	402 15.0	269 10.0	287 10.7	431 16.1	240 8.9	232 8.7	543 20.2	278 10.4
Wallace, 1972	551 20.6	275 10.3	207 7.7	312 11.7	178 6.7	178 6.7	481 18.0	494 18.5
Ford, 1976	791 27.7	515 18.1	434 15.2	397 13.9	228 8.0	108 3.8	283 9.9	95 3.3
Carter, 1976	641 22.5	540 19.0	418 14.7	420 14.8	237 8.3	149 5.2	238 8.4	203 7.1

*The entries in the table indicate the number and proportion of responses in each category to the statement," ———— as President, could be trusted."

Source: Data based upon Survey Research Center, Center for Political Studies of the Institute for Social Research, University of Michigan.

to a greater extent than the data in Table 5.1. In the construction of Table 5.1, trustworthiness was limited in such a way as to exclude basic competence, while Table 5.2 indicates the trustworthiness of each candidate as president. That competence is incorporated in the latter is indicated by the reversal in the ratings of McGovern and Nixon between the two tables. While McGovern was apparently rated as more honest and sincere in the first table, Nixon was rated as more trustworthy as president in the second.

These conclusions are amplified by comparison with other candidate ratings on the same surveys. Those items asking respondents to place candidates on similar scales representing positions on issues produce consistently higher proportions of "don't know." For example, when asked to identify the candidates' positions on busing to achieve integration on the 1972 survey, 17.9 percent could not place Nixon, while 31.9 percent and 25.3 percent were at a loss regarding the placement of McGovern and Wallace respectively. A more comparable set of candidate ratings involved placing the candidates on the familiar liberal/moderate/conservative continuum. Even after one-fourth of the sample in each survey were excused from rating the candidates because they indicated that they "had not thought much about it," the proportion of the remaining sample—already screened for salience—who responded "don't know" exceeded the proportion attained on trust ratings in all but one case.[12]

Additional evidence of the significance of trust issues in the 1976 election comes from a series of questions on the SRC/CPS survey that asked for evaluations of a set of ten given issues. First, respondents were asked to indicate whether each issue was important or not; on this test, honesty in government was rated as important by over 96 percent of the sample, second only to inflation.[13] Then each was asked, ". . . tell me how much responsibility you think the government in Washington has toward solving each problem—a great deal, some, or not much." Honesty in government was highest rated of the set on this criterion.[14] Finally, respondents were asked to rank the importance of each issue; honesty in government received the greatest number of first rankings and its overall ranking was rivaled only by inflation.[15] The other issues in the set were racial issues including busing, unemployment, high taxes, energy shortages, foreign relations, crime and drugs, consumer protection, and pollution.

The thrust of all of the available and applicable evidence is that voter concern with the trustworthiness of candidates—and with competence as well—is quite salient as a rule, and was exceptionally salient at the time of the most recent elections. Both hypotheses are corroborated and the evidence suggests a more substantial role for trustworthiness, and for candidate evaluations in general, then the voting behavior literature has recognized to date.

CORRESPONDENCE OF TRUST EVALUATIONS WITH VOTE CHOICE

If the data reported above constitute prima facie evidence that the trust dimension is meaningful for voters, it remains to be established that trust evaluations are relevant in the sense of being related to ultimate vote choice. The question here is whether trust evaluations are sufficiently consistent with candidate preference so that they may be presumed to be a factor in the preference decision. Consistency does not establish a factor as important, but repeated inconsistency between the two measures would be sufficient reason for rejecting the claims made here about the role of trust.

Evidence from the open-ended candidate evaluation series is offered in the section above to establish the salience of trust evaluations. Given that the questions ask respondents for vote-related criteria, the same evidence may be offered in support of the relevance of these concerns. However, another straightforward test is available: if a particular criterion does not afford more consistently accurate vote predictions than a random distribution of voters based on population proportions, then the criterion may be dismissed as irrelevant, or at least insignificant.* For this test trust is treated as a single variable predicting vote choice, and the vote-relatedness hypothesis is simply that trust is significantly associated with vote choice.

The data in Table 5.3 summarize the relationship between vote choice and a number of alternative bases of vote estimation. The independent variables include several operationalizations of trust and, for comparison, some more traditional indicators. The open-ended trust scores are based solely on those responses to the candidate like/dislike series that were coded as trust related, with direction determined by a net score of equally weighted remarks. The candidate trust scores are derived from respondents' self-placement on the agree/disagree scale accompanying the statements that each candidate could be trusted as president. The combined trust measure represents the differential placement of the candidates on the latter scales and is derived by simply subtracting one scale from the other. The proximity measures record a comparison of individuals' self-placement and their placement of the major candidates on seven-point scales representing issue positions and ideology on a liberal/moderate/conservative continuum, except for the inflation and unemployment issues in 1976, where respondents are merely asked for a party preference on the issue.

---

*The proper comparison in such a test is with a random distribution across the population, that is, with the distribution that would obtain if the two measures were independent. This random distribution is derived from the products of the marginals that intersect for each cell. In Table 5.3, this random distribution produces fewer than 60 percent correct predictions in every case, and every variable generates agreement at a significant level.

TABLE 5.3: Association of Various Measures of Trust with Vote and Comparison with Other Measures, 1972 and 1976

Year	Measure	Consistent Votes	Inconsistent Votes	Percentage Consistent
1972	Open-enedd McGovern Trust[a]	127	20	86.4
1972	Open-ended Nixon Trust[a]	136	32	81.0
1972	McGovern Trust[b]	508	129	79.7
1972	Nixon Trust[b]	578	110	84.0
1972	McGovern-Nixon Combined Trust[c]	607	65	90.3
1972	Party Identification[d]	553	204	73.1
1972	Proximity-Vietnam[e]	511	94	84.5
1972	Proximity-Minority Rights[e]	382	76	83.4
1972	Proximity-Ideology[e]	401	62	86.7
1976	Open-ended Carter Trust[a]	381	103	78.7
1976	Open-ended Ford Trust[a]	307	109	73.8
1976	Carter Trust[b]	908	392	69.8
1976	Ford Trust[b]	988	416	70.4
1976	Carter-Ford Combined Trust[c]	959	140	87.3
1976	Party Identification[d]	918	178	83.8
1976	Proximity-Inflation[f]	716	58	92.5
1976	Proximity-Unemployment[f]	636	115	84.7
1976	Proximity-Ideology[e]	707	143	83.2
1976	Open-ended Nixon Pardon[a]	161	31	83.9

[a]Based on volunteered responses to candidate like/dislike series.
[b]Based on seven-point agree/disagree response to candidate trustworthiness.
[c]Differential score on seven-point agree/disagree response to candidate trustworthiness.
[d]Independents excluded.
[e]Based on respondent's self-placement and placement of candidates on seven-point issue scales and liberal/moderate/conservative ideology scale.
[f]Based on respondent's designation of party that could best handle inflation, unemployment.

Source: Data based upon Survey Research Center, Center for Political Studies of the Institute for Social Research, University of Michigan.

The data in Table 5.3 record nothing more than the degree of correspondence between the various measures, taken singly and without screening for salience, and ultimate vote choice. But trust again is impressive on this simple test. The most consistent performance is that of the combined (differential) candidate trust evaluation, which produces more correct vote predictions in each election than the other measures of trust, the major issues, party identification and ideology, with but one exception. However, that exception, proximity on inflation for 1976, incorporates trust; for both inflation and unemployment, proximities are based on responses to the question of which party could do the better job, not which is closer. The accuracy of predictions based on the combined differential measure increases with the absolute differential between the candidates as well.

The inferences that may be drawn from Table 5.3 are limited, but sufficient for the immediate purpose. In particular, these data do not show that trust is important. But they do support the proposition that trust evaluations are demonstrably accurate indicators of vote preference and are clearly vote related.

SUMMARY

The necessary groundwork to establish that trust is a real concern of voters is presented in this chapter. It is argued that the American political system is so structured that the electorate must trust the president to follow through on his policy proposals where he can be specific, and that they must trust him with the management of the political system in all those areas where they are not informed and attentive. Again, the analogy between the president and the board of directors of a corporation is appropriate in terms of the functions of each, the degree of control exercised by the represented parties, and the requisite qualities for each. The evidence is clear and substantial that the matter of candidate trustworthiness is on the minds of most voters in every election, and that the same concern reached exceptional levels of salience in 1976. It also is clear that voters in the most recent elections have voted for the candidate whom they rated as the most trustworthy. In the following chapter, the meaning of trust is explored.

NOTES

1. James Madison, *The Federalist*, no. 10, ed. Edward Mead Earle (New York: Random House, n.d.), p. 59.
2. Madison, *The Federalist*, no. 57, p. 370.

3. Jean-Jacques Rousseau, *The Social Contract*, book II, chapter 4, trans. Maurice Cranston (Baltimore: Penguin Books, 1968), p. 75. Of course, representation was not a part of Rousseau's ideal.

4. Anthony Downs, *An Economic Theory of Democracy* (New York: Harper & Row, 1957), pp. 39-40.

5. Downs, of course, recognizes this distinction but holds to his ground. Instead of reinterpreting the current party differential as is done here, he compensates for the future by the addition of trend factors and performance ratings; cf. ibid., pp. 41-45.

6. Samuel Popkin, John W. Gorman, Charles Phillips, and Jeffrey A. Smith, "Comment: What Have You Done for Me Lately? Toward an Investment Theory of Voting," *American Political Science Review* 70 (September 1976): 799.

7. Morris P. Fiorina, "An Outline for a Model of Party Choice," *American Journal of Political Science* 21 (August 1977): 619-30.

8. Downs, *An Economic Theory*, pp. 132-39.

9. Roberta S. Sigel, "Image of the Presidency—Part II of an Exploration into Popular Views of Presidential Power," *Midwest Journal of Political Science* 10 (February 1966): 123-37.

10. Arthur H. Miller and Warren E. Miller, "Partisanship and Performance: 'Rational' Choice in the 1976 Presidential Election," paper presented at the 1977 annual meeting of the American Political Science Association, Washington, D.C., September 1-4, ms. p. 95.

11. Fiorina, "An Outline," p. 618. The coding of responses as relevant was based on a personal scheme, although it was not an overly generous one in the direction of relevance.

12. The proportion of the sample excluded in 1972 was 23.2 percent; in 1976, 28.8 percent were excluded. Of the remainder, when asked to rate Nixon in 1972, 5.2 percent responded "don't know." For the others the figures are: McGovern (1972) 9.8 percent; Wallace (1972) 18.6 percent; Ford (1976) 8.1 percent; and Carter (1976) 10.2 percent.

13. The lowest rated issue, however, was rated important by more than 80 percent of the sample: inflation—2,328 "important" to 69 "not important;" honesty in government—2,313 to 84; racial issues, including busing—1,939 to 458.

14. Honesty in government responses were: 1,936 "a great deal," 308 "some," and 27 "none." Lowest rated was racial issues, including busing, with 888, 788, and 217 respectively.

15. Honesty in government was ranked first, second, third, and fourth by 793, 239, 248, and 266 subjects; inflation was rated in the same order by 616, 546, 385, and 234.

6

THE MEANING OF TRUST

*U*nquestionably, one significant impact of the increasingly dominant role of the mass media in American presidential campaigns has been the oft-noted emphasis on creating the appropriate image for the candidate.[1] A great portion of the resources of the major party candidates is devoted to the media packaging of the candidate: the staging of events designed to associate the candidate with various symbols of his fine character and qualities for office, often quite independent of any particular issue position. The rapid rise to prominence in the hierarchy of campaign strategists of those concerned with media relations testifies to the respect that candidates hold for their images.

The 1976 presidential campaigns of Jimmy Carter and Gerald Ford demonstrated an emphasis on creating the appropriate image. Each candidate had a specific image problem to overcome. Carter, the newcomer to national politics, faced charges of political naiveté. His campaign attempted to turn this inexperience into an advantage by disassociating him from any responsibility—personal or through Democratic policies—for problems that national politicians might be expected to answer for, by stressing his independence of the networks of favors and personal relationships that characterize Washington politics, and by appealing directly to the voter who felt that it was time for a change. At the same time, Carter's administration as governor of Georgia was cited to reassure that he did possess the requisite skills for high administrative office. Ford, on the other hand, was clearly experienced in the ways of Washington politics, but suffered from an image of being not up to the job. Thus he was packaged to appear strong, decisive (he "stood up" to Congress with a series of vetoes), caring (the swine flu inoculation program), and possessed of valuable knowledge in foreign policy areas.

While the devotion of such substantial energies to image-producing activities belies at least a tentative faith among those directing media campaigns in the efficacy of their efforts, no such conviction is evidenced in the academic literature on candidate images. The conflict among image researchers arises from opposing positions on the sources of candidate images. To borrow an analogy, the question is whether beauty is "only skin deep" or "in the eye of the beholder."[2]

The skin-deep or image thesis holds that perceptions are stimulus determined. That is, the image of the candidate that voters hold is comprised of the attributes that the candidate projects. To the extent that communication is successful, the candidate is the source of his image in the sense that the same image is projected to all who will see it. Presumably, then, consistency in the messages about a candidate's attributes would insure a uniform perception of him among the electorate.

The eye-of-the-beholder school holds that perceptions are perceiver determined, in accord with the perceptual-balance principle. In other words, individuals bring to the act of communication any number of personal attitudes, values, and concepts that influence their reception of the message. In order to reduce the dissonance that might be produced by their reception of a message incompatible with their predispositions, the targets of the communication may distort the message, or they may engage in selective perception of compatible messages.

While the messages projected by the communicator constitute the raw material for selective perception, the target of the message may play a more creative role in the transaction in accord with the principle of assumed similarity. This principle captures the tendency of individuals to reduce the psychological distance between themselves and others toward whom they are positively disposed by assuming similarities in areas where there is no material basis for the assumption. Correspondingly, psychological distance from negatively evaluated objects is increased by assuming dissimilarities.

The upshot of the perceptual-balance thesis is that political candidates cannot successfully manipulate their images because the target audiences actively participate in the communication process, so that a single message produces a number of distinct responses. The principle predisposing agents in the electoral context are traditionally presumed to be party identification, ideology, and positions on certain issues.

The substantial body of research on this issue does not resolve it, probably because the attempt to isolate either the stimulus (candidate) or the perceiver (voter) as the sole source of candidate images is hopeless. There can be little doubt, for example, that Richard Nixon's final slide in the polls was a response to Watergate revelations and not a gradual deterioration of Republican party identification. At the same time, there are those whose partisanship caused them to misperceive the accumulating evidence against him. Thus, one can only ask of a given aspect of candidate image whether the stimulus or the perceiver has played the dominant role in its development.

This debate about the sources of candidate images is clearly relevant to the analysis of candidate trustworthiness evaluations. If trust is merely a projection by voters, that is, if it is simply attributed to candidates who hold compatible issue positions or party identification, then it is not likely to be of any value in explaining voting behavior. On the other hand, if trustworthiness is to some extent independent of other criteria of candidate evaluation, questions arise regarding the meaning and sources of trust evaluations. Thus, the first half of this chapter is devoted to an empirical examination of the degree to which trust is independent of traditionally recognized criteria of candidate preference, and the remainder of the chapter explores the meaning and sources of trust evaluations. The analysis of the data from the 1972 and 1976 elections does not resolve the conflict between the image and perceptual-balance schools. However, there is a sufficient evidentiary basis for two claims: trustworthiness is an independent criterion of candidate evaluation and is not simply a reflection of partisan predispositions; and voter evaluations of candidate trustworthiness can be linked to real political events.

THE RELATIVE INDEPENDENCE OF TRUST EVALUATIONS

If candidate images are perceiver determined, then evaluations of candidate trustworthiness must be conditioned by some antecedent, politically relevant attitude. The primary candidate for the attitude mediating candidate images is party identification. Parties, according to the preponderance of the voting literature, are the central symbols of politics for Americans, around which other political attitudes revolve. Identification with a political party represents more than mere membership in a politically active group, more than habit, and more than a source of political information. Rather, a party identifier is expressing a psychological tie, an affective relationship to a political entity.

Miller and Levitin describe the relationship of party identifier to party as analogous to that of a church member to a religion.[3] According to this analogy, the theology of the political party is its ideology, which distinguishes the good and true from the bad and false. Members consult the party ideology to give direction to their political lives.

The *American Voter* takes a more secular approach to party identification, emphasizing its influence on the internal consistency of the field of psychological forces bearing on the voter:

> Identification with a party raises a perceptual screen through which the individual tends to see what is favorable to his partisan orientation. The stronger the party bond, the more exaggerated the process of selection and perceptual distortion will be. Without this psychological tie . . . the Independent is less likely to develop consistent partisan attitudes.[4]
> . . . the influence of party identification on perceptions of political objects is so great that only rarely will the individual develop a set of attitude forces that conflicts with this allegiance.[5]

These examples are typical of a continuing tradition in the voting literature of work embodying the assumption that party identification is a manifestation of emotional attachment to a social group. This assumption is criticized in some detail in a previous chapter on the grounds that it is merely assumed based on the simple covariance of party and vote, it is inconsistent with the contemporary evidence, and it ignores the peculiarly political nature of parties as groups. Nevertheless, the status of this assumption in the literature behooves anyone who would introduce a new criterion of vote choice to address the question of its relationship to party.

The predisposing effects of attitudes are not limited to party identification. Nie and Verba, for example, speak of a "halo effect" whereby candidates known to hold certain compatible issue positions are presumed to hold compatible positions on other issues, whether or not they have ever addressed those issues.[6] The same phenomenon might well be observed in the relationship between trust evaluations and prior evaluations of issue positions or ideology. In fact, it is argued in the preceding chapter that trust in the generalized sense almost inevitably has substantive (that is, related to issues) content, and that voters will be forced to base their trust evaluations to some extent upon projection from familiar grounds to more mysterious areas.

If a trust evaluation is merely a summary index of the individual's appraisal of candidates' issue positions and party labels, in other words, a surrogate variable with no independent content, then it is of no concern here. If it is wholly derivative from those elements that have traditionally captured the attention of voting analysts, then it is only a new name for an expression of vote intention. It is essential to the case for trust to demonstrate its independence of these concerns. Complete independence of trust and issues is not to be expected, however. Because of the inevitability of issue content in trust evaluations, the question is one of the relative independence of trust. Nor is it to be expected that the relationship between trust and substantive variables will be constant across elections;

circumstances may emphasize or de-emphasize the relative importance of issue concerns.

There are several potential approaches to examining the relative independence of trust evaluations. The ideal methodology would be to employ panel data over the course of a candidate's political history, noting the changes in trust evaluations corresponding to particular events. In the absence of historical data, one must approach the question indirectly by observing the association of trust evaluations with other variables at a particular time.

The test criterion in this case is the degree of correspondence between the partisan direction of trust and the partisan direction of the other test variables. If trust is wholly derived from another attribute of the candidate, one should see perfect correspondence between the partisan directions of trust and the variable from which it is derived. Independence is indicated by a random distribution of the two variables relative to each other. A dependent relationship is not established by greater-than-random correspondence, however; some correspondence may arise spuriously or coincidentally. Dependence can be corroborated only in the context of a hypothesis assigning causal priority to the independent variable. Those cases where an apparently high degree of association obtains, then, should be evaluated in light of the previous arguments against the traditional notion of party identification.

In Table 6.1 the operationalization of trust evaluations is the combined differential trust evaluation, based on the differential rating of the major party candidates on the seven-point scales described earlier. Each individual's trust evaluation thus has a direction, favoring one candidate or the other, or neither. Similarly, each of the other variables in the table has a direction, and the degree of correspondence in direction between trust and other variables is indicated for each subgroup (row) by the percentages in parentheses. Party identification is based on respondents' self-placement with all independents excluded from the analysis. Direction on ideology and the Vietnam and minority rights issues is based on respondents' self-placement and their estimates of the candidates' positions on seven-point scales, with the more proximate (if any) candidate favored. The inflation and unemployment proximities are based on questions asking which party could better deal with each problem, and thus incorporate trust to some extent.

The proper interpretation of Table 6.1 is quite complex. Consider, for purposes of illustration, the figures, that describe the correspondence between party identification and the direction of the trust differential for 1972. The table entries indicate, for each row, the number and percentage of individuals in the sample whose trust differentials are in the same direction as their party identifications (agreeing), whose trust differentials

TABLE 6.1: Correspondence between Direction of Trust Evaluation and Direction on Various Other Dimensions, 1972 and 1976 (number and percent)

Dimension	Agreeing	Neutral	Disagreeing
Party Identification,[a] 1972			
All	432 (55.8)	145 (18.7)	197 (25.5)
Republicans only	237 (79.8)	37 (12.5)	23 (7.7)
Democrats only	195 (40.9)	108 (22.6)	174 (36.5)
Random	292 (37.7)	145 (18.7)	337 (43.5)
Vietnam-Proximity, 1972			
All	532 (67.3)	143 (18.1)	115 (14.6)
Closer to Nixon	371 (72.2)	85 (16.5)	58 (11.3)
Closer to McGovern	161 (58.3)	58 (21.0)	57 (20.7)
Random	355 (44.9)	143 (18.1)	292 (37.0)
Minorities-Proximity, 1972			
All	409 (68.7)	94 (15.8)	92 (15.5)
Closer to Nixon	276 (73.2)	50 (13.3)	51 (13.5)
Closer to McGovern	133 (61.0)	44 (20.2)	41 (18.8)
Random	268 (45.0)	94 (15.8)	233 (39.2)
Ideology-Proximity, 1972			
All	392 (67.8)	102 (17.6)	84 (14.5)
Closer to Nixon	271 (74.0)	60 (16.4)	35 (9.6)
Closer to McGovern	121 (57.1)	42 (19.8)	49 (23.1)
Random	260 (45.0)	102 (17.6)	216 (37.4)

TABLE 6.1 (continued)

Dimension	Agreeing	Neutral	Disagreeing
Party Identification,[a] 1976			
All	958 (58.3)	431 (26.2)	253 (15.4)
Republicans only	362 (61.0)	177 (29.8)	54 (9.1)
Democrats only	596 (56.8)	254 (24.2)	199 (19.0)
Random	618 (37.6)	431 (26.2)	593 (36.1)
Inflation Proximity,[b] 1976			
All	820 (70.6)	250 (21.5)	92 (7.9)
Republicans better	335 (71.7)	102 (21.8)	30 (6.4)
Democrats better	485 (69.8)	148 (21.3)	62 (8.9)
Random	468 (40.3)	250 (21.5)	444 (38.2)
Unemployment-Proximity,[b] 1976			
All	718 (62.3)	252 (21.9)	182 (15.8)
Republicans better	176 (75.2)	44 (18.8)	14 (6.0)
Democrats better	542 (59.0)	208 (22.7)	168 (18.3)
Random	513 (44.5)	252 (21.9)	387 (33.6)
Ideology-Proximity, 1976			
All	725 (60.7)	277 (23.2)	193 (16.2)
Closer to Ford	405 (59.1)	160 (23.4)	120 (17.5)
Closer to Carter	320 (62.7)	117 (22.9)	73 (14.3)
Random	462 (38.7)	277 (23.2)	456 (38.2)

[a] Independents excluded.
[b] Incorporates trust (see text).
Source: Data based upon Survey Research Center, Center for Political Studies of the Institute for Social Research, University of Michigan.

favor neither candidate (neutral), and whose trust differentials are in the opposite direction of their party identifications (disagreeing). Complete dependence, namely, the condition where trust evaluations are wholly derived from party identification, would be evidenced by perfect agreement between directions on each variable. Clearly, for party identification as well as for every variable pair tested, the percentage of agreement is far below 100 percent. On the other hand, complete independence would not be marked by zero percent agreement—then the two variables would be perfectly, negatively associated—but by the percentage agreement that would obtain if trust evaluations were distributed randomly relative to each variable. In the case of party identification for 1972, if the 53.1 percent of the sample who rated Nixon more trustworthy and the 28.2 percent who favored McGovern were distributed randomly across the sample of party identifiers, there would be 37.7 percent agreement and 43.5 percent disagreement between party identification and trust. These are the proportions that would obtain if Republicans and Democrats were equally likely to find Nixon the more trustworthy candidate, that is, if party identification had no predisposing effects on trustworthiness evaluations. The 55.8 percent agreement that actually obtains between the two variables should thus be compared with the 37.7 percent agreement that would obtain if the two were independent, rather than with zero.*

It may be objected to this procedure that it involves treating neutral evaluations as errors in prediction by comparing with perfect agreement. This, however, is in keeping with the formulation of the alternative hypotheses, for example, that party identification exercises a predisposing effect on trust evaluations, as they appear in the literature. To meet this objection, the alternative hypotheses may be reformulated as follows: the existence of a directional attitude on one of the assumedly causally prior variables is incompatible with trust evaluations of the opposite direction. This reformulation implies a weaker notion of the predisposing effects of

---

*The random distribution of the cases in a sample is that where the number of cases in each cell of the bivariate matrix has the same percentage of the row total as the percentage that the column has of the full sample, and the same percentage of the cases in the column as the row has of the full sample. The observed distribution may be compared to the random distribution in a variety of ways. For example, one may compare the percentage of agreement observed with the percentage of random agreement, and express the difference as a percentage of the difference between randomness and perfect dependence. In the case of party identification, this would indicate a 29.1 percent improvement over random, that is, 55.8 percent-37.7 percent/100.0 percent-37.7 percent. But this method ignores disagreements, and no other method seems clearly superior. Therefore, it is merely indicated what the random distribution is in the table.

party identification that resembles selective perception in application. In other words, the expectation of perfect agreement is replaced by the expectation of nondisagreement, and the neutral category is ignored in the calculation of percentages agreeing and disagreeing. In the case at hand, this would change the percentage agreeing to 68.7 percent, compared to a random expectation of 46.4 percent agreement. (These revised figures are obtained through the same steps outlined above, but ignoring the cases of neutral trust evaluation. The ratio calculated in this manner is symmetric as well, that is, the increased percentage agreement is equal to the decreased percentage disagreement.)

Table 6.1 includes data for subgroups of each variable's population defined by direction on the variable. Since the predisposing effects of attitudes are presumably similar in strength whatever the direction of the attitude, there should be only minor differences (attributable to sampling error) in percentage agreement between subgroups. Beyond these minor disturbances, differences between subgroups must be attributed to either innate differences in the members of the subgroups or to differences in the attitudes being measured. The latter would occur, for example, if Republicans were more enthusiastic about their party's candidate's trustworthiness than Democrats were about their party's candidate's trustworthiness. The fact that such differences do arise underscores the contribution of perceptions of the candidates themselves, apart from predisposing effects, to attitudes toward candidates.

With these considerations in mind, consider the evidence in Table 6.1 Clearly the strongest evidence in support of the hypothesized independence of trust evaluations is the comparison with party identification for 1972. The distribution of differential trust evaluations with respect to party identification for 1972 more closely approximates randomness than dependence. The greater proportion of agreement is attributed to Republicans who are relatively secure with their party's nominee. Democrats, by contrast, are quite divided and very nearly random in the designation of the more trustworthy candidate. This case alone provides corroboration for the independence hypothesis, as party identification had little, if any, predisposing effect upon Democrats in 1972.

Both parties moved closer to the mean in 1976, with more agreement among Democrats and less agreement among Republicans that their respective candidates were the more trustworthy. Overall, party identification and trust evaluations agree in direction 33.2 percent more than if the two were randomly distributed (57.2 percent, excluding neutrals). There remains a sizable difference in the percentage of disagreements between Republicans and Democrats.

The halo effects of the issue positions included in Table 6.1 are not greatly different from the predisposing effects of party identification.

Positions on both Vietnam and minority rights are aligned with trust differentials to about a 40 percent greater extent than they would be if they were randomly distributed. Of the 1976 issues, inflation is more highly associated with trust than are the 1972 issues, but unemployment is less so. However, both of the 1976 issues actually incorporate trust to some extent in that they are based on questions asking which party could do the better job, rather than which party's position is preferred. Ideological proximities do not determine perceptions of trustworthiness to any greater extent than do issues. Overall, the data record both some issue content in trust evaluations and some discrepancy between directions on issue positions and trust, as expected.

Another trend evidenced in the data in Table 6.1 is a greater prevalence of dissonant attitudes regarding the relatively obscure challengers than regarding the incumbents in each election. Unfortunately, both races pitted Republican incumbents against Democratic challengers, so it will be at least 1980 before one can see whether the relationship continues to hold when the parties are in the reverse positions. In the meantime, however, this reticence to accept newcomers is consistent with the argument that trust must be earned and does not simply attach to one's party's nominee.

Three additional points are in order before closing the discussion of these data. First, it is impossible to be definitive about the specific degree of noncorrespondence that constitutes evidence of relative independence. The degree of correspondence should vary with the political context (such as the issues, candidates, etc.) of elections in any case. Second, the test of independence in Table 6.1 is bivariate; it does not rule out the possibility that trust evaluations are wholly derived from party identification and most important issue, or any other combination of variables. Ultimately one doubtless could arrive at a set of variables that would account for variations in trust evaluations, but it is not likely that this process would contribute to understanding trust. More enlightening are the various tests in the following chapter that employ trust evaluations in multivariate statistical accounts of vote choice. Third, the question posed so far has been whether party, issue positions, or ideology predispose individuals to reach certain positions on candidate trustworthiness. But this formulation of the question excludes from consideration the very substantial numbers of voters who have no party identification, or no issue-based or ideological candidate preference, and who therefore must reach any conclusions about trustworthiness on the basis of criteria independent of these.

Taking into consideration the evidence in Table 6.1 and these various qualifications, there would appear to be a sufficient empirical basis for treating trust evaluations as separate, relatively independent elements of vote choice alongside the more traditional variables such as party identification and issues. It remains to be established that trust is of sufficient weight in voter calculations to merit the serious attention of psephologists; this question is addressed in the following chapter. The remainder of this chapter is devoted to a further exploration of the meaning of trust.

THE MEANING OF TRUST IN THE CONTEXT OF VOTE DECISIONS

The theoretical development of trust as a factor in vote decisions (in Chapter 5) involved the specification of two distinct roles, and hence two distinct meanings, for this element of candidate evaluation. With regard to specific issues that concern a voter, trustworthiness, including competence, serves as a discounting factor for a candidate's announced issue positions. Voters must sift through various candidate representations, along with whatever additional data seem appropriate, to arrive at some estimate of the probability that their relevant concerns will have an impact on the output of the political system. In its specific role, trust is an estimate of the reliability of candidate representations.

In its general role, trust has a broader meaning involving a candidate's intentions, capabilities, and values. By definition, the generalized component of a voter's candidate differential incorporates all of those presidential tasks to which the voter is neither attentive nor informed, and where consequently the voter alienates sovereignty (or a share in the public sovereignty) to the government in a very literal sense. From the perspective of the voter, this generalized portion of the political space is in effect a blind trust, with various government officials, including the president, acting as the voter's agents. Because these agents cannot be instructed, the voter is forced to base vote choices upon the characters of the candidates.

An illustration of the distinction between these roles is provided by the data in Table 5.1 for the 1964 election. Goldwater's reputation for sincerity is reflected in the more than ten-to-one balance of favorable to unfavorable trust comments in the open-ended series. Lyndon Johnson, by contrast, was noted more for political pragmatism than observance of principle, and he had nearly a four-to-one ratio of negative trust comments to positive ones. Despite the clear Goldwater advantage in this measure of sincerity, Johnson won a landslide victory in the election. This outcome can be explained by invoking both senses of trust. Goldwater's credibility, combined with his unpopular positions, led many voters to fear that, if elected, he would do exactly as he promised; he was perceived as an individual of such ideological rigidity that he could not be trusted with the management of the political system. Johnson, on the other hand, was the quintessential political manager, and his reputation for being adept at political wheeling and dealing actually enhanced his stock among certain groups. Blacks, for example, could look to the 1964 Voting Rights Act for assurance. Whether Johnson was sincere in his empathy for blacks or not was largely irrelevant when placed alongside the fact that he obviously considered them to be a key element of his political strategy, combined with his legislative omni-competence. Johnson was a president who could get things done, and the nature of his talents—compromise and negotiation within a relatively stable framework of power distribution—promised a greater degree of stability than those of Goldwater's.

An example with some evidentiary basis is the 1972 Nixon-McGovern contest. Although the outcome of the election was initially interpreted by academic analysts solely in terms of issues, subsequent research contains evidence that McGovern's crushing defeat was not only attributable to his extremist issue positions, but also to certain personal shortcomings of the type that are of concern here. (The issue-based interpretation of the 1972 election is described in detail in Chapter 3.) Popkin et al., for example, cite a variety of evidence that McGovern's dramatic descent in the polls and subsequent defeat were "due in great measure to McGovern's perceived incompetence rather than to his issue positions."[7] The evidence includes data from national polls showing that McGovern was at least a viable candidate in June 1972; that during the course of the campaign he lost support among numerous of his presumedly natural constituencies defined in terms of issue positions; and that this loss of support was paralleled by his decline in the polls on indexes of basic presidential competence. In addition, both Nixon's performance rating and McGovern's competence rating proved to be statistically significant and independent elements of vote choice.

Similar evidence is cited by Miller and Levitin, although they interpret the election in terms of issue positions. Again, McGovern was deemed to be a competitive candidate in terms of the issues at the beginning of the campaign.[8] But again, McGovern proved to be a weak candidate among his natural constituencies.

The Miller-Levitin analysis of the Vietnam issue is instructive on the role of personal factors in candidate preference decisions. They begin with the observation that:

> . . . many self-proclaimed doves did not perceive McGovern as closer than Nixon to their own Vietnam position. To the contrary, more than one-fifth (22 percent) of the doves who might have been expected to be included as part of McGovern's natural constituency on this issue actually saw Nixon as closer to their preferred position. One out of six (16 percent) saw no difference between McGovern and Nixon.[9]

The same apparent hesitancy to embrace McGovern is reported in connection with actual voting according to issue proximities. In order to account for these anomalies in an issue-oriented election, the authors invoke widespread confusion:

> These results were based on factual survey data; they seemed surprising because of our sense that McGovern's issue positions were closer to those of the electorate than the electorate perceived them to be. Our explanation of the discrepancy is that McGovern somehow failed to convince many of those who already shared his positions that they indeed did so, and he also failed to persuade the more indifferent in the electorate that he could better represent them.[10]

A more satisfying account of these findings, based on the investor-voter model, emphasizes the distinction between issue positions and political outcomes. First, it must be noted that treatment of the Vietnam war as a one-dimensional issue is inappropriate. In addition to those whose positions could accurately be represented on the single "military victory" to "immediate withdrawal" scale employed by the SRC/CPS, there were others who felt that decisive action one way or the other was preferable to continued muddling through. Additional complications, including international prestige, prisoners of war, and terms of peace, combined to give Vietnam positions a multidimensional character. Second, the Nixon position was not for escalation to achieve military victory. Instead, Republican pollsters Steeper and Teeter report that:

> The most widely held perception of Nixon's Vietnam policy was that he was "bringing the boys home". . . . Across our surveys in 1972, we consistently found Nixon's biggest asset was that a clear plurality of voters perceived him as successfully *de-escalating* the war.[11]

Apparently what the electorate saw in the Vietnam positions of the major candidates was a choice between two programs for withdrawal: one that was painfully slow but was at the same time cautious to preserve the best feasible outcome in terms of POWs and prestige, and another that was immediate, precipitous, humiliating, and did not promise to salvage any gains for all the sunken costs.

Now consider an alternative explanation of the anomalies in the issue-based account. First, the doves and middle-of-the-roaders who failed to perceive McGovern as their champion were not confused, but were expressing the multidimensionality of their concern. They were indicating proximity not to an abstract moral position, but to the preferred of two expected outcomes. While there were certainly grounds for confusion about some of McGovern's programs, particularly the $1,000 minimum-income plan, his position on Vietnam was precise and consistent through-out the campaign, and surely less confusing the Nixon's 1968 "secret plan" to end the war. Those who preferred withdrawal but perceived themselves as closer to Nixon may have been unprepared for the disastrous consequences that they saw as attendant to McGovern's plan.

The second set of anomalies—the lower-than-expected vote for McGovern from his natural issue constituencies—may well be a conse-quence of the electorate's general lack of faith in McGovern. Many who preferred McGovern's position were forced to discount the expected value of the position because they simply did not trust him to oversee the withdrawal. Those who were indifferent between the two positions were naturally inclined to support the more competent Nixon. Some of those who preferred McGovern's position but adjusted their expectations down-ward either found themselves closer to the net Nixon position or ab-stained. Finally, the fact that Nixon held the decisive edge across the elec-torate in generalized trust and competence, which is always a consideration of some weight, is also reflected in McGovern's failure to swing voters to his side on the single issue of the war.

SOURCES OF TRUST EVALUATIONS

The voter who would evaluate the trustworthiness of the candidates must project from the available data to the future performance of each candidate as president. The only data consistent with politically rational voting behavior are those attributes that affect the performance of the president as it bears on the output of the political system. This stipulation rules out of the rational voter's calculus all data that are not job related, such as eye color or an honest face. But it is not so easy to delimit the applicable data.

The most appropriate job-related information upon which to base a projection of future performance is the current performance of an incum-bent. Even in the case of an incumbent seeking reelection, there are inevitable difficulties posed by the fact that a president may pursue on strategy when he is eligible for reelection and another when he is in his final term, along with changes in at least some of the problems facing the president, but one could hardly ask for more reliable information. The major obstacle to employing incumbent performance rating is that candidates for the presidency are only occasionally incumbent. Of the 14 major party candidates in the past seven American presidential elections, only Eisen-hower in 1956 and Nixon in 1972 were full-term incumbents. Ford and Johnson were part-term incumbents, and two incumbent vice-presidents have sought the office. In Anthony Downs's idealized political system, one party is always incumbent and the other is always proposing alternatives so that voters may use performance ratings regularly, but it is argued in the foregoing that the independence of the president from his party and the inconsistency of American political parties make such comparisons largely irrelevant if not impossible in the American context.

Voters will use incumbent performance ratings whenever possible. Otherwise they must rely upon observations of the candidates in situations that provide some basis for projection to the presidency. Most of the viable presidential candidates have previously held positions of responsibility subject to public scrutiny. The quality of their performance in such areas is one source of expectations of the candidates, a very powerful source in some cases. But the audience for such performances is frequently much more circumscribed than the president's audience—the American public as a whole. Most voters, for example, were unable to appraise adequately Jimmy Carter's performance as governor of Georgia because their information was hearsay and contradictory. In addition, the job requirements for the presidency are distinct from those of the congressional representative or military hero or industrialist. Thus, such projections are incomplete as well as distant from the voter's experience.

The most underrated sources of candidate evaluations are the performances of the candidates in the election campaign itself. From *The American Voter* to the latest voting analyses, the campaign is lost in the party-versus-issues paradigm; either decisions are produced by long-held predispositions applied to particular candidates, or they result from impersonal comparison of issue positions. Neither party models nor issue models provide a major role for the candidates, so it is natural that both place the campaign in the background. But it is during the campaign that the candidates are most visible, are constantly faced with political problems, and bear personal responsibility for organization, administration, leadership, and substantive decision making. It is true that the performances of the candidates—or at least that of the challenger—are in many cases hypothetical during the campaign, a fact that has been adequately integrated into the present work. But there are real decisions to make as presidential candidate, and these actions must be taken at a time when voters are more highly attuned to such events than they are between elections, while they and their agents in the media and the opposition are consciously comparing candidates. Campaign observations of the candidates are immediate and frequently firsthand, or more so than the candidate's public record.

One aspect of the 1976 campaign that merits special attention is the series of debates between the major party candidates. The debates facilitated candidate evaluations by presenting the candidates in prolonged, face-to-face interrogation viewed by a substantial portion of the electorate and reported to millions more. Despite the wishes and expectations of many proponents of the debate format, however, neither the most recent series nor the 1960 Kennedy-Nixon debates seem to have substantially affected the incidence of issue voting among the electorate, nor, indeed, to have been perceived in terms of issues by most viewers. It could be that the candidates, in an attempt to be all things to all voters, failed to distinguish themselves adequately on the issues. One who ascribes to the investor-voter model, however, would argue that the debates are not necessarily about the issues. A candidate has ample opportunity to address the various issue publics more or less individually during the campaign. The debates present an excellent opportunity, instead, to appeal to the common, generalized concerns of the electorate, that is, to demonstrate one's competence, knowledge, decision-making abilities, and so on.

The data in Table 6.2 summarize the public response to the most recent debates, as recorded in the SRC/CPS survey. Four different questions capture four distinct sets of responses, but there are considerable regularities between the sets. Physical qualities, such as Carter's smile, were noted by only a very small percentage of respondents in each case. Qualities of personality, qualifications for office, and performance in the debates constitute the bulk of the responses in every case. References to a candidate's sympathies for various groups and positions on issues, that is, those observations relevant to the specific interests of certain voters, formed a much smaller proportion of the messages received by viewers of the debates. Whether these observations reflect the actual content of the debates or the limitations of the viewers is not definitively ascertainable from this evidence; to this observer the former seemed to be the case. In any event, the data support the conclusion that the debates were largely "about" the generalized qualities of the candidates and not specific issues.

In addition to the normal activities of the campaign and public life, there occur occasionally events of transcendent significance for the public images of the candidates. These are events where one or another attribute of the individual is so profoundly displayed that it becomes bound up with the individual's public image on a permanent basis, or at least for a time far exceeding the public memory of normal political events. Watergate has surely become a permanent component of the image of Richard Nixon, as has the Nixon pardon for Ford. To a lesser extent, the Mayaguez incident and the remark about Poland's freedom from Soviet domination, the most frequently cited memory of the debates, are part of the Ford image. McGovern is similarly linked with the Eagleton fiasco.

Each of these events has in common that it has become part of the definition of the public image of the character of the individual involved. It may well be that such events serve more as points of crystallization for

TABLE 6.2: Response to Ford-Carter Debates, 1976

Was there anything you learned about the issues or the candidates for the first time because of the debates? What was that?

	N	Percent
Physical Qualities	9	1.1
Personality Qualities	204	23.8
Qualifications	84	9.8
Performance	235	27.4
Group references, Issues	324	37.9
Total	856	100.0

Was there anything in particular you remember from the debates that impressed you either favorably or unfavorably about any of the candidates? What was that?

Physical Qualities	36	2.5
Personality Qualities	379	26.5
Qualifications	67	4.7
Performance	648	45.3
Group references, Issues	300	21.0
Total	1,429	100.0

Is there anything (else) from the debates that you remember about Mr. Ford?

Physical Qualities	31	2.0
Personality Qualities	538	35.6
Qualifications	106	7.0
Performance	670	44.3
Group references, Issues	168	11.1
Total	1,512	100.0

Is there anything (else) from the debates that you remember about Mr. Carter?

Physical Qualities	102	6.4
Personality Qualities	466	29.4
Qualifications	112	7.1
Performance	592	37.3
Group references, Issues	315	19.8
Total	1,568	100.0

Source: Tabulations include only coded responses, based on SRC/CPS coding scheme, and exclude miscellaneous categories.

attitudes than origins; it is quite possible that the Eagleton affair, for example, was more important for confirming the doubts of a large number of voters about McGovern's capabilities than it was for raising new doubts. In either event, such cases are difficult to stage or even to anticipate, and are thus relatively reliable and they are generally dramatic, which doubtless contributes to the long public memory of them.

There are any number of additional criteria for candidate trust evaluations with varying degrees of reliability. Jimmy Carter's fundamentalist religion may have been the basis for many people's trust in him, as well as for distrust of him by others. Demographic characteristics in general are readily verifiable, familiar to large numbers of voters, and have a significance based on personal experience, and so may be quite useful bits of information. The character of the candidate's associates, insofar as the candidate selects them, also gives clues to his character; witness the great attention directed toward the selection of running mates in the past two elections. It is impossible, for obvious reasons, to be exhaustive on the subject of sources of trustworthiness evaluations.

It is also difficult to establish the connection between any particular presumed criterion of trustworthiness and voter evaluations of the candidates. The ideal empirical basis for such an argument would be data from a panel study with repeated administrations of trust evaluation items before and after the event in question. A close approximation to this ideal is the regular presidential popularity poll; however, this captures a general performance approval rather than trust per se and does not provide the basis for establishing the contact that has occurred with the stimulus in question. One may safely assume, though, that Ford's plummeting in the ratings following the Nixon pardon, and his recovery following the Mayaguez incident, were largely related to these events.

In lieu of panel data, it is still possible to demonstrate the association at a single point in time of attitudes toward certain events and candidate trust evaluations. The impossibility of establishing the temporal ordering captured in these relationships renders this approach less than definitive, but it remains both worthwhile and suggestive.

Any number of real world events that might logically bear on candidate trustworthiness could be cited; only a sampling are reported in Table 6.3. Attitudes toward both McGovern's handling of the Eagleton incident and his handling of the campaign in general are moderately strong in their association with attitudes toward his trustworthiness, and attitudes toward the Nixon pardon exhibit a similar association with trust evaluations of Ford. The most impressive relationship in the table, however, is that between trust of Ford and rating of his incumbent performance. (The association between Ford performance approval ratings and Ford trustwor-

TABLE 6.3: **Association between Evaluations of Performance and Trust Evaluations of McGovern, 1972 and Ford, 1976**

At the time, what did you think of the way McGovern handled the whole question of Eagleton as his vice-presidential candidate?

McGovern Trust Evaluations

	Agreements		*Neutrals*		*Disagreements*	
	N	Percent	N	Percent	N	Percent
Overall	417	58.1	131	18.2	170	23.7
Poor	302	57.2	91	17.2	135	25.6
Well	115	60.5	40	21.1	35	18.4
Random	273	38.0	131	18.2	314	43.7

Do you think McGovern did a good job, or a poor job in running his campaign?

McGovern Trust Evaluations

	Agreements		*Neutrals*		*Disagreements*	
	N	Percent	N	Percent	N	Percent
Overall	469	54.1	151	17.4	247	28.5
Poor	306	52.9	99	17.1	173	29.9
Good	163	56.4	52	18.0	74	25.6
Random	351	40.5	151	17.4	365	42.1

Shortly after taking office, President Ford pardoned Richard Nixon for any wrongdoings he may have committed while he was president. Do you think that Ford should have pardoned Nixon?

Ford Trust Evaluations

	Agreements		Neutrals		Disagreements	
	N	Percent	N	Percent	N	Percent
Overall	1,385	55.0	355	14.1	780	31.0
Yes	886	83.8	83	7.9	88	8.3
No	499	34.1	272	18.6	692	47.3
Random	1,003	39.8	355	14.1	1,162	46.1

Do you approve or disapprove of the way Mr. Ford is handling his job as president?

Ford Trust Evaluations

	Agreements		Neutrals		Disagreements	
	N	Percent	N	Percent	N	Percent
Overall	1,737	72.9	301	12.6	346	14.5
Approve	1,279	84.9	136	9.0	91	6.0
Disapprove	458	52.2	165	18.8	255	29.0
Random	1,171	49.1	301	12.6	912	38.3

Source: Data based upon Survey Research Center, Center for Political Studies of the Institute for Social Research, University of Michigan.

thiness ratings is 46.7 percent stronger than random when neutrals are included, 62.1 percent stronger excluding neutrals.) This is to be expected, of course, because performance ratings are the most general and most reliable of criteria, as argued above.

The data in Table 6.3 bear a strong resemblance to the data in Table 6.1, and the interpretations and inferences are similar as well. Trustworthiness evaluations are associated with, but less than dependent on, the variables in each table. The causal links remain merely speculative, of course, but it appears roughly equally likely that any of the variables tested plays some role in the evaluation of candidate trustworthiness.

SUMMARY

In this chapter three separate approaches to the meaning of trust as a variable in candidate preference decisions are explored. The first is a demonstration that trust evaluations are relatively independent of party identification, attitudes toward issues, and ideology, and thus merit independent status as a criterion of vote choice. The second is a brief, largely speculative treatment of the roles that trust has played in some recent elections, which suggests some meanings that it may have for voters. Finally, tentative support is offered for the objective grounding of trustworthiness evaluations. Unfortunately, the empirical evidence is increasingly difficult ot interpret as one attempts to bring the concept of trust into sharper focus.

It is, of course, impossible to be definitive about the meaning of trust. In the investor-voter model, the precise meaning of the term is presumed to vary from election to election, from candidate to candidate, from voter to voter. In spite of these variations, there is sufficient overlap, or a sufficient common sense of the term, that individuals in conversation rarely feel called upon to define it. Ultimately, the grounds for dealing with trust as a common element of political competition are the same as those for dealing with any of the other factors—parties, candidate images, issue positions—that are perceived in unique ways by different individuals.

NOTES

1. The literary output of presidential campaigns always includes a generous sample of commentary on the packaging of the candiate. The most prominent work in this area is probably Joe McGinniss's *The Selling of the President 1968* (New York: Trident Press, 1969).

2. This analogy is taken from the summary of this debate in Dan Nimmo and Robert L. Savage, *Candidates and Their Images: Concepts, Methods, and Findings* (Pacific Palisades, Calif.: Goodyear Publishing, 1976), pp. 81–108.

3. Warren E. Miller and Teresa E. Levitin, *Leadership and Change: The New Politics and the American Electorate* (Cambridge, Mass.: Winthrop, 1976), pp. 31–33.

4. Angus T. Campbell, Philip E. Converse, Warren E. Miller, and Donald E. Stokes, *The American Voter* (New York: John Wiley & Sons, 1960), p. 133.

5. Ibid., p. 141. A more thorough treatment of the predisposing role of party identification in social-psychological models of voting appears in Chapter 2.

6. Norman H. Nie, Sidney Verba, and John R. Petrocik, *The Changing American Voter* (Cambridge, Mass.: Harvard University Press, 1976), p. 340.

7. Samuel Popkin, John W. Gorman, Charles Phillips, and Jeffrey A. Smith, "Comment: What Have You Done for Me Lately? Toward an Investment Theory of Voting," *American Political Science Review* 70 (September 1976): 799.

8. Miller and Levitin, *Leadership and Change*, pp. 120-22.

9. Ibid., p. 141.

10. Ibid., p. 145.

11. Frederick T. Steeper and Robert M. Teeter, "Comment on 'A Majority Party in Disarray'," *American Political Science Review* 70 (September 1976): 806.

7

TRUST AND THE VOTE

*T*he ultimate significance of the present analysis of candidate trustworthiness depends on the demonstration that trust is an important factor in vote decisions. In the preceding chapters it is argued that voters always attempt to evaluate the trustworthiness of presidential candidates, that this is a vote-related concern of relatively consistent and widespread salience, and that such evaluations are meaningful in the sense of being based on rationally employed criteria rather than on mere predispositions. It remains to be shown that trust is of sufficient weight in the decisions of voters to merit the subsequent attention of vote analysts. A variety of methodological devices frequently employed in voting studies are applied to this question below.

Underlying each of the various approaches to the weight of a factor is a theoretical understanding of the voter's decision process, in addition to assumptions behind the operationalizations of variables and the use of certain statistical techniques. Thus only in the case of the simulation model explicitly derived from the analysis of the investor-voter is the methodology appropriate to a test of the model. The use of the normal vote and six-factor models in the analysis below is consequently heuristic in this context, and does not constitute an endoresement of the associated theory. In the remaining cases, incomplete models are employed for specific, limited purposes with no theoretical implications.

None of the methodologies employed in this chapter has any claim to be definitive. At the end of the analysis, no conclusion is possible about the specific weight of trust in voter decisions. Each test is relevant only to a particular theoretical formulation and set of operationalizations and assumptions. Nevertheless, the performance of the trust dimension on these tests is consistently impressive, lending considerable support to the hypothesis that trust concerns are a relatively important factor in vote decisions, at least of comparable weight with parties, issues, and ideology.

TRUST AS A SINGLE VARIABLE ACCOUNT OF VOTE CHOICE

A considerable body of evidence is presented in the preceding chapters that, while not directly addressed to the question of the importance of the trust dimension, is adaptable to this purpose. Each of the applicable data sets, when applied to the question presently at hand, has the form of a model where a single variable is postulated to account for all of the variance in vote choice. While this formulation is clearly incompatible with the full investor-voter model, the evidence is suggestive of the importance attached to trust.

Table 5.1 indicates the proportion of responses to the open-ended candidate like/dislike series for elections since 1952 that are directly related to the trust dimension. The questions that elicited the recorded responses asked respondents to identify anything about the candidates "that might make you want to vote (for, against) him." The substantial proportions of responses tapping trust constitute prima facie evidence for its importance in candidate support calculations.

Table 5.3 incorporates no indication of the salience of various factors, but it does report the association of each with ultimate vote. These data constitute a series of one-variable models of vote choice. The great consistency between trust, especially as operationalized in the combined differential trust measure, and vote could arise for reasons other than that trust is an important component of vote choice. However, given the evidence in Chapter 6 that trust evaluations are relatively independent of other concerns more widely recognized as components of vote choice, these data are additional evidence that trust may be a very important factor as well. Again, the greater the trust differential between the candidates, the more likely it is that the voter will support the more trusted alternative.

TRUST AND CROSS-PRESSURED VOTERS

From the beginning of survey-based voter research, cross-pressured voters have been the objects of much concern in the explanation of voting behavior. Cross-pressured voters are those individuals who report holding simultaneously attitudes that incline them toward opposite courses of action, for example, a 1972 Democrat who preferred Nixon's Vietnam policy. The cases of cross-pressured voters are of particular significance for voting studies because the manner in which conflicting attitudes are resolved may indicate the relative weights of the competing forces.

The social-psychological model reviewed in Chapter 2, and particularly the version of the Columbia school, sees conflict in political attitudes as arising from simultaneous affiliation with groups holding conflicting attitudes. The consensus in these studies is that cross-pressures produce indecisiveness, postponement of preference decisions, and often abstention from voting if the conflict is not resolved. Resolution comes, if at all, through the restoration of perceptual balance; voters are not expected to maintain a set of conflicting attitudes.

Downsian and other rational models, by contrast, make no special provisions for cross-pressured voters. Conflicting attitudes are simply combined, appropriately weighted into a net attitude toward the competing parties. The investor-voter model is similar in this regard, except that the competing candidates are the foci of the relevant attitudes. In either case, to the extent that voters are cross-pressured, their incentives (party or candidate differentials) would be reduced, leading to lower turnout as a function of increased indifference to the outcome.

The analysis of cross-pressured voters is employed here to indicate the relative weight attached to the trustworthiness of the candidates as compared to another presumed influence on vote choice among those voters who are cross-pressured. A series of bivariate models of vote choice, including trust as one of the independent variables, are tested and the proportion of the cases of conflict that are resolved by an ultimate vote consistent with each variable is taken as an indication of the relative importance of the two variables. The implicit assumptions of this exercise are that both variables are in fact influences on the vote, that the two variables in question incorporate all of the influences on the vote, and that no changes in the direction of either attitude occur prior to the election. This particular assumption set is clearly incompatible with the full investor-voter model, as well as empirically dubious. The results of the exercise are thus merely suggestive, although not therefore trivial.

The hypothesis that trust is a matter of some considerable weight in candidate preference decisions implies that sizable proportions of cross-pressure dilemmas are resolved in the same direction as trust when it conflicts with attitudes toward party, ideology, and issues. The data in Table 7.1 summarize the outcomes for seven different classes of cross-pressures in the 1972 and 1976 elections. In every case but one, cross-pressures were resolved in the same direction as trust by sizable margins over its competitors. Again there is evidence of the reluctance of 1972 Democrats to support their candidate, as 102 of 117 cross-pressured Democrats voted for the more trusted Nixon. The single reversal of this trend is, significantly, the only case involving a screen for salience, that is, each respondent's most important issue is presumably so important because the respondent personally identified it as the most important issue. Even in this case, however, trust holds up as a significant factor as measured by the proportion of cross-pressured voters who voted contrary to their preference on their most important issue.

The evidence in Table 7.1 is rather strong support for the significance of the weight attached by voters to candidate trustworthiness. It is also one of the most straightforward demonstrations of the advantages accruing to the candidate who can establish the more trustworthy image in the eyes of the electorate.

A NORMAL VOTE EVALUATION OF THE TRUST DIMENSION

In slightly more than a decade since its introduction, normal vote analysis has achieved some prominence among voting study methodologies.[1] It is generally regarded as a way of measuring the importance of a particular issue (or group interest or any other dimension of vote choice) in a given election, and is presumed to be capable of straightforward interpretation and application across elections. In fact, the normal vote index values permit only a much narrower interpretation than that that is typically applied, and certainly justify no generalizations about the overall impact of an issue in a particular election or set of elections. Nevertheless, these measures, when properly interpreted, are relevant to the present concern and are presented below.

The normal vote was conceived in response to the need for a baseline against which aggregate votes could be registered in order to permit specification of the "meaning" of a particular electoral outcome.[2] The development of this concept begins with the assumption that the outcome of an election can be analyzed as the confluence of relatively stable, long-term political attitudes or predispositions and relatively transitory, short-term influences arising from the specific election. Because of its stability across elections, its presumed predisposing effect on other attitudes, and its demonstrably strong association with actual voting behavior, party identification defines the normal vote. On the other hand, political stimuli such as the issues of the day and the particular candidates of the major parties are representative of the stimuli that comprise the unique context of an election.

In the most common applications of normal vote analysis, the separate influences on the vote are represented by summary indexes of the long-term partisan effects and the short-term effects of the specific issue in

TABLE 7.1: Analysis of Cross-pressured Individuals, 1972 and 1976

For voters who were cross-pressured on:

Party Identification[a] v. Trust[b], 1972:	N	Percent
Voted with party	24	14.0
Abstained	41	24.0
Voted with trust	106	62.0
Ideology[c] v. Trust, 1972:		
Voted with ideology	22	31.0
Abstained	10	14.1
Voted with trust	39	54.9
Minority Rights Issue[d] v. Trust, 1972:		
Voted with issue	19	22.4
Abstained	19	22.4
Voted with trust	47	55.3
Vietnam Issue[d] v. Trust, 1972:		
Voted with issue	26	25.5
Abstained	27	26.5
Voted with trust	49	48.0
Party Identification[a] v. Trust, 1976:		
Voted with party	57	28.4
Abstained	58	28.9
Voted with trust	86	42.8
Ideology[c] v. Trust, 1976:		
Voted with ideology	39	25.2
Abstained	45	29.0
Voted with trust	71	45.8
Most Important Issue[e] v. Trust, 1976:		
Voted with issue	50	45.5
Abstained	22	20.0
Voted with trust	38	34.5

[a] Party identifiers only; independents excluded.
[b] Combined differential trust evaluation.
[c] Most proximate candidate on liberal/moderate/conservative scale.
[d] Most proximate candidate on seven-point issue position scale.
[e] Party likely to do best job on respondent's most important issue.

Source: Data based upon Survey Research Center, Center for Political Studies of the Institute for Social Research, University of Michigan.

question, designated L and S respectively.[3] The most accurate published interpretation of these measures is that of the originator, Richard Boyd:

> The partisan component (L) is the degree of party polarization on an issue. . . .
> The short-term component of an issue (S) is its relationship to defections from the normal party vote.[4]

The typical interpretation, consistent with the assumption set of the normal vote model, is that these indexes represent the separate effects of party identification and the issue on the vote.

Table 7.2 shows the normal vote index values for the trust dimension in both the 1972 and 1976 elections. For purposes of comparison, the index values for a number of issues in the 1972 election are reported as well.[5] The latter are taken from the SRC/CPS analysis of the 1972 election and contributed to their conclusion that issues were of unprecedented importance in that contest. However, by these measures trust is shown to be of greater importance than any of the 1972 issues. The L term for trust is not a great deal larger than those for other issues, although it is large, indicating that the partisan component of trust evaluations is only marginally greater than that for the issues examined in 1972. The S terms for trust in both 1972 and 1976 are far larger than any previously published short-term indexes for any issue in any election, and indicate a stronger impact on the vote for trust than for issues (according to the assumptions of the model).

The proper interpretation of the normal vote parameters must take into account the assumptions underlying the model, particularly those concerning the role of party identification. With these considerations in mind, the normal vote appears as a methodology peculiarly appropriate to a particular theoretical understanding of voter decision-making processes. Unless one is willing to grant the assumptions that allow the normal vote to be defined in terms of the distribution of party identifiers, the L term indicates only the degree to which there is partisan alignment on the issue, with no implication of causal relation in either direction. The S term expresses the greater degree of consistency between issue positions and vote than between party and vote. The S term is not a measure of the role of an issue in an election because any overlapping, reinforcing, or spurious impact of the issue is ignored by assumption, and S is, in any case, defined relative only to the influence of party.

In spite of these limitations on the interpretation of the normal vote values, the measures are applicable to this analysis of the trust dimension. In particular, the data in Table 7.2 support the hypothesis that trust is, relative to party identification, an independent and important basis of vote choice. The L terms for trust are not significantly larger than those for other issues, indicating that trust evaluations are about as independent of

TABLE 7.2: Normal Vote Index Values for Various Issues in the 1972 Election and for Trust in 1972 and 1976

Issue	L	S
Vietnam*	11.57	16.52
Liberal/Moderate/Conservative*	10.51	16.45
War Factor*	7.86	14.16
Economic Factor*	7.60	11.46
Social Factor*	8.26	14.81
Cultural Factor*	5.25	12.63
Trust, 1972	12.10	32.50
Trust, 1976	12.10	25.60

*Normal vote index values from Arthur H. Miller, Warren E. Miller, Alden S. Raine, and Thad A. Brown, "A Majority Party in Disarray: Policy Polarization in the 1972 Election," *American Political Science Review* 70 (September 1976): 753–78.

Source: Other than indicated above, data is based on Survey Research Center, Center for Political Studies of the Institute for Social Research, University of Michigan.

partisanship as positions on the major issues tested for 1972. The S terms for trust in 1972 and 1976, far larger than those for issues and absolutely quite large, indicate a stronger association for trust with vote than for party with vote.

TRUST IN MULTIVARIATE MODELS OF ELECTIONS

Multivariate models of elections combine a set of presumably significant influences on vote choice in a single model that explains vote. There are basically two families of multivariate models that are part of virtually every analysis of voting behavior. One family, adequately represented by the SRC six-factor model, employs multiple regression techniques to estimate the weight attached by voters to various factors in the preference decision. The other family—simulations—involves actual modeling of the voter's calculus, step by step, to predict vote choice. In the former case, the measure of success of the model is Pearson's r, the multiple regression coefficient; for the latter group, the performance of the model is measured by the proportion of correct predictions.

There are in principle any number of different multivariate models that could be tested here with substantial claim to propriety. There follows a representative sample of such tests. It perhaps may be objected that there are certain models of this type that remain unexamined here, and this is undeniably the case. However, it is the opinion of this researcher that, for the reasons explained below, the value of this approach is largely exhausted by the tests described.

The data in Table 7.3 are the product of a simple three-factor model of the 1972 election combining the combined differential candidate trust evaluation with proximity measures on the Vietnam issue and party identification as independent variables predicting vote choice. The model is quite successful overall, with trust clearly the most powerful component by every measure of factor importance.*

The data in Table 7.4 come from a variation on the SRC's traditional six-factor model applied to the 1976 election. In the seven-factor model, all trust-related responses are separated from the two candidate components and treated as a seventh, separate component. This new component has an unstandardized regression coefficient substantially larger than those attached to the other six components. On the other hand, the relatively small mean and standard deviation of trust render it less impressive by the net impact and polarization measures of importance.†

To the extent that multiple regression tests are capable of certifying the weight of a factor in vote choice, the trust dimension is shown by these two models to have been quite important in both 1972 and 1976. But there are certain assumptions underlying multiple regression models of vote choice—beyond those assumptions that permit the application of the statistical technique, such as the assumption that the independent variables are independent of each other—that limit the scope of the conclusions of such work. The assumptions combine to define an implicit theoretical model of vote decisions of dubious empirical relevance at best.

The multiple regression technique employs a number of designated independent variables to explain, statistically, variance in a single dependent variable. The explanation that is produced—that is, the set of regression coefficients for the independent variables—is relevant only to the particular set of independent variables employed and to no other, regardless of how similar the sets may be. For example, one cannot undertake a multiple regression analysis of trust, party, and Vietnam positions as variables explaining vote, produce a set of weights, and then draw any conclusion

---

*The various measures of importance are described in Chapter 2. The three-factor model described is the end product of a series of experiments employing five independent variables, including proximity on minority rights and ideology in addition to party, Vietnam, and trust. Neither minority rights nor ideology reached statistical significance in combinations with trust, and they were dropped from the final equation. The interpretation of this model should be tempered by the rather high correlation between trust and party identification.

†The very alert reader will note that the multiple regression coefficient for this seven-factor model is actually smaller than that for the closely related six-factor model in Chapter 2. While this could not occur if the former merely included an additional variable, it is quite acceptable when variables are reoperationalized as is the case with the candidate components in the seven-factor model. While references to each candidate were disaggregated, trust responses were combined into a net trust score.

TABLE 7.3: Multiple Regression of a Three-factor Model of the 1972 Election

	β	(t)	$\beta-_x$	$\beta\sigma$
Trust[a]	.0790	e	−.0814	.2696
Vietnam[b]	.0108	e	.0138	.0384
Party Identification[c]	.0538	e	.0135	.1122
r/r^2			.72 / .52	
$\beta\sigma$			.4122	
n[d]			827	

Intercorrelation Matrix

Trust			
Vietnam	.13		
Party ID	.47	.08	
Vote	.68	.17	.50
	Trust	Vietnam	Party ID

[a]Combined differential trust evaluation.
[b]Proximity to Candidate on Vietnam issue.
[c]Three-point scale.
[d]Voters only included.
[e]Statistically significant at .01 level.
Source: Data based upon Survey Research Center, Center for Political Studies of the Institute for Social Research, University of Michigan.

about the weight of trust except in combination with party and Vietnam positions. Each new set of variables produces a distinct set of weights.

There are two applications of this method for arriving at variable weights that overcome this objection. The SRC six-factor model, which was applied to a series of elections and supported certain conclusions about the relative impacts of the six factors, is an example of one appropriate application. The six-factor model represents a theory of voting behavior that postulates that attitudes toward the objects of politics (the six factors) are the determinants of vote choice. Thus the same model was applied to several elections to estimate the weights of the factors relative to the fixed set of six variables, an appropriate application because the conclusions do not exceed the range of the analysis. The other acceptable use of the technique is that employed here, namely, repeated applications to different variable sets in order to collect evidence for a general hypothesis that a particular variable is important or is a component of vote choice. Of course, no particular weight can be specified in general.

Another serious objection arises from the mechanics of the multiple regression technique as applied to vote choice. The set of regression coefficients produced is that set which, when the independent variables are thus weighted and summed for each case, yields the smallest total (squared) deviation from the value of the dependent variable. The dependent variable in this case is the choice of candidate, which is traditionally operationalized as a dichotomous variable with one value corresponding to a Republican vote and another to a Democratic vote. But if the technique is to measure the relative importance or influence of the various factors on the vote choices of the electorate, it should explain not vote per se, but preference or the incentive to vote for a particular candidate. It is clearly the case that individuals may vote with more or less enthusiasm for the same candidate. Because there is not available a reliable measure of incentive, a readily measured but discrete variable, the vote, is substituted for a dependent variable that is by nature continuous. It is apparent, from the

TABLE 7.4: Multiple Regression Analysis of a Seven-factor Model of the 1976 Election

	β	(t)	$\beta-$	$\beta\sigma_x$
Democratic Candidate	.0363	(2.1)	-.0034	-.0210
Republican Candidate	.0798	(5.1)	-.0005	.0512
Party Mgmt.	.0696	(10.2)	.0184	.0183
Groups	.0757	(10.6)	-.0606	.1106
Foreign Issues	.0437	(3.9)	.0051	.0399
Domestic Issues	.0701	(11.6)	.0179	.1233
Trust[a]	.1340	(9.53)	.0249	.1023
$\beta\sigma$		.5215		
r/r^2		.61 / .37		
n[b]		1631		

Intercorrelation Matrix							
Dem. Cand.							
Rep. Cand.	.02						
Pty. Mgmt.	.13	.05					
Groups	.14	.02	.14				
Foreign	.08	.03	.11	.10			
Domestic	.10	.04	.23	.26	.21		
Trust	.17	.15	.30	.20	.08	.14	
Vote	.17	.09	.38	.37	.19	.41	.35
	Dem. Cand.	Rep. Cand.	Pty. Mgmt.	Grps.	For.	Dom.	Trust

[a] Combined differential trust evaluation.
[b] Voters only included.
Source: Data based upon Survey Research Center, Center for Political Studies of the Institute for Social Research, University of Michigan.

description of the technique above, that this substitution may have profound effects on the outcome of the analysis.

Granting all of the assumptions underlying this use of multiple regression techniques, except that candidate preference is a discrete variable, it is not clear how one ought to interpret the regression coefficients. They are certainly not the weights attached to various considerations by everyone in the sample; if they were applied to a sufficiently large and diverse sample in order to predict vote choice, numerous errors would invariably result. The distortions that are introduced into the model by adopting a stand-in for the actual dependent variable render questionable any interpretation of the coefficients as average weights as well.

A different multivariate methodology, albeit one with its peculiar limitations as well, is simulation. In the present instance, a theoretical representation of the voter's decision-making process (that is, the investor-voter model) is operationalized using survey data from the 1976 election. The major advantage of the simulation approach over multiple regression tests is that the components and structure of the model are explicitly derived from the theory being tested. The relationships between the various factors included and their levels of inclusion are determined by the researcher and not by the statistical technique. The product of the step-by-step model is a score: a continuous predictor variable representing both the magnitude and the direction of each voter's preference between the major candidates. Thus, two objections to the multiple regression approach—the arbitrariness of the set of independent variables and the discrete misrepresentation of the dependent variable—are overcome with this technique.

The customary measure of success of the stimulation model is the proportion of the individual predictions that meet a discrete standard—agreement in direction of prediction and vote—but the standard is capable of application in a manner that utilizes the continuous nature of the predictor variable. If the theory that underlies the simulation model is correct, then any errors may be attributed to either inaccurate measurement or faulty operationalizations. If it is assumed that these failings are distributed randomly with respect to the size and direction of the predictor variable, that is, that the errors are not systematic, then the impact of the errors on the predicted direction of preference ought to be a decreasing function of the magnitude of the predictor variable.[6] In other words, if the theory is correct, the model should yield not only a high absolute proportion of correct predictions, but also an increasingly high proportion of correct predictions as a function of the magnitude of the predictor variable.

The simulation model tested here is a straightforward operationalization of the investor-voter model developed in Chapter 4. The predictor variable is the individual's candidate differential, composed of specific substantive (issue) concerns, generalized substantive concerns, and generalized candidate performance expectations. The specific issue component is operationalized by the individual's preferred party on the most important issue, if any, discounted by the rating of the individual's party's candidate's trustworthiness on the seven-point scale. The most important issue is weighted three and divided by the candidate trustworthiness rating (where one is the most trustworthy rating, seven the worst rating). The generalized substantive component is operationalized in terms of three variables: the Ford approval rating (namely, approve/disapprove) with a weight of 2.0; party identification, based on a seven-point scale with independents given a zero score, weighted 1.0; and ideological proximity, weighted 1.0. Generalized candidate performance expectations are operationalized by the combined differential candidate trust evaluation, which ranges from zero to six in absolute value. Except as indicated, each raw variable score has an absolute value of zero or one, with negative values signifying pro-Ford (anti-Carter) attitudes, and positive values pro-Carter (anti-Ford). Candidate differential is simply the sum of the three components and may assume values between 15.0 and –15.0. (The weights of the various factors are, within certain broad limits, arbitrary, and are discussed in the analysis of the model below.)

The outcome of this simulation is sunmarized in Table 7.5. By any of the measures of success that one might choose to apply, the model performs well. The percentage of correct predictions is absolutely high (74.3 percent of the full sample, 91.2 percent of predicted votes),* and the percentage correct increases as a function of the magnitude of the predictor variable. For purposes of comparison, a similar account is recorded for a simulation identical to the earlier one but excluding trust in both its discounting and generalized performance expectations roles. This simulation also is successful, although marginally less so than the full model.

While these simulations are relatively simple to construct, test, and understand, they are not so easy to appraise. Consider first the 91.2 percent rate of successful predictions for the full model. The full model is only 1.2 percent (about ten votes) more successful than the model excluding trust. How is one to appraise this result? One argument might be that trust adds 1.2 percent to the explanatory power of the model, a fairly trivial improvement. But surely a 1.2 percent improvement in a model that is 90 percent successful is more significant than the same improvement in a model that is only 50 percent successful. Instead it might be argued that the addition of trust accounts for 12 percent of the unexplained variance in vote in the

---

*Because turnout decisions are not strictly a function of the candidate differential in the investor-voter model developed here, no turnout predictions were included in this simulation. No preference predictions are made for those with zero candidate differentials.

TABLE 7.5: Results of Simulation of the 1976 Election (percent in parentheses)

Absolute Value of Candidate Differential	N	Votes Correctly Predicted	Abstentions	Votes Incorrectly Predicted	Percent Correct Excluding Abstentions
		Model Including Trust			
1.0–2.9*	167	93 (55.0)	37 (21.9)	39 (23.1)	70.5
3.0–5.9	324	204 (62.6)	85 (26.1)	37 (11.3)	84.6
6.0–9.9	381	327 (85.4)	51 (13.3)	5 (1.3)	98.5
10.0–15.0	237	202 (84.9)	35 (14.7)	1 (0.4)	99.5
1.0–15.0	1,106	822 (74.3)	205 (18.5)	79 (7.1)	91.2
		Model Excluding Trust			
1.0–3.0*	354	190 (53.5)	100 (28.2)	65 (18.3)	74.5
4.0–6.0	381	302 (79.1)	60 (15.7)	20 (5.2)	93.8
7.0–9.0	374	318 (84.8)	50 (13.3)	7 (1.8)	97.8
1.0–9.0	1,106	808 (73.1)	208 (18.8)	90 (8.1)	90.0

*No predictions made for zero candidate differentials. Discrepancies in totals due to rounding errors.

Source: Data based upon Survey Research Center, Center for Political Studies of the Institute for Social Research, University of Michigan.

trustless model, on the assumption that 100 percent of vote choices are capable of being explained by the available data.

In fact, neither of these conclusions is satisfactory. Two different models are tested here, making different predictions for different voters. The fact that the more complex model incorporating trust as a factor is only marginally more successful than a simpler model without trust provides no basis for rejecting the former as an explanation of vote. After all, the least sophisticated model employed in this work—the univariate model basing vote predictions on the trust differential alone—is just as successful as these models. But this is not a competition to find the simplest, most successful model; the point is to demonstrate the empirical relevance of a factor in an investor theory of voter decision making, a task adequately met by the data presented to this point.

There are additional qualifications on the application of the simulation method that merit mention. While the components of the model and their operationalizations are based upon the theory of the investor-voter, the weights attached to the various elements of the model are arbitrary. It would be permissible to vary the weights in an effort to identify the optimal set, but the exercise would be pointless. The weights cannot be interpreted in the context of a theory that predicts that actual weights will vary as a function of the interests of individual voters. In any case, the real locus of the action in a simulation is the set of cross-pressured voters; predictions do not change for those voters with consistent attitudes, unless weights are permitted to change sign.

Because voting simulations generally share the characteristics of the present model (namely, a set of independent variables each of which is strongly associated with vote, a small subset of cross-pressured voters, and no independent measure of intensity of preference), it would appear that simulation is of limited value for the testing of theories of vote choice.[7] The major benefits of the approach are that it demands a clarification and operationalization of theoretical concepts, and that these then may be used to establish the prima facie empirical plausibility of the theory. But the heart of the simulation is the resolution of cross-pressures, a matter dealt with directly in the bivariate analysis earlier in this chapter.

CANDIDATE TRUST AND THE TURNOUT DECISION

In the first chapter of this work it is argued that individual turnout decisions are in part a function of the individual's trust in the political system. That is, the rational individual's decision to expend the resources necessary to vote is based on the expectation that the election will, in one way or another, affect the output of the political system. While the notion of trust implied in that analysis is not the same as the notion of candidate trust that is the primary focus of this examination of the preference decision, there are important areas of overlap. Specifically, the candidates may be regarded as the (potential) agents of the political system whose responsibility it will be to lend meaning to the election through their subsequent actions. Thus, it is reasonable to hypothesize certain general effects of untrustworthy candidates on individual turnout decisions.

The investor-voter theory offers no hypothesis regarding those who rate one versus those who rate both candidates as trustworthy. The turnout decisions of these individuals depend on their candidate differentials in this theory, and consideration of candidate trustworthiness may affect differentials in a variety of ways.

When a candidate takes an ideal position from the perspective of a particular voter, lack of trustworthiness will reduce the value of the candidate's election for that voter.[8] But in other cases, untrustworthiness may move a candidate closer to the ideal. For example, a candidate who promised to promote integration would be more highly rated by an ardent segregationist if the candidate is perceived as being unlikely to keep that promise. Thus no systematic consequences for turnout decisions could be expected to follow from the instance of one untrustworthy candidate.

For those who rate neither candidate as trustworthy, two general effects should be noted. First, the expected value of the election of each candidate should be lowered by the individual's negative evaluation of each on the generalized performance criterion. Second, the likelihood that the election will be meaningful, in the sense that future policy outputs will be affected by votes, would be reduced as neither candidate could be expected to be constrained by election campaign promises. Each would have the effect of decreasing the value of the election for the individual, with a consequent decrease in the incentive to vote. Thus, just as turnout is lower among those who lack trust in the political system, there ought to be lower turnout among those who are unable to rate one of the major candidates as trustworthy.

The turnout among groups classified according to the number of candidates whom they rate as trustworthy is summarized for the 1972 and 1976 elections in Table 7.6. The candidate trust ratings are based on the same seven-point scales that have been employed throughout this work. The hypothesis that those who rate neither candidate favorably will vote in smaller proportions than those who rate at least one candidate positively is supported by the data. The difference is less than spectacular for 1972, but it is quite substantial for 1976. In both cases, only one dimension of the turnout decision is examined.

TABLE 7.6: Candidate Trust Evaluations and Turnout, 1972 and 1976

1972 Election Ratings	Voted	Abstained	Turnout (percent)
Both candidates trustworthy	138	60	69.7
One candidate trustworthy	471	133	78.0
One or both trustworthy	609	193	75.9
Neither candidate trustworthy	40	21	65.6
1976 Election Ratings			
Both candidates trustworthy	637	216	74.7
One candidate trustworthy	537	212	71.7
One or both trustworthy	1,174	428	73.3
Neither candidate trustworthy	74	87	46.0

Source: Data based on ratings based on responses to the questions: "_____, as President, could be trusted." On seven-point agree/disagree scale, positions 1,2,3, coded as trustworthy; positions 5,6,7 coded as "not trustworthy. Compiled by the author.

SUMMARY

A variety of univariate, bivariate, and multivariate empirical tests of the strength of the relationship between trust and the candidate preference decision are examined in this chapter. Each of these tests is found wanting because each necessitates invoking a set of assumptions or a model of the voter decision-making process that is intuitively unappealing and theoretically unacceptable. Each of these tests falls short of the ideal because there is no definitive test of the weight of an issue. But it has not been necessary to avoid all conslusions. Instead, the set of evidence presented in this chapter is sufficient to establish that trust is a matter of some considerable concern to members of the electorate, notwithstanding the fact that no particular measure of its importance is identified. Among the tests that are reported here, the most telling is, for reasons outlined in the text, the analysis of cross-pressured voters.

Overall, the evidence in the three empirical chapters of this work would appear to constitute strong evidence of the validity of the theoretical analysis of trust and of the important but overlooked role of trust in elections. It has been shown that trust is salient, that its salience is enduring although it may be heightened by events, and that it is a vote-related salience. Trust evaluations of the candidates are not simple reflections of party identification, ideology, or issue positions; but they do reflect individual's evaluations of certain relevant events. It is further demonstrated that this salient, independent concern also matters to voters in their choice of candidates to support. Finally, evaluations of the trustworthiness of the candidates seem to play a role in turnout decisions as well.

All of this is significant not only for the academic study of voting behavior, but also for the political system and the role of the citizen in democratic theory. The conclusions that may be based upon this analysis are treated in the next chapter.

NOTES

1. Among the recent applications of the normal vote methodology are several articles appearing in the *American Political Science Review*'s quadrennial presidential election symposia: Richard W. Boyd, "Popular Control of Public Policy: A Normal Vote Analysis of the 1968 Election," *American Political Science Review* 66 (June 1972): 429-49; Richard A. Brody and Benjamin I. Page, "Comment: The Assessment of Policy Voting," *American Political Science Review* 66 (June 1972): 450-58; John H. Kessel, "Comment: The Issues in Issue Voting," *American Political Science Review* 66 (June 1972): 459-65; Arthur H. Miller, Warren E. Miller, Alden S. Raine, and Thad A. Brown, "A Majority Party in Disarray: Policy Polarization in the 1972 Election," *American Political Science Review* 70 (September 1976): 753-78; David RePass, "Comment: Political Methodologies in Disarray: Some Alternative Interpretations of the 1972 Election," *American Political Science Review* 70 (September 1976): 814-31.

2. The seminal work is Philip E. Converse, "The Concept of a Normal Vote," in Angus T. Campbell, Philip E. Converse, Warren E. Miller, and Donald E. Stokes, *Elections and the Political Order* (New York: John Wiley & Sons, 1966), pp. 9-39.

3. The L and S indexes were developed by Boyd, "Popular Control," and have been widely employed in subsequent published normal vote applications.

4. These brief descriptions and amplification thereof appear in ibid., p. 431. The formula for each is in Boyd's Appendix II, ibid., pp. 448-49.

5. The normal vote index values for the trust dimension are based on the three-point combined differential candidate trustworthiness scale described in Chapter 4. The three-point issue values for 1972 are based on proximity-to-candidate's-position scales, and are thus directly comparable. The war, economic, social, and cultural factors are the products of a factor analysis of the issues in the 1972 election. All of the issue scores were published in Miller et al., "A Majority Party in Disarray." All of the normal vote indexes were based on the revised parameter values revealed in Arthur H. Miller and Edward J. Schneider, "Normal Vote Analysis: Sensitivity to Change over Time and Place" (unpublished manuscript). The trust values were estimated using the linear approximation method since the distribution of party identifiers on trust was well within the acceptable bounds outlined by Miller and Schneider.

6. This is an adaptation of the argument made in Norman Frohlich, Joe A. Oppenheimer, Jeffrey A. Smith, and Oran R. Young, "A Test of Downsian Voter Rationality: 1964 Presidential Voting." *American Political Science Review* 72 (March 1978): 186.

7. An exception to this problem is the simulation model developed by Frohlich et al., "A Test of Downsian Voter Rationality." The Downsian model employs party differential in the prediction of both the turnout and preference decision, thus affording an opportunity to test

estimates of the magnitude of party differential (as a measure of incentive to vote) separately from estimates of direction.

8. The expected utility valuation of a lottery around the ideal point would ordinarily be expected to be lower than the expected utility of the ideal point; cf. Benjamin I. Page, "The Theory of Political Ambiguity," *American Political Science Review* 70 (September 1976): 747.

8

THE INVESTOR-VOTER
AND AMERICAN
DEMOCRACY

*T*he American political system has recently experienced an extended period of exceptional volatility. From the civil rights movement through the Vietnam era and the Nixon resignation, Americans have witnessed and participated in a series of unprecedented and dramatic political events. Even if they disagree about the causes, most observers concur that these events marked fundamental changes in the U.S. political tradition.

The turmoil of American politics has been reflected, appropriately, in American political science. In recent years a great number of publications have challenged the traditional wisdom about political institutions and behavior, and argued that a fresh understanding is needed to replace the misguided or outmoded models of the past. The analysis of voting behavior has seen its share of revisionist activity in response to the events of the 1960s and 1970s; the present work is one more contribution to this process.

The investor-voter model is rich with implications for the study of voting behavior per se. Acceptance of the model entails not only a new understanding of American voters and their choices, but also necessitates a reinterpretation of the elections of the 1950s and 1960s, previously understood in the terms of other models. In addition, the model may be applied to the analysis of the broader topics surrounding voting research. In particular, the model offers a different perspective on voters and their relationship to their political environment. Some of the ramifications of this perspective are explored in this chapter.

The investor-voter model is detailed in the foregoing with particular attention to the nature of the concerns voters are likely to bring to presidential elections, the types of information likely to be brought to bear on those concerns, and the influence of certain institutional arrangements on the ways they address their concerns. A special emphasis is placed on the various elements of trust that have been slighted by vote analysts in the past. Because the development of these topics has consumed a substantial number of pages, the first section of this chapter is devoted to a brief recapitulation of the investor-voter model, with commentary directed to certain selected and heretofore underemphasized implications.

It is not unusual for voting analysts to cap their endeavors with a set of assertions about the operation of the political system and the relationships between voters and public officials. Typically, such comments involve a static, functionalist analysis treating voting behavior as largely independent of political context. In the present model, however, voters in a particular contest reflect their political context in such a way that, if the voter's portrait is drawn accurately, the impact of changes in political context may be read in the behavior and attitudes of the electorate. This idea is developed in the second section of this chapter.

Finally, various images of the voter are set in the contexts of broader theories of democracy in the previous pages. In particular, the pervasive influence of Joseph Schumpeter's reformulation of democratic theory on two generations of voting studies and the scientific status accorded to certain modern pluralist/elitist notions of democracy by those voting studies are emphasized. The model developed here places the behavior of citizen-voters in an altogether different perspective by disentangling the rational from the good in evaluating their actions. This formulation thus provides a basis for the reconsideration of the claims of advocates of nonparticipatory "democracy." An exploration of the implications of investor-voter theory for democratic thought and reform occupies the third section of this chapter.

THE IMAGE OF THE INVESTOR-VOTER

The image of the investor-voter is a sharp contrast to those associated with the social-psychological and issue-based models. The social-psychologists' voter, whom Pomper appropriately dubbed the "dependent voter," engages in political activity the meaning of which is devoid of political content; the investor-voter is assumed to be politically rational. Rather than concentrating upon the social-psychological mechanisms that tend to produce short-run consistency in attitudes, this model stresses the structure of rationality within which those mechanisms operate. While theoretically descended from the rational voter model, the emphasis on the peculiarities of the American political system in the model developed here places the quality and character of the candidates—apart from their issue positions—in a central position in the voter's calculus. The curious and inconsistent amalgam of rational and nonrational elements here labeled the new issue voter marks the introduction, through new issues or political enlightment, of political meaning to voter behavior. By contrast, investor-voters do not change, although their responses to a given election vary with the political context, so that the elections of the past must be reexamined, rather than merely set aside, as modern evidence contradicts standing assumptions. The investor-voter model, while drawing heavily from its predecessors, in no sense occupies a middle ground between them.

To begin with, investor-voters view political activity, particularly voting, as a marginal activity no more central to their lives (except in certain rare circumstances) than any of their nonessential consumer goods. The predominant liberal individualism of their cultural milieus tends both to reinforce this appraisal of politics and neutralize early socialization in voting as citizen duty. Nevertheless, they may find it worthwhile to absorb the minimal costs involved in voting based on their belief that voting meaning-fully influences the output of the political system. With their votes they contribute to a collective good (the quality of government during the next interelection period) or a number of collective goods (in the form of specific aspects of future policy) that are, at the time of the election, of inestimable value to them.

If they decide to vote, investor-voters do not set out to do so with reckless enthusiasm but, as befits a marginal activity, attempt to conserve by striking an appropriate balance between their efforts and their expected returns. Weighing against the incentive to vote are at least three kinds of costs: the costs involved in voting per se, the opportunity costs of undertak-ing political activity rather than other pursuits, and information costs. Beyond the turnout decision, the costs of acquiring, analyzing, and weight-ing information bearing on the vote choice are the most significant for their effects on voters. In the face of these costs, combined with the limited choice set available to them and structural limitations on their capacity to affect policy by voting, voters typically employ economical but less-than-reliable bits of information and do not aspire to a fully informed vote.

Investor-voters, while exhibiting rational behavior in the context of American presidential elections, are not well informed by an ideal standard. Most individuals probably gather more information to support the purchase of a new car than to pick a president. Called upon to justify their prefer-ences for a particular candidate, they typically offer a set of vaguely meaningful party and ideological labels, demographic characteristics (age, religion, regional associations, wealth, education) and personality traits, projections from past positions, performances, and group sympathies, and an occasional specific issue position. They appear to be best informed when queried on areas where the incentive to be informed is boosted by a direct, personal impact of government policy on their daily lives; they are less informed on more remote or generalized issues.

The nature of the information possessed by voters is well established in empirical studies of voter attitudes. The investor-voter theory differs from most accounts of voting in ascribing to party labels, trust evaluations, and the like a rational quality and political content, based on an explicit analysis of the voter's decision-making context. Empirical evidence for this interpretation vis-à-vis the social-psychological model is provided by the underlying objective rationality of voter attachments as well as the apparent willingness of voters to abandon cues that become unreliable or change their meanings. The foregoing chapters contain both theoretical arguments and empirical evidence for the rational consideration of nonissue-based candidate evaluation criteria.

The structural imperative in the American political system of investing the president with a substantial degree of autonomous authority, his position as manager of the political system through future issues and crises, prohibitive information costs, and government secrecy all combine to attach great importance to personal characteristics of the candidates quite apart from the immediate policy consequences of the election. At the broadest level these attributes comprise the trust factor, incorporating evaluations of basic competence, honesty, reliability, and responsiveness, as well as general political orientations. A major proportion of the preceding work is devoted to showing that concern with trust is rational, has political content, is of widespread and frequently great importance in vote choice decisions, and provides the basis for a consistent account of recent elections.

An implication of the investor-voter theory that is corollary to the importance of trust is the significance of the campaign period. In no other model of elections is the campaign performance of the candidates central; rather, the campaign is viewed merely as the period during which issue-based coalitions are assembled and parties disseminate nonrational associations with the candidates. But the campaign period is frequently the first opportunity for voters to evaluate personally the performance of the candidates as future presidents. The campaign places both contenders in similar situations, forcing each to deal, on a day-to-day basis, with an assortment of political, administrative, and leadership challenges. Obviously, incumbent candidates are in a different situation, with a long period of public exposure in office behind them. Nevertheless, they are usually forced to confront their challengers in the campaign. No empirical evidence on the matter has been examined here, but the impact of certain events in recent campaigns that had little direct issue content, and the often dramatic fluctuations in candidates' relative standings in the polls attest to the significance of the preelection period.

Although the arguments in this work have concentrated upon a single model of the investor-voter, there is no implication that the electorate may be understood as an undifferentiated mass. On the contrary, it should be clear from the discussion that there are many different types of investor-voters when considered from the perspective of, for example, the strategists for a political campaign. Thus a set of equally rational voters may fall into any number of distinct categories depending upon their personal evaluations of the stakes in a given election. Those who feel that the political system has consistently failed to address their needs, regardless of the party affiliation of the successful candidate, or that political institutions are corrupt or inept may constitute a contingent of chronic nonvoters. This group would be expected to exhibit little interest in the campaign and to devote their scarce resources to activities other than the gathering of political information.

Those who are inclined to vote in a given election may form several distinct groups defined in terms of the information they employ in their vote choices or their most important concerns. Those who perceive the political system to be benevolent, responsive, and effective, but who do not perceive themselves to have a significant interest in the resolution of particular ongoing policy conflicts, will base their vote choices on the personal qualities of candidates and very broad political considerations such as party and ideology. Those who regard the favorable resolution of one or another policy conflict as a matter of great personal significance, and who see the outcome of the election as bearing—in a predictable direction—on the ultimate policy decision, constitute the issue public for that policy. Members of an issue public are likely to be better informed than the general public on existing policy and the positions of the candidates on that issue. Still, even those who expect significant policy implications to follow from the outcome of the election may find their concerns adequately summarized in terms of the relative responsiveness of the candidates to the interests of various groups.

Although substantial variations can be expected in the amount of information possessed by different members of the electorate, the overall picture is not an impressive one. This analysis of the investor-voter model is not meant to challenge the strictly empirical findings of past voting studies relevant to the typical voter's stock of political information. Instead, it has been suggested that the limited information that voters do possess may be sufficient to guide their vote choices with a reasonably high degree of correctness and to lend political meaning to their actions.

It would be a mistake to read this work simply as an argument that ignorance is rational. Rather, substantial ignorance is a rational response to the limited possibilities for affecting policy change that voters have available to them through elections. The American political system forces voters to personalize political conflict by the very structure that vests so much authority in individuals who act almost totally independently of public control and oversight, and removes the personal responsibility for policy from the individual citizen.

Nor is it the case that the concept of rationality has been emptied of content in the analysis here. Even though investor-voters are no more ideal democratic citizens than the voters of earlier models, their shortcomings in this regard are not entirely attributable to personal limitations. The better educated and otherwise sophisticated members of the electorate may possess a richer conception of American politics than is the norm, but this in itself does not justify the evolutionary flow of power away from the public to remote institutions over which they exercise little more than nominal control. Further consideration of this issue occupies the third section of this chapter.

THE CHANGING INVESTOR-VOTER

The assumptions that constitute the foundation of the investor-voter theory are that voters are rational, personally and politically, and that the voter's rational behavior is determined by the relevant contextual features of elections. If these assumptions and the subsequent analysis are correct, then changes in behavior observed in the electorate should be related to changes in the political context.* It follows that periodic reviews of citizen attitudes may provide the basis for a sort of moving-average evaluation of the American political system. This is not to say that one may deduce changes in the political system from changes in behavior, but rather that behavior reflects changes when they occur, and that one may cite such behavioral changes as evidence for hypotheses concerning broad political change.

The implications of this argument are explored in the present section Many of the remarks that follow are speculative and should be regarded with the appropriate degree of skepticism. Nevertheless, the significance of the relationship between voter behavior and political context warrants some tentative comments.

As an initial example, consider the changing role of party identification in vote choice. Numerous analysts have identified a pair of related trends: a

---

*Changes in individual behavior may be related to changing personal circumstances, for example, a new job or more free time. Barring major social change, the electorate as a whole will not reflect these individual shifts. Increased educational level of the electorate may alter the quality of voter response, although such effects have not been empirically demonstrated to date.

greater reluctance on the part of party identifiers to support the party's candidate and a general decline in the number of party identifiers. The predominant explanation of these trends is that voters have changed, becoming more issue oriented and thus been liberated from their former loyalties to parties. The investor-voter model offers a different account, based on the political interpretation of party labels as information cues summarizing the historical adherence of a set of politicians to certain broad principles, positions, or social groups. Voters employing party as a piece of information would have no great qualms about not supporting their favorite party's candidate when the nominee takes positions that violate the meanings voters attach to party labels, or when other considerations—such as the character of the candidate—outweigh the concerns summarized by party. The return to "party-line" voting in the 1976 election may simply reflect the absence of these factors (for most voters) in the most recent contest.

Of greater significance in the long run is the overall decline in party identification. A number of reasonable explanations, consistent with a political interpretation of the parties, can be offered for this decline. First, the national integration of American politics, especially through the influence of the mass media, may expose contradictions in the meanings that different groups attach to party labels. This strain would be felt to some extent in the South, for example, where "Democrat" historically meant someone more like George Wallace than like Ted Kennedy. Second, the increasing independence of the president from his party elevates consideration of the personal attributes and positions of the candidates to a relatively more central position than their party affiliations. The growing importance of the mass media as nonpartisan political reporters undermines the dependence of voters on party labels at the same time as the media supplant the parties as information sources. Finally, the decline in party identification may reflect the opinions of many voters that the meanings attached to party labels are irrelevant to their most important concerns. The repeated failure of the major parties to take any clear positions on the war in Vietnam between 1964 and 1972 would surely contribute to such a conclusion. Similarly, there are no definite party positions on contemporary environmental and consumer issues. In general, the alignment of the parties on the issues of the New Deal becomes less significant as New Deal institutions become a permanent part of the political structure, and the social divisions on new issues do not always conform to the old alignments. In the judgment of the electorate, the parties are apparently becoming increasingly irrelevant. (That is, the parties as representatives of political positions are becoming irrelevant. The two parties have maintained and perhaps strengthened their virtual duopoly on access to public office.)

Another example of apparent qualitative change in the electorate, albeit one with less substantial empirical corroboration to date, is the increasing use of ideology by voters. Many models of the new issue voter rely rather heavily on assertions that voters employ ideological labels to a greater extent than in the past, and that their issue positions exhibit greater ideological constraint. These developments are in turn interpreted to mean that voters are thinking in terms of abstract political principles and thus are better prepared to take positions on issues than they were when they organized politics according to their party affiliations.

This analysis of ideology exhibits the curious inconsistency in the interpretations of party and ideological labels commented upon previously. That is, whereas the organization of issues by party labels is assumed to represent nonrational, affective attachment to a social group, the use of ideological labels in the same way represents political enlightenment. In the investor-voter model, both party and ideological labels are viewed as cost-conservative information cues, and the shift by a number of voters from reliance on the former to reliance on the latter bears no implications for the quality of voter response to issues. Instead, the trend toward ideology may imply no more than that voters find one set of labels more useful than another set. It is suggested above that party labels are apparently becoming less valuable as an organizing scheme. The enormous inconsistencies that remain in the positions of self-professed ideologues further suggest that liberal and conservative may refer to something other than universal political principles. The new ideologues may be simply a reflection of the current fashion among the mass media of organizing political reporting in liberal/conservative terms.*

A third modern political phenomenon worthy of comment is the well-documented recent increase in the number, activity, and membership of so-called single-issue constituencies. Thousands of voters have aligned themselves with one or another group that threatened to punish any elected official who takes positions contrary to their own on abortion, gun control, the Panama Canal treaties, or some other issue. Those who align themselves with such groups claim, in effect, to have subordinated all of their policy interests to a single, decisive one.

The rise of single-issue publics may be accounted for in at least two ways. The most popular account sees this phenomenon as a consequence

---

*That issues are grouped rather arbitrarily into liberal/moderate/conservative terms, rather than according to principle, is seen in the increasing constraint evidenced between domestic and foreign policy issues, while analysts are hard pressed to link these domains on principle. How, for example, does one link the liberal position in Vietnam with the liberal position on aid to education?

of extremism, just the sort of suspension of rationality that so concerned Schumpeter and his disciples. This explanation holds political system performance constant, while attributing dysfunctional behavior to the shortcomings of individuals or social control mechanisms. Those who believe the policymaking process to be dominated by special interests, unresponsive to the average person, and largely crooked or inept have little incentive to engage in normal politics. On the other hand, a coalition of similarly inclined individuals who focus their political energies on a single policy may be effective in creating a structure of accountability where none otherwise exists. Even if the truth lies somewhere between these alternative accounts, the latter at least raises the possibility of a real decline in system responsiveness or a failure to impress on the public the real limitations of political performance. One need not automatically assume that reason has deserted large portions of the electorate.

Finally, a change that is perhaps more fundamental than any of these is the apparently decreasing faith of the citizenry in the whole political system. Surveys of the electorate have recorded for two decades increasingly cynical attitudes toward the intentions and competence of public officials and the responsiveness of political institutions. (A sample of this trend in attitudes is reported in Table 1.5.) While analysts can hardly ignore such a consistent pattern, there is considerable disagreement about the interpretation and significance of this trend.

Arthur Miller sets the explanation in the context of the arrival of the new issue voter. Examining the relationship between political cynicism and positions on racial issues, the war in Vietnam, and the "social issue," he finds that those who place themselves at either end of various issue scales exhibit greater cynicism than those in the center. This prompts the conclusion that policy divisiveness is the source of declining trust, as extremists dissatisfied with specific government policy decisions become "sore losers":

> By 1970, Americans to a considerable degree had withdrawn some of their trust from the government because they had become widely divided on a variety of issues, for in the normal attempt to satisfy the greatest numbers, the government had generally followed a more or less centrist policy which in reality appears to have displeased a substantial proportion of the population.[1]

Jack Citrin dismisses such findings as merely offering confirmation of the familiar generalization that: "We tend to trust and like those who agree with us."[2] In many ways, although not in any precise and consistent sense, this critique invokes the social-psychological approach against Miller's issue-based model.[3] It is demonstrated, for example, that attitudes toward the in-party, and especially toward particular political actors, are associated with the degree of cynicism expressed by individuals. In addition, there is evidence that "a diffuse sense of pride in and support for the ongoing 'form of government' can coexist with widespread public cynicism about 'the government in Washington' and the people 'running' it."[4] Citrin interprets this evidence as support for the conclusion "that many cynical responses merely record opposition to incumbent officeholders or largely ritualistic expressions of fashionable cliches."[5] One implication of this analysis is to ameliorate the political content of widespread public dissatisfaction with government, that is, to reduce it to mere partisan politics and fad.

The investor-voter theory provides the basis for a more significant and coherent analysis of attitudes toward the political system. Politically rational individuals who choose to bear the costs associated with voting must expect to receive a return on their investment; they must, then, believe that the outcome of the election bears a relationship to the future quality of their political environment in some predictable manner. The latter relationship is, in turn, a function of the democratic nature of the political system, or the extent to which its processes are governed by those who vote, and the efficiency of the political system in translating intentions into policy effects. These are the principle dimensions of trust in the political system. It follows that declining trust in the political system is a function of perceived decline in the democratic nature and/or the efficiency of government. Indeed, these seem to be exactly the dimensions of evaluation that are tapped in the series of survey items traditionally used to measure system trust. (The items reviewed in several tables in Chapter 1 are the same ones employed by Miller and Citrin. These ask, for example, whether government is run for a few big interests or for all the people, and how many public officials are crooked.)

It is a curious theoretical position to hold the assumption that people cannot distinguish between the political values of a particular policy and the manner in which it is formulated and implemented. This is not to argue that there is no partisan component to system trust evaluations; there is no doubt some evidence of the sore-loser syndrome, and there are those who are so removed ideologically from American politics that the system cannot be trusted to respond to them. But it would be a mistake to ignore the nonpartisan component of system trust; this, after all, is what democratic theorists mean when they emphasize the need for consensus on the rules of the game.

Consider the evidence that distrust is associated with extreme issue positions. It is not surprising that both those advocating integration and those advocating segregation are among the cynical portion of the population. American policy on integration has been among the most muddled and inconsistent policies pursued by the U.S. government in the recent past. It has been marked by shifting policy proposals, delays, retreats, and attempts to apply uniform policies to diverse local situations with fluctuating levels of commitment. Further, it has been handled largely in the court system, where little claim can be made to weighing the popular will, and where the perception of arbitrariness in policy is abetted by the remoteness of the decision-making authority. It may well be argued that, rather than expressing disapproval of centrist government policy, these cynics are expressing their frustration with a series of presidents and governments that have failed to pursue any specific policy on integration at all.

The case of attitudes toward the war in Vietnam may be similarly analyzed. Both hawks and doves were found to be more cynical than those who supported the centrist policies of the Johnson and Nixon administrations. Again, these policies were not comprehensibly designed to meet the goals of either group, and policy decisions were made at points remote from the public. But whereas integration policy has unfolded (or collapsed) publicly, Vietnam policy was designed and often executed secretly. The administrations, rather than exhibiting a lack of resolve, frequently demonstrated the willingness to defend their policies with force if necessary. On the other hand, none of the institutions of the political system that presumably offered the public some measure of democratic control, or that could have demanded an accounting for Vietnam policy, was willing to address the issue. Thus abandoned by Congress, the courts, and both parties, kept in the dark when they were not being deliberately misinformed by the Johnson and Nixon administrations, and frustrated by apparently incompetent sets of war policies, it is no wonder that many hawks and doves were cynical about the political system as well as the policies it produced.

The issue-based account ties the recent increase in cynicism to the polarization of the public on issues. But the Vietnam issue faded with American involvement, and it has been argued that the recent increase in issue polarization was and is a methodological illusion. Both the results of the six-factor model and the SRC/CPS analysis of the Ford-Carter election point to a decline in the weight of issues in 1976. If the issue-based analysis were correct, then a decrease in cynicism should have been observed in 1976. The evidence in Chapter 1 clearly contradicts that implication.

The partisanship-based account of increasing distrust is similarly unconvincing. It should not be surprising that attitudes toward the political system are correlated with attitudes toward the in party and not with attitudes toward the out party. After all, the ins are the current personification of the political system, while the outs represent a plethora of hypothetical alternatives.

There is one sense in which cynicism should be linked to partisan attitudes. Assuming that everyone positively values a more trustworthy political system, one consequence of declining trust would be an increase in the weight of that portion of the candidate differential reflecting trustworthiness. Thus the populist appeals of certain candidates such as Carter, McGovern, and Wallace, the moral appeals of the first two, and the outsider images of Carter and possibly Wallace, should be effective with cynics, albeit on a rational rather than a merely partisan basis.

It is frequently argued that distrust can be overcome with results, and competence has been identified as an important dimension of trust. The history of attitudes on the Vietnam war suggests that policymakers had greater latitude during the early years of the war to pursue any reasonably justifiable policy. As the war dragged on, however, attitudes crystallized in opposition to a policy that was an apparent failure. Early success may well have averted the decline in faith that may be attributed to the experience of the war. The failure of government to control inflation, reduce crime, and arrest social decay—particularly in the face of politicians claiming to know the solutions to these problems—may contribute to still further declines. But it would be a mistake to ignore the other dimensions of trust, particularly after the experience of Watergate. Results did not save the Nixon administration, nor do results give potential voters any reason to participate if they feel that it is bribery and deceit that shape policy rather than elections.

It is easier in the era of post-Watergate morality to identify nonpartisan, rational bases for cynical attitudes about politicians and the political system. It should not be forgotten, however, that the credibility gap was a product of the Johnson administration, and that ample evidence to justify cynicism has been provided by many politicians other than Richard Nixon. There are also any number of institutional developments that may foster such attitudes, for example, the greater proportion of public policy produced by bureaucracies and the courts rather than legislatures, the growing secrecy around and isolation of the president, and the decline in the roles of Congress and parties. There is also the evidence of a series of failed policies, from Vietnam to LBJ's war on poverty and Nixon's war on crime. Indeed, in the light of all the modern evidence, one must ask of Citrin and those who take his position: Which—the trusting or the cynical—is the ritualistic response?

THE INVESTOR-VOTER AND DEMOCRATIC THEORY

Even a cursory comparison of modern democratic theory with classical democratic thought reveals a substantially smaller role for the average citizen in the former. The institutions of representation that form the heart of modern models are a sharp contrast to the direct personal participation of citizens in Athenian democracy. In many other ways as well, the modern citizen is typically allocated a very limited role in directing the course of democratic government. The restricted status of participation is most stridently expressed in those theories that attribute to the apathetic citizen a functional role in guaranteeing the stability of the democratic political system.[6]

The justification for the limited role of the modern citizen in government decision making is typically derived from one or both of two somewhat overlapping arguments.[7] The first invokes certain technical or practical objections to mass participation: logistical problems in assembling the people, the scale of modern American government, and the requirement of technical expertise for dealing with many modern issues. The Greeks, it is said, lived in simpler times when government dealt with problems familiar to the average citizen. Such considerations are of obvious relevance to the contemporary political experience.

A second line of argument that has appeared in virtually every critique of participatory democracy, and that invariably serves as a cornerstone of modern elitist theories of democracy, involves an attack upon the decision-making capacities of the average citizen. Plato, in *The Republic*, expressed his doubts that the masses could restrain their appetites in democracy. The image of the mob activated by a momentary passion is contrasted throughout *The Federalist Papers* with the reasoned deliberations of republican institutions in Hamilton and Madison's scheme for limiting public control of government.

Schumpeter's redefinition of democracy turns on his rejection of the classical theory of democracy, in part on the ground that that theory involves "the practical necessity of attributing to the will of the individual an independence and a rational quality that are altogether unrealistic."[8] Writing at the outset of World War II, Schumpeter had little scientific evidence on which to base his conclusion that the modern citizen failed to meet the requirements of democratic citizenship. It was but a few years before voting analysts filled this gap.

The social-psychological analyses of voting behavior and the Schumpeterian reformulation of democratic theory proved to be mutually reinforcing in the 20 years following the publication of the latter. The findings of the Columbia and Michigan schools and others confirmed Schumpeter's dismal appraisal of the voter's interest and information. The revision of democratic theory provided a ready-made framework for the interpretation of these findings, at least insofar as their implications for democratic government were concerned.[9] Because voters are so poorly informed and apathetic, it was argued, democracy must be restricted to the popular selection of competing individuals who will bear the direct responsibility for making decisions.

Investor-voter theory—or more specifically, the set of assumptions from which the theory is derived—calls into question these links between the capacities of the individual and the structure of the political system. Whereas Schumpeter based his work in part on the assumption that expecting rational behavior is "altogether unrealistic," the investor-voter is assumed to be rational. Building upon this assumption, a set of hypotheses or standards of rational behavior for voters in American presidential elections are derived, which are demonstrably consistent with the empirical regularities identified in earlier studies and the specific tests applied in the present work. In effect, the entire assumption set, including the rationality assumption, is empirically corroborated.

The discrepancy between this claim that voters are rational and the conventional wisdom that voters are not rational arises from different applications of the notion of rationality. Schumpeter's rationality is an ideal standard applied to a specific context. Whether or not they actually are to be found in the classical literature, the expectations of behavior captured in the naive model of the democratic citizen are peculiar to a classical democracy. In Schumpeter's argument, these standards are lifted from their classical context and invested with a universal status.

In the investor-voter theory, it is not only assumed that individuals are rational, but also that the content of rational behavior is specific to its context. Thus the standards of rational behavior for the investor-voter are derived from the cultural setting and institutional structure of American presidential elections. Not surprisingly, given the vast differences in the cultural settings and institutional structures of classical and American democracies, the investor-voter's rational behavior is quite distinct from the ideal. (Although expectations of rational behavior are shaped by context, the notion of rationality per se is a transcendent one; that is, the form, but not the content, of rationality is the same in any context.)

It is important to be specific here about the relationship between rationality and good citizenship, especially with regard to the role of self-interest. Self-interest may be distinguished from selfish interest; one may recognize a personal interest qua community member in a good society and behave accordingly quite rationally, even when a form of altruism or self-sacrifice is required. Standards of good citizenship ought to bear an identifiable relationship to the promotion of a good society, namely, they ought to have a rational quality.

The author would argue that the institutions, processes, and cultural setting of Athenian democracy lent a rational quality to the expectations of its citizens. Where policymaking and administration was the direct, personal responsibility of each citizen, and where the activities of the whole society were central to the lives of individual members, the links between the informed, active participation of all and the quality of the individual's life could be easily apprehended. Indeed, participation per se was valued for its effects in promoting the widespread development and distribution of civic virture. (If this is an idealized image of ancient Athens, and the American case is similarly simplified, there still remains much substance to the comparison.)

For classical democracy, standards of good citizenship encouraged individual contributions to the collective goods that were realized through political activity. In contemporary American politics the connections between such behavior and its putative benefits do not emerge with the same force. First, activity in the public sector is as frequently regarded as an obstacle to the good society as it is a means of achieving the same. Second, the average citizen does not bear personal responsibility for policy choices; the choice of a republican form of government two centuries ago ensured this quality and subsequent developments have extended it. Finally, the possibility of affecting policy through informed voting appears quite doubtful to a large proportion of the American public.

All this is not to say that it is inappropriate to employ ideal standards of democratic citizenship in evaluating the American voter, but rather that the behavior of citizens should not be judged apart from its context. The investor-voter described here falls far short of any reasonable expectations of a democratic citizen. One does not economize on information costs without sacrificing some measure of scope or reliability, and the low level of information at the command of the typical voter certainly restricts whatever capacity that voter might otherwise have to influence policy. This, in turn, renders problematic the presumed benefits of popular government in providing a check against tyrannical rulers.

What this analysis does suggest is that it is inappropriate to draw the conclusion that Schumpeter and others find in the gap between the actual behavior of voters and the ideal, namely, that the American electorate must be regarded as a fixed quantity and the political system must be designed to accommodate their shortcomings. Instead, one may properly regard the electorate as a product of its cultural setting and institutional context. One should not expect—although it may be desirable for other reasons—that American voters will act as if they were part of a democracy in the classical sense. In order for the U.S. to see more voters who meet the standards of democratic citizenship, it may be necessary to provide the democratic context where such behavior is rational.

The recent discovery of the new issue voter has carried some form of this message and stimulated many voting analysts to reexamine the relationship between voter behavior and institutions. Unfortunately, this rethinking process typically has concentrated on marginal reform of the existing institutional structure and ignored the possibility (or the necessity) for more fundamental change. Most frequently, the recommendations call for the realignment of parties and voters in a way that will facilitate the integration of political conflict in a coherent framework, with strong (responsible) parties able to exercise greater influence over their office-holding members, the better to interpret the outcome of elections and thus facilitate voter control of policy.

Consider, for example, the program offered by Gerald Pomper. He argues that a new era of responsive politics is possible in the United States because:

> Issue preferences have . . . become more coherent. Voters grasp the connections between different policy questions, rather than reacting to each matter separately. Their outlook on politics is more integrated, as they can more readily place preferences on individual issues into a general ideological framework and also can see parties in the same framework.[10]

It is noted in the preceding pages that these changes in voter attitudes have not been established empirically, that the notion of ideology among voters is typically treated quite primitively by vote analysts, and that ideological consistency is neither inherently desirable nor a basis for reading policy mandates into election outcomes.* All of these are, or should be, important considerations in the evaluation of proposals that recommend increased voter control through ideology. Instead of repeating these arguments, consider Pomper's recommendations for institutionalizing ideological voter control:

> The vigor of the party system must be restored in order to provide effective and responsible institutions. Parties are . . . the most effective democratic institutions available. . . . If election finance were centralized in the party organization, there would be a strong incentive for candidates to achieve a united platform . . . it would be preferable to funnel most funds through the Democratic and Republican organizations. . . . A similar step would be to provide equal and free time in the mass media for the parties, rather than for the individual candidates. . . . The parties should move toward . . . reliance on the support of a dues-paying membership. . . . Greater reliance on mass financing . . . reflecting the [fact] of national integration. . . .
>
> Party leaders must also be restored to a central role in the nominating process. While presidential primaries need not be abolished, they certainly should not be extended. . . .

---

*(On the latter points, see the discussion of a similar proposal by Miller and Levitin in Chapter 3 of this work.)

These reforms constitute a partial program for the renewal of American democratic institutions. The alternatives are grim, including demagogic movements, continued drift and social division.[11]

One effect of the implementation of these proposals may well be, as Pomper suggests, to present the voter with a choice of two coherent programs. But the price of this increased coherence would be an increasingly rigid political system, constrained to competition along a single dimension of ideological conflict, and increasingly dominated by two sets of party leaders with no claims to democratic legitimacy of their own.* Political activity independent of the leaders of the major parties would be significantly handicapped. Increased ideological coherence would either sharpen the lines separating the coalitions of social groups advocating different policies, or would fail to do so because both parties offered very nearly the same (coherent) ideology. Popular participation within the parties would suffer as each organization became more nationally integrated—that is, centralized and remote—for the sake of coherence. Costs such as these must be weighed before one designates a particular proposal as, on balance, a move toward greater democracy.[12]

From the perspective of the investor-voter model, the Pomper program would have the effect of increasing the security of the voter's investment in the sense that predictable results would follow from a given election outcome. But consideration of the model in all of the aspects that bear on the quality of voters' behavior would recommend a more wide-ranging agenda of reform. At least some attention should be addressed to the costs and values of an informed vote.

If the analysis of the limitations of two-party politics in Chapter 4 is accurate—and others have made the same arguments—then any program that enhanced two-party dominance would only exacerbate those limitations. Despite the fundamental differences between the parties on a number of issues, they have operated so as to restrict the range of issues and alternatives that enter public debate and have consequently lowered the value of elections for many Americans. This suggests that moves to open the electoral process to greater competition may be more effective in generating incentive to participate than those that tighten the grip of the current duopoly.

One proposal that meets with some favor among political scientists is to move, through whatever policies are appropriate, to a multiparty system

---

*The single dimension of conflict is that defined by the opposition of two integrated party platforms. Only if all participants accept this arrangement of opposed interests will politics achieve the desired coherence. Otherwise, if American politics is pluralistic, two-party politics will always foster ideological incoherence.

on the European models. The most successful implementation of this plan could offer society the advantages of a modified pluralistic politics with ideologically coherent parties. A wider variety of interests could be addressed at some point in the system, the scope of public debate would be extended, and the stakes in the outcome would correspondingly increase. If policy outcomes could not be predicted, at least the policy implications of a given vote would increase with the ideological coherence and consistency of the parties. Short of this, efforts to enhance the viability of third-party challenges could have similar but limited effects.

Information costs are a significant factor affecting the quality of individual participation. It is often alleged that the impact of the mass media has been to increase greatly the quantity of free information available to citizens. But while the quantity of information to which individuals have free access has increased, many cost barriers to a well-informed public remain. For example, increased public exposure has led many government decision makers to restrict in various ways the information available, especially on controversial or embarrassing decisions. The conduct of foreign policy has become increasingly secretive, as evidenced by the experience of the Vietnam war. This trend led Pomper to conclude that:

> Ultimately, foreign policy questions can become, for the electorate, questions only of personal competence. Which man can be trusted with the nuclear trigger? Which candidate can negotiate better or stand up to the Russians?[13]

At the same time, the increasingly technological nature of many of the questions placed before the public, such as whether the B-1 bomber would be a significant, cost-effective addition to the American arsenal, more than offsets the advantages of free access to information with prohibititive costs of assimilation.

If citizens are buried under an avalanche of information, they are little better off than they would be in the dark. A comprehensive program of institutional reform would include mechanisms for subordinating technological issues to more fundamental policy considerations in a way that would both enable the nonexpert to direct the experts and obviate the technocratic objection to citizen participation in such questions as nuclear power development and economic policy. At the same time, citizens must be encouraged to pay the costs of informing themselves on such issues.

The return side of the participation investment is a function of both the stakes in the decision and the efficacy of the individual. Thus more widespread, active, and informed participation could be expected to follow from reforms that broaden the scope of decisions affected by public participation, tighten or make more direct the links between the public's registration of preference and the specific policy outcome, and/or decentralize the decision points in such a way as to increase visibly the efficacy of the individual. Unfortunately, it is in these very areas that the size and complexity of modern society have their greatest impact on political processes. As certain problem areas become certifiably technological questions beyond the expertise of the average citizen—at the point, that is, where experts in the field are recognized—the administration of the area is typically delegated to an agency yet another step removed from the public (and frequently from congressional oversight as well). Uniformity and efficiency are achieved through nationalization of administration, bureaucracy, and secrecy.

The gradual shift of power away from individuals and communities and toward national institutions has certainly promoted national integration and has contributed to the dissemination of certain good values—for example, the removal of formal barriers to racial desegregation. But these benefits have exacted their costs in terms of removing policy decisions from effective public participation and responsibility. For both these reasons, any effort to decentralize or return policy to public control would be painful.

These remarks imply an imposing agenda for institutional reform that many observers of American society would reject out of hand. It is not the author's purpose to propose a specific program for such reform, or even to argue that it is feasible; these matters must be reserved for another opportunity. The point is to suggest that voters would respond to changes in their environment, but that the type of institutional reform necessary to affect significantly the participation of the citizenry is more fundamental than mere tinkering with campaign finance laws and the like, and comprehensive reform must involve multiple dimensions of the political context.

There is, finally, an even more significant determinant of the investment value of political activity: its cultural setting. Just as individuals' valuations of various nonessential goods is affected by the cultural milieus (for example, through the effects of advertising), so too are their evaluations of political activity at least partially determined by its place in their culture. These effects are well captured in a pair of quotations from individuals representing quite different cultures who attempted to put into words the place of political activity in their respective societies. The first is a relic of the ancient Greek democracy, circa 439 B.C., from the famous funeral oration of Pericles:

> Our citizens attend both to public and private duties, and do not allow absorption in their own various affairs to interfere with their knowledge of the city's. We differ from other states in regarding the man who holds aloof from public life not as "quiet" but as useless; we decide or debate, carefully and in person, all matters of policy, holding, not that words and

deeds go ill together, but that acts are foredoomed to failure when undertaken undiscussed.[14]

The second quotation is a description of contemporary American society by a noted student of political participation, Lester Milbrath:

Modern society . . . has evolved a very high division of labor, not only in the economic sector but also in politics and government. Political roles have become highly differentiated and specialized. This enables some persons (elected and appointed officials) to devote their full attention to the complex public issues facing modern society. This division of labor allows others (most of the citizens) to pay relatively little attention to public affairs. Politics and government are a peripheral rather than a central concern in the lives of most citizens in modern Western societies. As long as public officials perform their tasks well, most citizens seem content not to become involved in politics.[15]

Of course Pericles was a politician, while Milbrath is a social scientist. But compare the tone of Pericles's rhetoric with that of a recent American politician who claimed the mandate of the Great Silent Majority and the distinctions will be just as clear.

The fundamental reasons why the American investor-voter falls so far short of the ideal of active, informed participation are to be found in the cultural attitudes displayed in these descriptions. There is, first, the communitarian sentiments expressed in the Greek priority of social over individual affairs, and the reversal of those priorities in the modern case. Second, there is the personal responsibility of the individual for political activity in Athens, contrasted to modern society's "division of labor." Finally, there is the implicit Greek conception of the public space as the arena for the community's pursuit of consensual solutions affecting the whole community, versus the modern cultural conception of the political system as the locus of competition between groups pursuing policies enhancing their own interests.

Whether meaningful reforms of institutions can be realized independently of changes in the cultural setting of American politics, or whether one must precede the other, is not readily apparent. It does seem clear, however, that while individuals may be motivated to more active participation by institutional reforms that promise to increase the returns from their investments in elections, or by an outsider candidate promising such reform, the possibilities of realizing an ideal democratic citizenry are inextricably tied to the cultural setting of political activity. (Local organizers like Saul Alinsky managed to stimulate participation among their clients by creating for them, on a small scale, a new cultural setting for their political action within an organization.) For those who would encourage a more democratic American politics, it would seem that the greater challenge lay not in the reform of institutions, but in the reform of more fundamental values.

NOTES

1. Arthur H. Miller, "Political Issues and Trust in Government: 1964–1970," *American Political Science Review* 68 (September 1974): 963. As implied by the title, Miller's analysis predates the Watergate revelations.

2. Jack Citrin, "Comment: The Political Relevance of Trust in Government," *American Political Science Review* 68 (September 1974): 973.

3. While Citrin explicitly dissociates himself from sociological explanations (ibid., pp. 973–74), he consistently emphasizes the psychological over the rational-evaluative interpretation of trust and the partisan basis of these attitudes.

4. Ibid., p. 975. The data cited in support of this conclusion demonstrate a strong and consistent inverse relationship between pride in and support for the government and cynicism, however.

5. Ibid., 984, italicized in the original. The designation of cynical attitudes as "ritualistic responses" based on Americans' ambiguous attitudes toward power is a familiar theme; cf. Herbert McClosky, "Consensus and Ideology in American Politics," *American Political Science Review* 58 (June 1964): 370.

6. Samuel Huntington offers an example of this position significant for the prominence of the source if little else: "the effective operation of a democratic political system usually requires some measure of apathy and noninvolvement on the part of some individuals and groups." Samuel P. Huntington, "The United States," in Michel Crozier, Huntington, and Joji Watanuki, *The Crisis of Democracy: Report on the Governability of Democracies to the Trilateral Commission* (New York: New York University Press, 1975), p. 114.

7. In addition to the two arguments noted below, many authors point to the difficulties involved in translating an election outcome into a social preference for particular policies; cf. Joseph Schumpeter, *Capitalism, Socialism, and Democracy* (New York: Harper & Row, 1950), pp. 254–56, or Robert A. Dahl, *A Preface to Democratic Theory* (Chicago: University of Chicago Press, 1956), pp. 39–44. However, these problems are not resolved—although they may be overcome—by removing the locus of decision making from the public at large.

8. Schumpeter, *Capitalism, Socialism, and Democracy*, p. 253. These requirements are detailed in Chapter 2 under the rubric of the naive model of the democratic citizen.

9. The most explicit example is Bernard R. Berelson's Chapter 14 in Berelson, Paul F. Lazarsfeld, and William M. McPhee, *Voting* (Chicago: University of Chicago Press, 1954). This and other instances are cited in Chapter 2.

10. Gerald Pomper, *Voter's Choice: Varieties of American Electoral Behavior* (New York: Dodd, Mead, 1975), p. 214.

11. Ibid., pp. 223–24.

12. In this regard it is worthy of note that Huntington identifies the weakening of the parties as both a symptom and a contributing cause of "democratic distemper," an *excess* of participatory democracy; Huntington et al., *The Crisis of Democracy*, pp. 55–91.

13. Pomper, *Voter's Choice*, p. 216.

14. From the funeral oration of Pericles, as quoted in Alfred Zimmern, *The Greek Commonwealth* (New York: Oxford University Press, 1969), p. 204.

15. Lester W. Milbrath and M. L. Goel, *Political Participation* (Chicago: Rand McNally, 1977), pp. 145–46.

APPENDIX: THE CITIZEN DUTY SCALE

*T*he SRC/CPS survey and the scores of analysts who employ the data have attempted to measure a respondent's sense of the citizen's duty to vote circuitously rather than directly. A series of statements is intended to tap feelings of obligation by positing situations where voting to influence the outcome is meaningless. Citizen duty scales are then developed by combining responses (agree or disagree) to the series. The following statements comprise the citizen duty series for 1976:

(1) It isn't so important to vote when you know your party doesn't have any chance to win.
(2) So many other people vote in the national elections that it doesn't matter much to me whether I vote or not.
(3) If a person doesn't care how an election comes out, he shouldn't vote in it.
(4) A good many local elections aren't important enough to bother with.

Disagree responses are presumed to indicate citizen duty.

Because of certain ambiguities in the series of questions above, the construction of a citizen duty scale must proceed cautiously. A disagree response to the first two statements may reflect an obligation to vote or a purely pragmatic evaluation of the impact of a vote; beyond determining the ultimate winner in an election, the vote totals also affect the extent of the winner's popular mandate, the size of the following of the loyal opposition, and the credit given to various candidate support groups. The fourth statement measures respondents' evaluation of the relative importance of local issues as well as their orthodoxy in the application of citizen duty.

For the first, second, and fourth statements, disagreement was recorded in the neighborhood of 90 percent. The third statement, in contrast, gained only 54 percent disagreement. It seems likely that this anomaly may be attributed to the conditional clause that posits an antecedent violation of citizen's duty—that is, not caring—and that produces a statement somewhat analogous to asking whether agnostics ought to pray (cf. Table 1.3). On the other hand, the near unanimity on three of the statements suggests that respondents may be making the acceptable response; a similar phenomenon has been noted with respect to the consistent overreporting of turnout in the same surveys.

These drawbacks in the citizen duty series are readily overcome for the limited purpose at hand. For Tables 1.3, 1.6, and 1.7, two groups are defined by responses to the first three statements above. The citizen duty group is all those who answered disagree to all three questions; the no citizen duty respondents are those who consistently agree. The fourth statement is ignored because of the ambiguity noted above and because the present interest is only in national elections. Further ambiguities are reduced by ignoring those with mixed responses to the first three statements.

This attempt to purify the measure of citizen duty is not without a small, but not prohibitive, cost. The skewed distribution of responses to the citizen duty series is reflected in a wide disparity in sample size for the two groups. The citizen duty group is of ample size with 1,398 members (93.1 percent); the no citizen duty group contains only 103. Because the sample sizes for the two groups vary with elimination of inappropriate responses on other variables, these figures represent the maximum sample size for each group. Nevertheless, the trends in the data are clear despite the larger confidence interval for the no citizen duty sample.

BIBLIOGRAPHY

BOOKS

Arrow, Kenneth J. *Social Choice and Individual Values*. New York: John Wiley & Sons, 1951.

Berelson, Bernard R., Paul F. Lazarsfeld, and William M. McPhee. *Voting*. Chicago: University of Chicago Press, 1954.

Campbell, Angus T., Philip E. Converse, Warren E. Miller, and Donald E. Stokes. *The American Voter*. New York: John Wiley & Sons, 1960.

Campbell, Angus T., Gerald Gurin, and Warren E. Miller. *The Voter Decides*. Evanston, Ill.: Row, Peterson, 1954.

Campbell, Angus T., and R. L. Kahn. *The People Elect A President*. Ann Arbor: Institute for Social Research, 1952.

Dahl, Robert A. *A Preface to Democratic Theory*. Chicago: University of Chicago Press, 1956.

Downs, Anthony. *An Economic Theory of Democracy*. New York: Harper & Row, 1957.

Frohlich, Norman, and Joe A. Oppenheimer. *Modern Political Economy*. Englewood Cliffs, N.J.: Prentice-Hall, 1978.

Hamilton, Alexander, John Jay, and James Madison. *The Federalist*. Edward Mead Earle, ed. New York: Random House, n.d.

Hartz, Louis. *The Liberal Tradition in America*. New York: Harcourt, Brace, and World, 1955.

Hess, Robert D., and Judith V. Torney. *The Development of Political Attitudes in Children*. Chicago: Aldine Publishing, 1967.

Key, V. O., Jr. *The Responsible Electorate*. Cambridge, Mass.: Harvard University Press, 1966.

Lazarsfeld, Paul F., Bernard Berelson, and Hazel Gaudet. *The People's Choice*. New York: Columbia University Press, 1944.

McGinniss, Joe. *The Selling of the President 1968*. New York: Trident Press, 1969.

Milbrath, Lester W., and M. L. Goel. *Political Participation*. Chicago: Rand McNally, 1977.

Miller, Warren E., and Teresa E. Levitin. *Leadership and Change: The New Politics and the American Electorate*. Cambridge, Mass.: Winthrop, 1976.

Mueller, Claus. *The Politics of Communication*. New York: Oxford University Press, 1973.

Nie, Norman H., Sidney Verba, and John R. Petrocik. *The Changing American Voter*. Cambridge, Mass.: Harvard University Press, 1976.

Nimmo, Dan, and Robert L. Savage. *Candidates and Their Images: Concepts, Methods, and Findings*. Pacific Palisades, Calif.: Goodyear Publishing, 1976.

Pateman, Carol. *Participation and Democratic Theory*. Cambridge: Cambridge University Press, 1970.

Pomper, Gerald M. *Voter's Choice: Varieties of American Electoral Behavior*. New York: Dodd, Mead, 1975.

———. *Elections in America: Control and Influence in Democratic Politics*. New York: Dodd, Mead, 1968.

Pool, Ithiel de Sola, Robert P. Abelson, and Samuel Popkin. *Candidates, Issues, and Strategies*. Cambridge, Mass.: MIT Press, 1964.

Scammon, Richard, and Benjamin Wattenberg. *The Real Majority*. New York: Coward McCann Geoghegan, 1970.

Schumpeter, Joseph A. *Capitalism, Socialism, and Democracy*. New York: Harper & Row, 1950.

ARTICLES

Berelson, Bernard R. "Democratic Theory and Public Opinion," *Public Opinion Quarterly* 16 (Fall, 1952).

Boyd, Richard W. "Popular Control of Public Policy: A Normal Vote Analysis of the 1968 Election." *American Political Science Review* 66 (June 1972).

Brody, Richard A., and Benjamin I. Page. "Indifference, Alienation and Rational Decisions: The Effects of Candidate Evaluations on Turnout and the Vote." *Public Choice* 15 (Summer 1973).

———. "Comment: The Assessment of Policy Voting." *American Political Science Review* 66 (June 1972).

Bruner, Jerome S., and Sheldon J. Korchin. "The Boss and the Vote: Case Study in City Politics." *Public Opinion Quarterly* 10 (Spring 1946).

Burdick, Eugene. "Political Theory and the Voting Studies," in American Voting Behavior, edited by Eugene Burdick and Arthur J. Brodbeck, (Glencoe, Ill.: Free Press, 1959).

Campbell, Angus T. "Voters and Elections: Past and Present." *Journal of Politics* 26 (November 1964).

Campbell, Angus T., and Henry Valen. "Party Identification in Norway and the United States." In Angus T. Campbell, Philip E. Converse, Warren E. Miller, and Donald E. Stokes, *Elections and the Political Order*. New York: John Wiley & Sons, 1966.

Citrin, Jack. "Comment: The Political Relevance of Trust in Government." *American Political Science Review* 68 (September 1974).

Converse, Philip E. "Change in the American Electorate." In Angus T. Campbell and Philip Converse, eds., *The Human Meaning of Social Change*. New York: Russell Sage Foundation, 1972.

———. "The Concept of a Normal Vote." In Angus T. Campbell, Philip E. Converse, Warren E. Miller, and Donald E. Stokes, *Elections and the Political Order*. New York: John Wiley & Sons, 1966.

———. "The Nature of Belief Systems in Mass Publics." In David Apter, ed., *Ideology and Discontent*. Glencoe, Ill.: Free Press, 1964.

Converse, Philip E., Warren E. Miller, Jerrold Rusk, and Arthur Wolfe. "Continuity and Change in American Politics: Parties and Issues in the 1968 Election." *American Political Science Review* 63 (December 1969).

Ferejohn, John A., and Morris P. Fiorina. "The Paradox of Not Voting: A Decision Theoretic Analysis." *American Political Science Review* 68 (June 1974).

Fiorina, Morris P. "An Outline for a Model of Party Choice." *American Journal of Political Science* 21 (August 1977).

Frohlich, Norman, Joe A. Oppenheimer, Jeffrey A. Smith, and Oran R. Young. "A Test of Downsian Voter Rationality: 1964 Presidential Voting." *American Political Science Review* 72 (March 1978).

Huntington, Samuel P. "The United States." In Michel Crozier, Samuel P. Huntington, and Joji Watanuki, *The Crisis of Democracy: Report on the Governability of Democracies to the Trilateral Commission.* New York: New York University Press, 1975.

Kessel, John H. "Comment: The Issues in Issue Voting." *American Political Science Review* 66 (June 1972).

Lane, Robert E. "The Fear of Equality." *American Political Science Review* 53 (March 1959).

McClosky, Herbert. "Consensus and Ideology in American Politics." *American Political Science Review* 58 (June 1964).

McGrath, Joseph E., and Marion F. McGrath. "Effects of Partisanship on Perceptions of Political Figures." *Public Opinion Quarterly* 26 (Summer 1962).

Margolis, Michael. "From Confusion to Confusion: Issues and the American Voter (1952–1972)." *American Political Science Review* 71 (March, 1977).

Miller, Arthur H. "Rejoinder to Comment by Jack Citrin: Political Discontent or Ritualism?" *American Political Science Review* 68 (September 1974).

———. "Political Issues and Trust in Government: 1964–1970." *American Political Science Review* 68 (September 1974).

Miller, Arthur H., and Warren E. Miller. "Ideology in the 1972 Election: Myth or Reality—A Rejoinder." *American Political Science Review* 70 (September 1976).

Miller, Arthur H., Warren E. Miller, Alden S. Raine, and Thad A. Brown. "A Majority Party in Disarray: Policy Polarization in the 1972 Election." *American Political Science Review* 70 (September 1976).

Natchez, Peter B. "Images of Voting: The Social Psychologists." *Public Policy* 18 (Summer 1970).

Page, Benjamin I. "The Theory of Political Ambiguity." *American Political Science Review* 70 (September 1976).

Pierce, John C., and Douglas D. Rose. "Nonattitudes and American Public Opinion: The Examination of a Thesis." *American Political Science Review* 68 (June 1974).

Popkin, Samuel, John W. Gorman, Charles Phillips, and Jeffrey A. Smith. "Comment: What Have You Done for Me Lately?: Toward an Investment Theory of Voting." *American Political Science Review* 70 (September 1976).

Prewitt, Kenneth, and Norman Nie. "Review Article: Election Studies of the Survey Research Center." *British Journal of Political Science* 1 (October 1971).

RePass, David. "Comment: Political Methodologies in Disarray: Some Alternative

Interpretations of the 1972 Election." *American Political Science Review* 70 (September 1976).

—— . "Issue Salience and Party Choice." *American Political Science Review* 65 (June 1971).

Riker, William H., and Peter C. Ordeshook. "A Theory of the Calculus of Voting." *American Political Science Review* 62 (March 1968).

Rossi, Peter H. "Four Landmarks in Voting Research." In Eugene Burdick and Arthur J. Brodbeck, eds., *American Voting Behavior*. Glencoe, Ill.: Free Press, 1959.

Schneider, William. "Issues, Voting, and Cleavages: A Methodology and Some Tests." *American Behavioral Scientist* 18 (September 1974).

Shepsle, Kenneth A. "The Strategy of Ambiguity: Uncertainty and Electoral Competition." *American Political Science Review* 66 (June 1972).

Sigel, Roberta S. "Image of the Presidency—Part II of an Exploration into Popular Views of Presidential Power." *Midwest Journal of Political Science* 10 (February 1966).

—— . "Effect of Partisanship on the Perception of Political Candidates." *Public Opinion Quarterly* 28 (Fall 1964).

Steeper, Fredrick T., and Robert M. Teeter. "Comment on 'A Majority Party in Disarray'." *American Political Science Review* 70 (September 1976).

Stokes, Donald E. "Spatial Models of Party Competition." In Angus T. Campbell, Philip E. Converse, Warren E. Miller, and Donald E. Stokes. *Elections and the Political Order*. New York: John Wiley & Sons, 1967.

—— . "Some Dynamic Elements of Contests for the Presidency." *American Political Science Review* 60 (March 1966).

Stokes, Donald E., Angus T. Campbell, and Warren E. Miller. "Components of Electoral Decision." *American Political Science Review* 52 (June 1958).

MANUSCRIPTS

Burnham, Walter Dean. "Contributions of the SRC to the Development of Voting Theory." Paper presented at the annual convention of the American Political Science Association, September 1976.

Kagay, Michael R., and Greg A. Calderia. "I Like the Looks of His Face: Elements of Electoral Choice 1952–1972." Paper delivered at the annual meeting of the American Political Science Association, San Francisco, September 1975.

Miller, Arthur H., and Warren E. Miller. "Partisanship and Performance: 'Rational' Choice in the 1976 Presidential Election." Paper presented at the 1977 annual meeting of the American Political Science Association, Washington, D.C., September 1–4.

INDEX

ability to deliver, 106–7, 126
ambiguity, 98–101, 126–27
The American Voter, 38, 39, 42–43,
    46–47, 48, 78–79, 140–41, 152
Attitude Structure, 40–42, 52–60, 64–65,
    65–66, 67–69, 69–70

Berelson, Bernard R., 2, 30–31, 33
Boyd, Richard, 163–64

campaign, role of, 113–14, 152–54,
    181–82
Campbell, Angus, 39, 79, 100
candidates, role of, 43–45, 60, 64–65, 68,
    69, 73, 78–79, 79–80, 114–15
candidate differential, 103–9
candidate image, 44–45; source of,
    138–40, 153–55
Carter, Jimmy, 1, 97–98, 128, 130,
    138–39, 152, 154, 189
Center for Political Studies (*see* SRC)
citizen duty, 6–8, 10–11, 12–13, 19, 20,
    60–61, 103, 180, Appendix
Citrin, Jack, 186–87, 189–90
collective goods, 89
competence, 22, 126, 128, 132, 133–34,
    149, 153, 189, 195
Converse, Phillip, 42, 46, 79
costs of voting, 86–87
cross-pressured voters, 32, 161–63,
    172–73

debates, 152–53
dependent voter, 70, 179
democracy, 2, 10–11, 11–12, 20, 22,
    26–27, 67–69
democracy, classical, 26–27, 189–90,
    191, 191–92, 196–97
democracy, economic model, 56–57

demographic characteristics, 16–19,
    111, 154, 180–81
dependent voter, 70, 79
dilution thesis, 16
Downs, Anthony, 8, 54–61, 83, 84, 99,
    106, 114–15, 125, 151–52

ecological analysis, 31–32
education and attitude structure, 65,
    69–70, 73, 74, 77, 78
education and turnout, 17–19, 63–64
education and voting behavior, 46,
    78–79, 79–80, 183
Eisenhower, Dwight D., 44, 45, 124, 126,
    128, 129
elitist theory of democracy, 29, 38,
    41–43, 46–47, 190–91
expected value of vote, 6

Fiorina, Morris P., 126, 128
Ford, Gerald R., 73, 97–98, 128, 130,
    138–39, 153, 155
foreign policy, 94, 97–98, 110–11, 195
free information, 87, 90, 195
fun information, 87

general management, 108, 112–14
general policy, 107, 110–12
generalized component of voting
    decision, 58
Goldwater, Barry, 63, 129, 148–49
group interests as a factor in voting, 39,
    95, 110–11, 122, 153

halo effect, 141, 146–47

ideological constraint, 40–41, 46, 59–60,
    64–65, 67–69, 69–70, 72, 184–85,
    194; critique of, 68–69,

ABOUT THE AUTHOR

JEFFREY A. SMITH is president of the Austin-based opinion polling and market research firm Opinion Analysts, Inc. He is also a member of the faculty of the Government Department of the University of Texas.

Dr. Smith's previous work has appeared in the *American Political Science Review*.

Dr. Smith holds a B.B.A. and a Ph.D. from the University of Texas.